Deleted Material

Television in American Society

Almanac

Television in American Society

Almanac

Laurie Collier Hillstrom

Allison McNeill Gudenau, Project Editor

U·X·L

An imprint of Thomson Gale,
a part of The Thomson Corporation

THOMSON
★
GALE™

Detroit • New York • San Francisco • New Haven, Conn. • Waterville, Maine • London

Television in American Society: Almanac

Laurie Collier Hillstrom

Project Editor
Allison McNeill Gudenau

Rights and Acquisitions
Shalice Shah-Caldwell,
Emma Hull

Imaging and Multimedia
Leitha Etheridge-Sims, Lezlie Light,
Dan Newell

Product Design
Kate Scheible, Deborah van Rooyen

Composition
Evi Seoud

Manufacturing
Rita Wimberley

LIBRARY OF CONGRESS CATALOGING-IN-PUBLICATION DATA

Hillstrom, Laurie Collier, 1965–
  Television in American society. Almanac / Laurie Collier Hillstrom; Allison McNeill,
project editor.
    p. cm. -- (Television in American society reference library)
  Includes bibliographical references and index.
  ISBN-13: 978-1-4144-0222-2 (hardcover : alk. paper) -- ISBN-13: 978-1-4144-0221-5
(set : alk. paper)
  ISBN-10: 1-4144-0222-8 (hardcover : alk. paper) -- ISBN-10: 1-4144-0221-X (set : alk. paper)
  1. Television broadcasting -- Social aspects -- United States -- Juvenile literature. I. Title. --
II. Series.
  PN1992.6.H53 2006
  302.23' 450973 -- dc22
                                                                    2006011890

This title is also available as an e-book.
ISBN-13: 978-1-4144-1075-3, ISBN-10: 1-4144-1075-1
Contact your Thomson Gale sales representative for ordering information.

Printed in the United States of America
10 9 8 7 6 5 4 3 2

Contents

Reader's Guide

Television in American Society: Almanac presents a comprehensive overview of the development of television technology, the growth of the broadcast and cable industries, the evolution of television programming, and the impact of television on American society and culture. The volume's eleven chapters cover all aspects of television in the United States, from the invention of the technology in the 1920s to programming trends in the 2000s. The main emphasis of the volume concerns the many ways in which television has both reflected and influenced American life throughout its history.

Television in American Society: Almanac begins by describing the early efforts of various scientists, engineers, and inventors to transmit visual images across a distance. It then details the formation and growth of the American broadcasting industry. The volume continues by covering the development of television programming, with separate chapters devoted to prime-time series, children's and daytime shows, sports broadcasting, and news and political coverage. It then provides an assessment of television's impact on various aspects of American society, including its treatment of minorities, its influence on the political process, and its role in advertising. The volume concludes by offering a look at possible future trends in television.

Features

Television in American Society: Almanac includes informative sidebars, some containing brief biographies of influential people in the world of television, and others providing descriptions of technical features or interesting facts about the television industry. Approximately seventy black-and-white photographs enliven the work. *Television in American Society: Almanac* also includes a timeline of important events, a section defining important words to know, and a list of research and activity ideas with suggestions for study questions, group projects, and oral and dramatic presentations. *Television in American Society: Almanac* concludes with a bibliography of sources for further reading and a subject index.

Television in American Society Reference Library

Television in American Society: Almanac is only one component of a three-volume Television in American Society Reference Library. The other two titles in this multivolume set are:

- *Television in American Society: Biographies* presents profiles of twenty-six men and women who influenced the development of television in a significant way. The volume covers such key figures as inventors Philo T. Farnsworth and Vladimir Zworykin; industry leaders David Sarnoff and William S. Paley; cable TV pioneers Ted Turner and Robert L. Johnson; program producers Joan Ganz Cooney and Norman Lear; TV news journalists Walter Cronkite and Barbara Walters; and television personalities Lucille Ball, Bill Cosby, and Oprah Winfrey.

- *Television in American Society: Primary Sources* presents fifteen full or excerpted documents relating to the development and impact of television. These documents range from notable speeches that mark important points in TV history to critical analyses of television's influence on American culture. The documents are arranged chronologically, beginning with longtime RCA chairman David Sarnoff's 1936 remarks to the press at his company's first demonstration of television technology, and ending with former vice president Al Gore's 2005 speech about the effects of television on democracy.

- A cumulative index of all three titles in Television in American Society Reference Library is also available.

Comments and Suggestions

We welcome your comments on *Television in American Society: Almanac* and suggestions for other topics in history to consider. Please write: Editors, *Television in American Society: Almanac*, U*X*L, 27500 Drake Road, Farmington Hills, MI 48331-3535; call toll-free 800-877-4253; fax to 248-699-8097; or send e-mail via http://www.gale.com.

Timeline

1835 Samuel Morse invents the telegraph.

1876 Alexander Graham Bell invents the telephone.

1880 *Scientific American* magazine runs an article about the possibility of distance vision (television).

1884 German scientist Paul Nipkow invents the optical scanning disk used in mechanical television systems.

1887 Heinrich Rudolph Hertz discovers radio waves.

1895 Guglielmo Marconi develops a wireless or radio telegraph.

1897 German scientist Karl Ferdinand Braun develops the first cathode ray tube.

1900 Russian scientist Constantin Perskyi coins the term "television" at the Paris World's Fair.

1900 David Sarnoff immigrates to the United States from Russia.

1901 Guglielmo Marconi sends and receives radio signals across the Atlantic Ocean.

1907 Russian physicist Boris Rosing designs an electronic television receiver with a cathode ray tube.

1911 Boris Rosing and his assistant, Vladimir Zworykin, achieve the first successful transmission of crude television images, using a mechanical transmitter and an electronic receiver.

1912 The Radio Act of 1912 allows the U.S. government to issue licenses to people who wish to broadcast signals over radio waves.

1912 David Sarnoff, working as a telegraph operator, claims to have received distress signals from the sinking luxury oceanliner *Titanic*.

1919 The Radio Corporation of America (RCA) is formed.

1921 American inventor Philo T. Farnsworth, age 14, has a vision of an all-electronic television system.

1921 Commercial radio broadcasting begins in the United States.

1922 Philo T. Farnsworth explains his television system to his high school science teacher.

1923 Vladimir Zworykin applies for a patent on an all-electronic television system.

1925 Vladimir Zworykin demonstrates a TV system for his bosses at Westinghouse, but they decide against funding further TV research.

1926 Philo T. Farnsworth gathers investors and opens a television research laboratory in San Francisco, California.

1926 The National Broadcasting Company (NBC) is formed as a radio network.

1926 American Charles Francis Jenkins and Scotsman John Logie Baird independently invent working mechanical television systems.

1927 Philo T. Farnsworth builds his all-electronic TV system and successfully transmits an image.

1927 The Columbia Broadcasting System (CBS) is founded as a radio network.

1927 Secretary of Commerce Herbert Hoover appears in the first long-distance transmission of television signals, between Washington, D.C., and New York City.

1927 The Radio Act of 1927 first mentions broadcasters' duty to serve the public interest.

1928 The U.S. government issues the first permits for experimental TV stations.

1928 Philo T. Farnsworth demonstrates his TV system for the press.

1929 Vladimir Zworykin goes to work for RCA and begins developing his Kinescope electronic television receiver.

1929 The Great Depression begins in the United States.

1930 David Sarnoff becomes president of RCA.

1930 Philo T. Farnsworth receives a patent for his Image Dissector television camera.

1931 CBS begins experimental TV broadcasting.

1932 NBC begins experimental TV broadcasting.

1934 The Communications Act of 1934 established the Federal Communications Commission (FCC).

1935 Philo T. Farnsworth wins the patent battle against Vladimir Zworykin, preventing RCA from gaining total control over electronic television technology.

1935 David Sarnoff announces RCA's million-dollar television research and testing program.

1936 RCA demonstrates an all-electronic television system.

1936 Philo T. Farnsworth begins experimental TV broadcasts from his Philco laboratory in Philadelphia, Pennsylvania.

1936 The Olympic Games in Berlin, Germany, are televised using both RCA and Farnsworth equipment.

1936 About 200 television sets are in use worldwide.

1938 Vladimir Zworykin and RCA introduce an improved Iconoscope television camera that is ten times more sensitive to light than the original version.

April 20, 1939 David Sarnoff introduces television to the public at the New York World's Fair.

April 30, 1939 Franklin D. Roosevelt becomes the first U.S. president to be televised.

May 1, 1939 RCA begins selling television sets to the public, followed by DuMont, General Electric, and Philco.

October 2, 1939 RCA pays a licensing fee to Philo T. Farnsworth for use of his television patents.

1940 Peter Goldmark of CBS develops the first working color television system, which uses both mechanical and electronic elements.

March 1941 The FCC's National Television Standards Committee (NTSC) announces a technical standard for monochrome (black-and-white) television sets.

July 1, 1941 NBC makes the first commercial television broadcast in the United States.

December 7, 1941 Japanese fighter planes attack the U.S. naval base in Pearl Harbor, Hawaii, drawing the United States into World War II.

1942–45 Most television broadcasting and manufacturing stops for the duration of the war.

1942–45 About 10,000 television sets had been sold, and 23 TV stations exist in the United States.

1943 The American Broadcasting Company (ABC) is formed when NBC is forced to sell its Blue radio network.

1946 Postwar production of television sets begins.

1946 CBS demonstrates its color television system for the FCC.

1948 The first cable TV systems (known as Community Antenna Television or CATV) are installed to improve reception in rural areas of the United States.

1948 The FCC places a temporary freeze on new broadcast licenses in order to study interference between stations and develop an orderly system for assigning licenses.

1948 There are 107 television stations operating in 63 markets.

1949 Philo T. Farnsworth sells his company, Farnsworth Radio and Television, to ITT and leaves the television industry.

1949 The Academy of Television Arts and Sciences creates the Emmy Awards to honor excellence in TV performance and production.

1950 The FCC approves the CBS mechanical-electronic color television system.

June 1951 CBS begins broadcasting TV programs in color; only a few hundred TV sets can receive the broadcasts.

June 1951 RCA demonstrates its all-electronic color television system.

October 1951 Color TV production stops during the Korean War (1950–53).

December 1951 The National Association of Broadcasters (NAB) adopts its Code of Practices for Television Broadcasters.

1952 The FCC ends its freeze on new broadcast licenses and approves broadcasting on UHF channels.

1952 The first political campaign advertisements appear on television.

1953 The FCC reverses its 1950 decision and approves the RCA color television system.

1953 NBC begins broadcasting in color.

1956 Ampex Corporation demonstrates videotape recorder (VTR) technology, which makes it possible to record television programs for immediate viewing.

1959 The U.S. Congress uncovers the quiz show scandal, in which producers and sponsors provided answers to some game show contestants in advance.

1959 Congress adds the Fairness Doctrine, written by the FCC in 1949, as an amendment to the Communications Act of 1934.

1960 John F. Kennedy and Richard M. Nixon take part in the first televised presidential debates.

1960 Approximately 87 percent of American homes contain at least one television set.

1961 Newton N. Minow becomes chairman of the FCC under President John F. Kennedy.

1962 The Telstar communications satellite is launched into orbit, allowing for the first international transmission of television images.

1962 The All-Channel Receiver Act requires all new television sets to be equipped to receive both UHF and VHF broadcasts.

1962 The FCC decides that it has the authority to regulate cable television.

1963 President John F. Kennedy is assassinated; television news provides around-the-clock coverage of the story for four days.

1967 ABC Sports introduces slow-motion and stop-action features to sports telecasts.

1967 Most television broadcasts are now in color.

1967 The Public Broadcasting Act of 1967 creates the framework for public radio and television in the United States.

1969 A worldwide television audience estimated at 600 million watches American astronaut Neil Armstrong become the first human being to set foot on the Moon.

1970 The Public Broadcasting Service (PBS) is established.

1970 The invention of fiberoptic cable increases the amount of information that can be transmitted through wires.

1972 The FCC issues its open-skies decision, allowing commercial use of satellites.

1972 The U.S. government releases the results of a large-scale study which shows that viewing violent programs on television tends to increase children's aggressive behavior.

1975 The pay-cable channel Home Box Office (HBO) broadcasts a heavyweight championship fight between Muhammad Ali and Joe Frazier live via satellite from Manila, in the Philippines.

1976 The first videocassette recorders (VCRs) are introduced for home use.

1976 Ted Turner turns his Atlanta-based independent TV station into the national cable network Superstation TBS by arranging to deliver his signal to cable systems across the country via satellite.

1978 PBS becomes the first network to deliver all of its programming via satellite.

1979 The Entertainment and Sports Programming Network (ESPN) becomes the first sports network on cable TV.

1980   Ted Turner launches the Cable News Network (CNN), television's first twenty-four hour news channel.

1981   Electronic News Gathering (ENG) technology gives a boost to local television newscasts.

1981   Mark S. Fowler becomes chairman of the FCC under President Ronald Reagan.

August 1, 1981   Cable channel MTV (Music Television) makes its debut.

1982   The FCC authorizes Direct Broadcast Satellite (DBS) services.

1984   The FCC deregulates broadcasting under President Ronald Reagan, eliminating rules about the number of commercials allowed per hour of programming and increasing the limits on ownership of TV stations.

1984   The FCC authorizes stereo TV broadcasting, and sales of stereo TV sets begin.

1984   The U.S. Supreme Court rules in favor of Sony in the *Betamax* case, making VCR technology legal for home use.

1987   Fox becomes the fourth broadcast TV network operating in the United States.

1989   The FCC eliminates the Fairness Doctrine.

1990   General Instrument (GI) develops the world's first all-digital TV broadcasting system.

1990   The U.S. Congress passes the Children's Television Act (CTA), which requires all television networks to broadcast at least three hours of educational/informational (E/I) programming per week and limits the amount of advertising allowed during children's programs.

1992   The broadcast networks adopt a ratings system, modeled after that used for theatrical films, to inform parents about program content that might be inappropriate for younger viewers.

1994   The FCC establishes technical standards for high-definition television (HDTV) in the United States.

1995   The first television program is delivered over the Internet.

1995 Broadcast networks WB (the Warner Brothers Network) and UPN (the United Paramount Network) are formed.

1996 The Telecommunications Act of 1996 reduces limits on TV station ownership and removes barriers between different areas of the communication industry, leading to increased media consolidation.

1996 Approximately one billion television sets are in use worldwide.

1997 The FCC establishes a schedule for the transition to digital television broadcasting.

2000 All new television sets sold in the United States are required to contain a V-chip to allow parents to block programs electronically based on their content ratings.

2000 Television news comes under criticism for its coverage of the 2000 presidential election, after several broadcast and cable networks report results before they have enough information to do so accurately.

2004 During the presidential campaign, Democratic Senator John Kerry and Republican President George W. Bush, combined, spend more than $600 million on television and radio advertising.

2006 The ABC network charges advertisers $2.5 million for each 30-second commercial that airs during Super Bowl XL; these ads reach more than 100 million people in the United States and hundreds of millions more around the world.

2006 The WB and UPN networks merge, forming a new network, The CW.

Words to Know

affiliate: A local television station that is connected or grouped together with a major network. Local affiliate stations are required to carry the network's programs according to a regular schedule.

airwaves: Naturally occurring waves of electromagnetic energy that travel through the air and can be used to carry information, such as television signals. In the United States, the airwaves belong to the American people, and the FCC grants individuals and companies the right to use the public airwaves by issuing broadcast licenses.

American Broadcasting Company (ABC): One of the major U.S. broadcast television networks, formed in 1943.

analog: A naturally occurring form of electromagnetic energy that is composed of waves and can be used to carry information, such as television signals.

anchor: The main host or presenter on a television news program.

animated: A type of television program that features cartoon characters rather than live actors.

bandwidth: A measurement of the amount of space on the airwaves needed to carry a television signal, based on the frequency and wavelength characteristics of that signal.

Big Three: The major networks (ABC, CBS, and NBC) that controlled television broadcasting in the United States from the 1940s until the 1980s.

broadcast: The act of sending communication signals, such as radio or television programs, over a large area to be received by many people. The term is also used to distinguish television networks that deliver their signals over the airwaves from those that deliver their signals by cable or satellite.

broadcast license: A permit granted by the FCC that gives an individual or company the right to operate a radio or television station that sends communications signals over the public airwaves.

cable television: A type of service that delivers television signals to customers through cables, or long wires buried underground or strung along electrical poles, rather than through the airwaves.

cathode ray tube: The part of a television set that makes it possible to see an image on the screen. Invented in 1897, it works by shooting a beam of electrons (tiny, negatively charged particles) toward the inside of the TV screen, which is coated with a substance that glows when struck by the beam of radiation. Also known as a picture tube.

coaxial cable: A type of line or wire used to transmit electronic communication signals, consisting of a copper wire surrounded by insulation, with an aluminum coating.

Columbia Broadcasting System (CBS): One of the major U.S. broadcast television networks, formed in 1927 as a radio network.

commercial television broadcasting: A type of service, approved by the FCC in 1941, in which television networks sell commercial time to advertisers. The networks use advertising money to create and distribute programs according to a regular schedule. Before 1941, television broadcasting was experimental, and it was paid for by the television networks and TV set manufacturers.

Communications Act of 1934: The first major U.S. law that covered television. It created the Federal Communications Commission to oversee and regulate all forms of electronic communication, including radio, television, telephone, and telegraph.

consolidation: The combination or merger of several different companies that each operate in one part of the media industry to form a large communications firm that controls many types of media outlets.

content: The topics or subject matter included in a television program.

content ratings: A labeling system for television programs that provides viewers with information about the types of subject matter they contain. The system in effect in 2006 included warnings about violence (V), strong language (L), and sexuality (S).

deregulation: The process of reducing or eliminating government rules and regulations affecting a business or industry.

digital: A method of storing and transmitting electronic information as a binary code consisting of long strings of the digits zero and one. The main advantage of digital television signals is that they can be understood, changed, and enhanced by computers.

digital video recorder (DVR): A device that saves television programs onto a computer hard drive, making it easy for users to record shows for later viewing.

Direct Broadcast Satellite (DBS): A technology that allows television signals to be sent from satellites orbiting Earth directly to small, individual dish antennas on the roofs of houses and buildings.

electronic television: The type of television system used in the United States, which has no moving parts and works using the properties of electricity.

Emmy Awards: Annual honors presented by the Academy of Television Arts and Sciences for excellence in television programming. There are separate Emmy Awards for prime time and daytime programs.

experimental television broadcasting: A type of service provided by early television networks and manufacturers in order to test their facilities and equipment and try out different kinds of programming. It was used in the United States until 1941, when the

FCC approved commercial (advertiser-supported) television broadcasting.

Fairness Doctrine: An FCC rule, in effect from 1949 to 1989, that required broadcasters to present opposing viewpoints on controversial issues of public importance.

Federal Communications Commission (FCC): The U.S. government agency, created in 1934, charged with regulating all forms of electronic communication, including television, radio, telephone, and walkie-talkie.

fiberoptic cable: A type of line or wire consisting of clear rods of glass or plastic, which transmits electronic communication signals as rapid pulses of light.

Fox: The fourth major U.S. broadcast television network, formed in 1987 by Australian businessman Rupert Murdoch.

frequency: A characteristic of radio waves that refers to how often the wave pattern repeats itself. The entire range of frequencies is called the radio spectrum. The FCC assigns every television station a specific operating frequency within the radio spectrum to broadcast its signal.

game show: A type of television program in which contestants answer questions, solve puzzles, or complete physical challenges in an effort to win money or prizes.

genre: A general type or format of television program, such as a drama, situation comedy, talk show, or soap opera.

high-definition (HD): A technology that scans and transmits a visual image at a higher resolution, or number of horizontal lines per screen, than the original U.S. technical standard of 525 lines. The U.S. standard for high-definition television established in 1994 divides a TV screen into 1,080 lines, creating a picture twice as sharp as the old system.

interactive: A technology that allows two-way communication between the sender and receiver of TV signals. It gives viewers more control over programming by enabling them to select, respond to, and change the content of shows.

Internet Protocol Television (IPTV): The process of delivering television signals over the vast computer network known as the Internet.

market: A geographic area that is served by a distinct group of television stations.

mechanical television: An early type of television system that used a spinning disk with holes punched in it to measure the light reflected off a moving image and turn it into an electrical impulse. It required extremely bright lights to create a decent image, and it was replaced by electronic television in the 1940s.

media: Plural of medium; often used to refer to all sources of news and information, or all types of mass communication.

media outlets: Specific modes or systems of mass communication, such as radio and TV stations, cable TV systems, newspapers, and magazines.

medium: A mode or system of communication, information, or entertainment.

miniseries: A type of television program in which the story continues over several episodes, but then ends rather than extending for a full season.

National Association of Broadcasters (NAB): An industry organization made up of representatives of U.S. radio and television networks and local stations.

National Broadcasting Company (NBC): One of the major U.S. broadcast television networks, formed by the Radio Corporation of America (RCA) in 1926 as a radio network.

network: A business organization that creates programs and distributes them to a group of affiliated or linked local stations.

news magazine: A type of television program that features several different segments, like the articles in a print magazine, ranging from investigative news reports to celebrity interviews.

on the air: Short for "on the airwaves," referring to the airwaves that carry television and radio signals. Slang term for the broadcast of a program.

patent: A form of legal protection that gives an inventor the exclusive right to use or make money from an invention for a period of seventeen years.

pilot: An initial test episode of a television program, which is used to determine whether the program will attract enough viewers to become a continuing series.

prime time: The evening hours, roughly between 8 P.M. and 11 P.M., when television programs generally reach the largest number of viewers.

Public Broadcasting Service (PBS): A national nonprofit organization, consisting of more than 350 member stations, designed to air TV programs that serve the public interest. Instead of selling commercial time to make money, PBS stations receive funding from individual viewers, businesses, charities, and the federal government.

public interest: A phrase that was included in the Communications Act of 1934, which said that people who received licenses to use the public airwaves had a duty to serve the public interest. Although never fully defined by the U.S. government, the phrase was generally taken to mean that the broadcast industry had a responsibility to benefit American society by providing informative and educational programming.

Radio Corporation of America (RCA): A company that was formed in 1919 and became the nation's leading producer of televisions, operator of TV stations, and broadcaster of TV programs (through its ownership of the NBC network) in the 1940s and 1950s.

radio spectrum: The entire range of frequencies, or repeating patterns, in which radio waves exist. Television signals are broadcast over a small part of the radio spectrum.

radio wave: A form of electromagnetic energy that travels through the air and can be used to carry communication signals.

ratings: Measurements of the percentage of all television viewers who watched a particular program. A program's ratings determine how much money the network can charge advertisers to place commercials on that program. Ratings also influence whether programs are renewed for another season or canceled.

reality TV: A type of program that features regular people, rather than actors, who compete against one another or experience unusual situations together, while television cameras film their interactions. Reality shows are also known as unscripted programs, because the participants use their own words instead of reading lines from a script.

regulate: To establish rules or guidelines to control the operation of a business or industry.

rerun: A repeat showing of a television program that has already been broadcast.

satellite: A man-made object that orbits around Earth and can be used to relay television signals.

signal: A set of instructions that tells a television set how to display an image. A TV set can receive video signals from a broadcast network, a cable box, a satellite dish, or a VCR/DVD player. A complete video signal consists of three parts: picture, color, and synchronization (which forces the TV set to lock onto the signal in order to reproduce the image correctly).

situation comedy (sitcom): A type of television program that draws humor from continuing characters and their environment.

soap opera: A type of television program, also known as serial drama or daytime drama, that involves continuing characters and a complex story line.

spin-off: A television series that centers around a character who first appeared on another TV series.

sponsor: An individual or business that provides the money to create or broadcast a television program. Sponsors want their products and services to be associated with a television program for advertising purposes.

standard: A basic rule or guideline established by the U.S. government that applies to an entire industry.

syndication: The process of selling the legal rights to a television program to customers other than the major broadcast networks, such as independent TV stations and cable channels. First-run syndication describes programs that are created especially for independent distribution, or are syndicated when they appear on television for the first time. Off-network syndication occurs when programs that originally ran as network series are sold for a second time in syndication.

talk show: A type of television program that features a host, whose name often appears in the title, and includes some discussion of current events in the fields of news and entertainment.

transmit: To send or broadcast.

Ultra-High Frequency (UHF): A portion of the radio spectrum used to broadcast television signals. When most TV signals were sent over the airwaves, rather than by cable or satellite, UHF channels were generally considered technically inferior to VHF channels because they sent a weaker signal over a smaller area.

variety show: A type of television program that features a wide range of entertainment, such as music, comedy, and skits.

Very-High Frequency (VHF): A portion of the radio spectrum used to broadcast television signals. When most TV signals were sent over the airwaves, rather than by cable or satellite, VHF channels were generally considered technically superior to UHF channels because they sent a stronger signal over a wider area.

videocassette recorder (VCR): A device that saves television programs on videotape enclosed in a plastic cassette, allowing users to record shows at home for later viewing. By the 2000s it was being replaced by digital video recorder (DVR) technology.

wavelength: A characteristic of radio waves that refers to the time or distance between waves.

Research and Activity Ideas

The following research and activity ideas are intended to offer suggestions for complementing social studies and history curricula; to trigger additional ideas for enhancing learning; and to provide cross-disciplinary projects for library and classroom use.

- With the help of your family, track the television viewing time in your household for one week. Note how many hours each television set is turned on, and how many commercials appear during that time. Multiply your results by 52 weeks to estimate your family's TV viewing time for one year. Discuss and compare your results with the class.

- Imagine that television producer Mark Burnett, creator of the reality TV series *Survivor* and *The Apprentice,* offers to pay your family not to watch television for one year. Would you agree? How much money would he have to pay you? If Burnett filmed your family's interactions before and during the television-free year, how do you think they would change? What kinds of things would you do to fill the time you normally would have spent watching television? What would you miss the most and least about television? Would you be willing to give up television permanently?

- As a class, make a list of some of the ways that television has influenced or changed American society. Consider such areas as politics, family life, gender roles, perceptions of racial and ethnic minorities, views of other nations and cultures, and attitudes about violence. Following the discussion, ask students to vote about whether the overall impact of television has been positive or negative.

- Select a topic in the news. Collect information on that topic from at least three different media outlets (television, radio, newspapers, magazines, online sources, etc.). Compare how the different sources of information cover the topic. Research the ownership of each media outlet you used. Does media ownership seem to influence the presentation of news?

- As a class, discuss what it means to be an informed citizen of the United States. What kind of information does a person need to participate in a democracy? Think about the main ways in which television provides information about current events and political issues, such as news programs, press conferences, speeches, debates, and campaign advertisements. Does TV help American voters identify the differences between candidates for office and make good choices as citizens?

- In the United States, the airwaves used to broadcast television programs belong to the American people, and broadcasters are allowed to use this public property through a system of licenses. Some people, such as former FCC chairman Newton N. Minow, argue that this system gives broadcasters a responsibility to operate in ways that serve the public interest. Do you agree? Should the U.S. government intervene to make sure that broadcasters meet this responsibility? In what ways might government regulation limit the rights and freedoms of broadcasters? Can you think of other cases in which the government regulates the activities of private businesses in order to protect individual rights or promote the public interest?

- Divide the class into two groups. Hold a debate on the topic of reinstating the Fairness Doctrine. This FCC policy, which was in effect from 1949 to 1989, required television news programs to present both sides of controversial issues in a fair and accurate manner. One group should represent the National Association of Broadcasters (NAB), which argues that any government effort to control the content of television news programs violates broadcasters' right to free speech. The other group should represent Congresswoman Louise Slaughter and other supporters of the Fairness Doctrine, who claim that a law is needed to ensure that minority opinions are represented on the public airwaves.

- Evaluate how a specific group of people—such as women, children, families, African Americans, doctors, athletes, or police officers—has been presented on television over time. Write a paper outlining the changes you notice, examining whether these changes have been generally positive or negative.

- Choose a decade in the history of television, from the 1950s through the 2000s. Make a list of the most important events and issues of that decade, then make a list of the most popular prime-time television shows of that decade. Compare the two lists. In what ways did television programming reflect the major events of the decade? In what ways did television serve as a release or escape from the realities of the decade?

- Present a skit based on real or imaginary interactions between important historical figures in the development of television. Some possible situations to dramatize include: RCA president David Sarnoff visiting the television laboratory of independent inventor Philo T. Farnsworth in 1930; CBS president William S. Paley arguing with broadcast journalist Edward R. Murrow about whether to cover controversial topics on the 1950s news program *See It Now*; and Ted Turner trying to convince advertisers to support CNN, the twenty-four-hour cable news channel he launched in 1980.

- Cable and satellite television services have given American viewers more channel options than ever before. Yet studies have shown that most households only watch an average of fifteen channels regularly, and the broadcast networks that dominated television in the 1950s continued to attract the largest percentage of viewers in the 2000s. How many TV channels does your family watch on a regular basis? Do you think that the increase in the number of available TV channels has caused the quality of programming to improve or decline? Has it become easier or more difficult to find something good to watch on TV?

- Does television programming include too much sex, violence, and profanity? Who should decide what type of material is appropriate or inappropriate to put on television? What role should the U.S. government play in controlling television content?

- Political candidates try to create an appealing image on television. What are the most important qualities a candidate must possess in order to create a positive media image? What are the most important qualities a candidate must possess in order to be an effective leader? Are these qualities the same, or are there significant differences between the two lists? Pretend that you have been invited to question candidates during the next presidential debate. What questions would you ask to help voters see beyond the candidates' image and understand their leadership qualities and views on important issues?

- Write a one-page paper predicting what television technology and programming will be like fifty years into the future.

Television in American Society

Almanac

The Invention of Television Technology

It is hard for Americans in the twenty-first century to envision a world without television. According to U.S. Census Bureau statistics from 2004, 98 percent of households in the United States contain at least one TV set, and the average household has 2.4 sets. TV sets in the 2000s often have large screens (at least 32 inches across) that show high-definition color images. Cable and satellite systems, which are available to about 80 percent of U.S. homes, give viewers hundreds of programs from which to choose. Typical Americans spend more than four hours each day watching television. They depend on TV for entertainment as well as news and information, and they expect to see instantaneous, live coverage of various types of events from around the world.

Yet television is a relatively new invention. The technology that allowed people to send moving images across great distances did not become available until the 1920s, and most commercial development of TV took place after 1945. In fact, the grandparents of young people in school in 2006 can probably remember the first time they ever saw a TV set. That set almost certainly had a tiny screen (between 4 and 10 inches across) that showed grainy, black-and-white images. In the early days of TV, there were only three television networks. These networks broadcast programs only a few days each week, for an hour or two in the evening. For many years, television viewing was such a special event that people who owned TV sets often invited friends and neighbors over to watch the shows. Over the course of just a few decades, however, television has become a constant presence in people's lives and one of the most influential forces in American culture.

Dreaming of distance vision

Television did not arise out of the work of a single inventor. Instead, a number of inventors, scientists, and engineers made important contributions to the development of TV technology. Perhaps the first invention

Origins of Television Terminology

The word "television," which means "seeing at a distance," was first used to describe the futuristic technology at the 1900 World's Fair by Russian scientist Constantin Perskyi. It combined two root words of different origins: the Greek word "tele," meaning "distant," and the Latin word "visio," meaning "sight." Once television technology became a reality in the late 1920s, some critics did not like the term. The editor of the British newspaper *Manchester Guardian,* for instance, once famously wrote: "Television? The word is half Greek and half Latin. No good will come of it."

More complaints were heard in England in 1936, during a competition to decide what television system would be adopted as standard by the British Broadcasting Corporation (BBC). Some people claimed that, given the roots of the word, the verb "televise" should actually refer to the act of watching a program rather than the act of broadcasting one. People suggested a wide variety of alternative names that they felt better described TV technology, including radioscope, farscope, mirascope, optiphone, and lustreer.

The early days of television also saw many arguments over what to call television viewers. During the 1936 competition, for example, London newspapers generally referred to people watching the test broadcasts as "lookers" or "lookers-in." Some people felt that this term was too narrow, since people not only watched but also listened to TV. A number of alternative terms were suggested—such as perceptors, audiobservers, telegazers, teleseers, inviders, and audivists—but the simpler term "viewers" eventually caught on.

that contributed to the later development of TV was the telegraph. Introduced by Samuel Morse (1791–1872) in 1835, the telegraph allowed people to exchange coded messages by transmitting (sending) a series of tapping sounds over electrical wires. Although the telegraph did not allow for the transmission of voices or pictures, its invention opened the door to long-distance communication. The next step in the development of communication technology was the 1876 invention of the telephone by Alexander Graham Bell (1847–1922). Unlike the telegraph, which limited communication to codes made up of dots and dashes, the telephone enabled people to send live voice messages across many miles of wires.

Almost as soon as the telephone was introduced, scientists began dreaming about the possibility of transmitting visual images of people, objects, and events. They referred to this exciting potential technology as distance vision or seeing at a distance. Bell himself spent time working to develop a picture phone that would enable people to see each other as they talked on the telephone. The idea of viewing live, moving pictures across a distance also captured the public's imagination during the late nineteenth century. *Scientific American* magazine, for instance, ran its first articles about the potential for distance vision in 1880. Futuristic cartoons of the period showed people sitting at home watching sports and current events projected on a wall or a small screen. The topic of distance vision generated so much public interest that it was featured at the 1900 World's Fair (major events held in large cities around the world that gave people an opportunity to see and experience new technologies) in Paris, France, where Russian scientist Constantin Perskyi became the first person to use the word television.

Another important step in the development of long-distance communications technology came in 1887, when Heinrich Rudolf Hertz (1857–1894) discovered radio waves. Radio waves are electromagnetic energy that travels through the air (see sidebar "Broadcasting over Radio Waves"). In 1895 a scientist named Guglielmo Marconi (1874–1937) used Hertz's discovery to develop a wireless telegraph. Also known as a radio telegraph, this invention allowed telegraph messages to be sent through the air on radio waves instead of through wires. Marconi first demonstrated his invention in 1899 by sending a message across the English Channel (a twenty-mile-wide body of water separating Great Britain and France). The wireless telegraph soon led to the development of broadcast radio, which allowed voices, music, and other sounds to be transmitted wirelessly through the air. Lee DeForest (1873–1961) demonstrated this new technology in 1908 by broadcasting from the top of the Eiffel Tower in Paris, France. Some 500 miles away listeners with radio receivers were able to hear DeForest's broadcast. It was only a matter of time before inventors figured out how to use similar technology to broadcast pictures.

Experimenting with light

While all of these inventions were paving the way for television, a number of scientists and engineers were actively trying to develop the technology to transmit moving images. The earliest efforts involved the chemical element selenium. In 1873 scientists discovered that selenium responded to variations in the intensity of light. In other words, the element's ability to conduct electricity changed depending on whether it was exposed to bright light or dim light. For several years, inventors tried to use selenium's light sensitivity to convert moving images into electrical impulses, but they eventually found that the element responded too slowly for this purpose.

In 1884 German scientist Paul G. Nipkow (1860–1940) applied for a patent (a form of legal protection that gives an inventor exclusive rights to use and market an invention for a certain number of years) on an invention he called an electric telescope. Nipkow's invention successfully scanned the light reflected by a moving image, turned it into an electrical signal, and transmitted it across a wire. His system used a set of spinning metal disks with holes arranged in a spiral pattern to scan the image. Inside each hole were photosensitive cells (cells sensitive to light) that, as the disks spun, repeatedly measured the amount of light hitting the hole.

Broadcasting over Radio Waves

Television broadcasting, along with all other types of wireless communication, relies upon radio waves. Radio waves are made up of electrical and magnetic energy that travels through space. These electromagnetic waves have two main characteristics: amplitude, which is a measure of the strength or height of each wave; and frequency, which is a measure of how quickly the wave repeats itself, or occurs at any given point.

Both of these characteristics of radio waves vary. Waves that are stronger, or taller, have a higher amplitude. Waves that occur more rapidly have a higher frequency. The frequency of radio waves is measured in hertz (named after the German physicist Heinrich Rudolf Hertz [1857–1894], who discovered radio waves in 1887). Using metric prefixes, the term kilohertz or KHz means one thousand hertz, while megahertz or MHz means one million hertz.

Not all electromagnetic energy takes the form of radio waves. At higher frequencies, the waves become infrared light. At even higher frequencies, they appear as visible light. At other, increasingly high frequencies, they turn into ultraviolet light and X rays. Some people are surprised to learn that the type of energy in radio waves is actually related to light rather than to sound. Radio waves occur in a continuous spectrum, like the colors of the rainbow in the spectrum of visible light. Each part of the radio spectrum provides a different frequency, or broadcast channel.

Radio waves can be used to carry many types of communication signals, including music, television programs, cellular phone calls, and wireless Internet data. In order to transmit such information from one place to another, it must be attached to the radio waves through a process called modulation. Modulating a radio wave involves changing one or both of its basic characteristics. Changing the strength of the wave is called amplitude modulation, which is commonly abbreviated AM. Changing the repetition pattern of the wave is called frequency modulation, abbreviated FM. There are many other types of modulation, but they are all variations or combinations of AM and FM. For example, one of the types that is often used to carry television broadcast signals, Vestigial Sideband (VSB), is a form of AM.

Although the spectrum of useful radio waves is large, it is not unlimited. If two radio or television stations in the same area broadcast on the same frequency, their signals may interfere with each other, causing poor reception. In order to prevent interference between different types of communication signals, the Federal Communications Commission (FCC) divides up the radio spectrum and assigns frequencies to broadcasters through a system of licenses.

The cells then sent electrical signals that varied in strength depending on the amount of light hitting them. These signals were transmitted across a wire to a similar device at the other end, which reversed the process and turned the electrical signals back into light. The light source varied in intensity depending on the strength of the electrical signals it received and thus created a crude representation of the moving image at the other end of the wire. Nipkow's system of spinning disks provided the

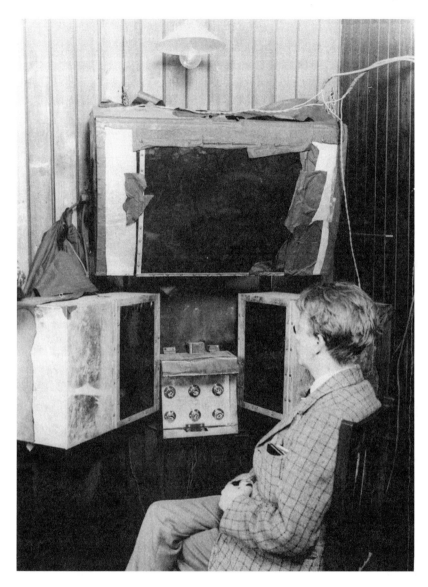

foundation for mechanical television sets. Mechanical TV sets were perfected in 1926 by two independent inventors, American Charles Francis Jenkins (1867–1934) and Scotsman John Logie Baird (1888–1946).

Other scientists followed a different path to develop electronic television sets. Electronic TV systems were based on cathode rays—the light rays that were emitted when an electrical current was forced through a vacuum tube. This technology served as the foundation for modern

TV (see sidebar "How TV Works"). German physicist Karl Ferdinand Braun (1850–1918) invented the first cathode ray tube in 1897. The technology was further developed a decade later by English inventor A. A. Campbell-Swinton (1863–1930) and Russian scientist Boris Rosing (1869–1933).

The two men who are arguably considered the fathers of American television—Philo T. Farnsworth (1906–1971) and Vladimir Zworykin (1889–1982)—succeeded in using cathode ray tubes to create the first working electronic television systems. Farnsworth came up with his first ideas about electronic television systems in 1921, at the age of fourteen. He later claimed that a vision of the technology appeared to him while he was plowing hay on his family's Idaho farm. He began experimenting while still in high school and demonstrated various systems for his teachers. After graduating, he gained the support of investors and created the first complete electronic TV system, which he called the Image Dissector. Farnsworth applied for a patent on his system in 1927 and demonstrated it to members of the media in San Francisco, California, the following year.

In the meantime, Zworykin immigrated to the United States from Russia, where he had worked as an assistant to Boris Rosing. After taking a research job at the electrical equipment manufacturer Westinghouse, Zworykin received a patent in 1923 for a television camera tube, which he called the Iconoscope or electric eye. He then developed a screen he called the Kinescope for displaying images captured by his electric eye. Zworykin combined the two inventions to achieve the first successful electronic transmission of images in 1925. The following year, Westinghouse management decided that there was no future in television technology. They ordered Zworykin to work on projects that they considered more valuable. Yet Zworykin remained committed to television and continued his research on his own time.

Demonstrating TV's potential

The American people in the 1920s knew very little about the early research into television systems that was taking place. Farnsworth, Zworykin, and other inventors conducted their experiments outside the public eye, and no TV sets were produced for sale at this time. Most Americans were not aware that television had become a reality until April 7, 1927, when the first public demonstration of television in the United States took place. On that day, Bell Laboratories and the U.S.

Herbert Hoover, seated, participates in the first long-distance transmission of a TV broadcast, April 7, 1927. HULTON ARCHIVE/ GETTY IMAGES.

Department of Commerce staged the first simultaneous long-distance transmission of a live image and voice.

The speaker was Herbert Hoover (1874–1964), who was then the secretary of commerce and later became president of the United States (served 1929–33). In his historic transmission, as quoted in *The Broadcast Century,* Hoover said: "Today we have, in a sense, the transmission of sight for the first time in the world's history. Human genius has now destroyed the impediment [barrier] of distance in a new respect, and in a manner hitherto [until now] unknown."

The *New York Times* covered the event in the following day's newspaper, under a large headline reading: "Far-off Speakers Seen as Well as Heard Here in a Test of Television." According to *The Broadcast Century,* the *Times* reported that "Herbert Hoover made a speech in

Washington yesterday afternoon. An audience in New York heard him and saw him. More than 200 miles of space intervening between the speaker and his audience was annihilated [destroyed] by the television apparatus...demonstrated publicly for the first time yesterday...It was as if a photograph had suddenly come to life and begun to talk, smile, nod its head and look this way and that."

Experimental television broadcasts began the following year. In 1928 inventor Charles Francis Jenkins received the first license awarded to a television station in the United States. His station, W3XK, broadcast from Wheaton, Maryland, using a mechanical TV system. The first broadcasts were so weak that the images appeared on screen as shadowlike pictures or silhouettes. According to David E. Fisher and Marshall Jon Fisher in *Tube: The Invention of Television,* "the entertainment value lay solely in the miracle of seeing these flickering images in your own home, transmitted as if by magic through the air." At that time, television receiver sets were tiny and expensive. The screens were only about four inches across, and they cost the equivalent of a month's pay for an average worker. Since the only programming available consisted of test broadcasts, few people were willing to make the investment in the new technology.

The golden age of radio

Another reason that television failed to catch on right away was the growing popularity of radio. Broadcast radio originated in 1908, but its initial use was limited to sailing ships and the military. The U.S. government authorized the first commercial radio station in 1921. From that time on, radio's popularity increased rapidly, and the number of radio stations, programs, and receivers increased as well. Throughout the 1920s, in fact, Americans bought radio receiver sets as quickly as they could be manufactured. Two million sets were sold in 1925 alone, and by the end of that year one out of every six homes in the country contained a radio.

Radio became America's main source of entertainment and news. The first broadcasts originated in live performances at local radio stations. Soon two major radio networks emerged: the Columbia Broadcasting System (CBS) and the National Broadcasting Company (NBC). One of the nation's largest radio manufacturers, the Radio Corporation of America (RCA), launched NBC with much fanfare in 1926. The network's first broadcast included live coverage of a star-studded event in the grand ballroom of the Waldorf-Astoria Hotel in New York City.

Featuring leading singers, orchestras, and humorists of the day, it was heard by millions of people in the city and surrounding areas.

Both NBC and CBS quickly developed large networks of local radio stations that covered much of the United States. Programs originated in the network studios in New York and were sent to local stations over telephone lines. The rapid increase in radio stations led to overcrowding of the air waves, which caused interference between stations. The U.S. government addressed this situation by passing the Radio Act of 1927, which created the Federal Radio Commission (FRC) to oversee and regulate, or control, broadcasting. The FRC took responsibility for issuing radio licenses and assigning specific broadcast frequencies (operating space on the air waves) to individual stations. "Laws of physics tell us that only a limited number of frequencies can carry [radio or] television signals," William F. Baker and George Dessart explained in *Down the Tube*. "That limitation brought about the Radio Act of 1927: the government, to ensure that the air waves were efficiently used in the public interest, had somehow to choose among those who wished to own stations, selecting some and rejecting others."

The Radio Act of 1927 included several requirements that had important effects on the later development of broadcast television. For instance, it required that radio stations operate in the "public interest, convenience, or necessity." In effect, the act ensured that no individual or company could own the air waves. Instead, it said that the air waves belonged to the American people, and it granted broadcasters temporary licenses to use those air waves. People with radio receivers were allowed to tune into broadcasts for free, while the stations were encouraged to pay their operating costs by selling advertising time to sponsors. All of these provisions also applied to broadcast television when it became established.

Car radios were introduced in 1927, which led to further increases in the number of listeners. By 1928 there were 677 broadcast radio stations on the air and eight million radios in use across the United States. In 1929, however, the United States entered a long period of extreme economic hardship known as the Great Depression (1929–41). Businesses failed by the thousands, and a significant percentage of Americans found themselves unemployed. At the same time, a severe dry spell hit the farmlands of the Midwest and South, leading to sharp declines in crop production and widespread food shortages.

By providing free news and entertainment to struggling Americans, radio became even more popular during the 1930s. People gathered around their radios to listen to concerts, variety shows, comedies such as "Amos 'n' Andy," and multi-part dramas. As stated in *The Broadcast Century,* "The principal escape for millions of homeless, hungry, and ill Americans—and for millions more on the edge of poverty—was radio."

TV technology continues to develop

Since radio seemed to fulfill Americans' needs for news and entertainment, especially during the Great Depression, many people doubted whether a market really existed for television. Despite such doubts, a number of inventors and entrepreneurs continued working to develop television technology. Frustrated by Westinghouse's negative view of television, Zworykin left the company in 1929 and took his ideas to RCA. The visionary leader of RCA at this time was David Sarnoff (1891–1971). Sarnoff had first become famous in 1912 when, as a young telegraph operator, he had supposedly picked up distress signals from the famous ocean liner *Titanic* as it was sinking. He was a rising executive at RCA when the company created its NBC radio network in 1926, and four years later he became president of the company.

Sarnoff understood emerging communications technologies better than most people of his day, and he eagerly agreed to support Zworykin's efforts to build an all-electronic television system. In his biography of Sarnoff, titled *The General: David Sarnoff and the Rise of the Communications Industry,* Kenneth Bilby called the meeting between Sarnoff and Zworykin "one of the most decisive in industrial annals [history]. It brought together television's leading inventor with the executive who would guide its development."

Unwilling to be left behind, the major radio networks got involved in early TV broadcasting. These broadcasts were considered experimental, rather than regular or commercial, until TV sets went on sale to the public in 1939. The radio networks used these broadcasts to test and improve their equipment and programming. CBS began making experimental television broadcasts in 1931, for example, and by the end of that year fifteen experimental TV stations were on the air. NBC launched its first experimental television broadcasts the following year, helping to increase the total number of experimental TV stations to thirty-eight.

The early experimental TV stations did not broadcast regularly scheduled programs. Instead, the stations usually sent out postcards to inform potential viewers of the time and date of an upcoming program. Most programs were limited to half an hour, because that was how long performers could endure standing under the hot studio lights. Since only a few people had television sets in their homes at this time, the experimental TV stations often set up receivers in public places to demonstrate the new technology.

As the number of experimental television stations grew, the U.S. government decided to step in to regulate the new form of broadcasting. The Communications Act of 1934 created the Federal Communications Commission (FCC) to oversee and regulate all types of communications, including radio, television, telephone, and telegraph. The FCC thus took over the responsibilities of the FRC and also gained new, expanded responsibilities. The Communications Act of 1934 affirmed the public ownership of air waves and free access to broadcast programming that had been granted by the Radio Act of 1927. This arrangement meant that the broadcast networks depended on paid advertisements to finance their operations.

Some critics complained about this system, claiming that it forced networks to create programming with mass appeal (of interest to the majority of people) in order to attract the large audiences required by advertisers. They argued that this limited the potential for special interest and educational programming. Some people recommended that the United States adopt the British system of broadcasting, in which all TV and radio stations were owned by the government and financed through taxes. But the National Association of Broadcasters (NAB), which represented the commercial radio and experimental TV networks, objected to this plan. Its members looked forward to making money from television broadcasting.

Television saw a number of technological improvements during the 1930s. In 1936, for instance, the first coaxial cable was laid between New York City and Philadelphia, Pennsylvania. This type of cable—which consisted of copper wire surrounded by insulation, with an aluminum covering—could be used to transmit TV, telephone, and data signals. Many years later, it would make cable television possible. The first coaxial cables had the capacity to carry one television program or 480 telephone calls (by the 1970s, according to the FCC History Project, improved coaxial cables could carry 200 television programs or 132,000 telephone calls). In 1937, brothers and physicists Russell Varian (1898–1959) and Sigurd Varian (1901–1961) introduced a high-frequency amplifier called the Klystron. Their invention is credited with vastly expanding the frequencies available for TV broadcasting.

A number of broadcasting firsts also occurred during the 1930s. TV equipment produced by both RCA and Philo Farnsworth was used to broadcast the 1936 Olympic Games in Berlin, Germany. The German government set up twenty-five large screens around the city so that residents could watch the events as they occurred. Back in the United States, 1938 saw the first telecast of a Broadway play, Rachel Crothers's *Susan and God*. That year also featured the first live television coverage of an unscheduled news event. An NBC mobile TV camera unit happened to be nearby when a fire broke out on Ward's Island in New York. Since the TV camera was the first on the scene, several newspapers ran photographs of television screens showing footage of the event, rather than pictures of the fire itself.

RCA pushes commercial television

By the mid-1930s, electronic television systems had basically overtaken mechanical systems as the basis for future technological development efforts.

Inventor Philo Farnsworth demonstrates his all-electronic television receiver. © BETTMANN/CORBIS.

Electronic systems could scan images faster than the mechanical systems' rotating disks and thus produced clearer pictures on the TV screen. In 1935, RCA announced a million-dollar research program aimed at producing affordable electronic television systems for American homes.

David Sarnoff announced a three-part strategy to bring TV to the American people. First, RCA planned to mass-produce sets on a factory assembly line to make them affordable for consumers. Second, the company decided to expand the original programs offered on its NBC network to make TV ownership more appealing. Finally, RCA organized a major demonstration of television to expose large numbers of people to the exciting new technology.

Before Sarnoff could follow through on his plans, however, RCA had to clear up some legal complications. RCA researcher Vladimir

Zworykin and independent inventor Philo Farnsworth had developed working electronic television systems independently at around the same time. Both men applied to the U.S. government for patents to protect their inventions. In 1939 the U.S. Patent Office ruled in Farnsworth's favor, granting him the legal rights to produce and market several key components of television systems. After losing the patent lawsuit, RCA was forced to pay Farnsworth a licensing fee, or royalty, in order to use his patented components in its TV sets. Paying this fee marked the first time that RCA, which was famous for its own research and development, had ever paid to use someone else's technology since the company's founding in 1919.

Once RCA gained access to Farnsworth's patents, Sarnoff put his plan into action at the 1939 World's Fair in New York. The RCA pavilion contained twelve television sets representing the various new products the company planned to sell to consumers. Each set featured a small screen that was between five and nine inches across diagonally. Some of the sets had to be hooked up to a separate radio receiver in order to provide sound.

On the first day of the fair, NBC televised opening remarks by President Franklin D. Roosevelt (1882–1945; served 1933–45). This event marked the first presidential speech ever aired on television. It was broadcast to around two hundred TV sets within a 40-mile radius of the exhibition. As the fair continued, NBC broadcast different types of programs each day to appeal to a wide audience, including puppet shows, a circus, sporting events, cooking demonstrations, and coverage of the star-studded world premiere of the movie *Gone with the Wind*.

RCA advertised its World Fair exhibition as the first major public demonstration of television technology. Although this was not strictly true, since experimental stations had been offering programs for a dozen years by this time, huge crowds gathered to see TV for the first time. Visitors to the RCA pavilion could even step in front of a camera and see themselves on a nearby TV set. The memorable exhibit succeeded in creating a wave of public interest in television technology.

Shortly after the World's Fair, NBC switched from experimental to regular programming. It broadcast a regular schedule of dramas, variety shows, sports, and special events over its network of local stations. CBS followed suit in 1941, airing about fifteen hours of shows per week. As the programming options improved, television sets became widely available for the first time. Eight different companies—including RCA, GE,

NBC broadcasting from the 1939 World's Fair. For most attending the fair, this was the first time they had seen TV.
© BETTMANN/CORBIS.

DuMont, and Philco—offered TV sets for sale to the public in 1939. The price of the sets ranged from $200 to $600, or the equivalent of about two months' salary for an average worker. This put the technology out of reach for many consumers, since millions of Americans were still out of work due to the Great Depression. Nevertheless, about five thousand television sets were sold by the end of 1939.

TV screens go black during World War II

While commercial television made its debut, however, most Americans remained glued to their radios. By 1940 there were fifty million radios in use in the United States, and more than 80 percent of American

How TV Works

The technology that makes television sets work remained basically the same for eighty-five years after the invention of television in the 1920s. Although more sophisticated types of display screens became more popular in the early 2000s, such as liquid crystal and plasma screens, most traditional televisions continued to rely on cathode ray tubes—also known as picture tubes—to display images.

A cathode is a filament inside a sealed glass tube, similar to those found in light bulbs. When the filament is heated, it forms a vacuum, or an empty space that does not contain any matter, inside the glass tube. A cathode ray is a stream of electrons, or negatively charged particles, that pour off the cathode into the vacuum. These electrons are attracted to a positively charged terminal called an anode. The anode focuses the electrons into a tight beam and shoots them toward a flat screen at one end of the tube. The inside of the screen is coated in phosphor, a substance that emits light, or glows, when struck by the beam of radiation.

If the beam of electrons were allowed to hit the screen without any interference, it would appear

A cathode ray tube, circa 1927. THE LIBRARY OF CONGRESS.

as a tiny dot in the middle. Instead, the cathode ray tube is wrapped in copper wires called

homes contained at least one radio. Radio proved its place in people's lives the following year, when the United States became involved in World War II (1939–45). On December 7, 1941, Japanese fighter planes launched a surprise attack on the U.S. naval base at Pearl Harbor, Hawaii. The following day, President Roosevelt declared war on Japan and its allies, Germany and Italy, which had been conquering various countries in Europe for the previous two years. Some sixty-two million people—the largest audience ever up to this time—listened to Roosevelt's speech on the radio.

Television development, as well as most broadcasting, came to a halt during World War II. At that time, there were twenty-three television stations in the United States, and about ten thousand TV sets had been sold.

steering coils, which create magnetic fields inside the vacuum. One set of coils deflects the beam vertically, and another set deflects it horizontally. Electronic circuits inside the TV control the movement of the beam. These circuits cause the beam to move across the phosphor-coated screen in high-frequency patterns, effectively painting the screen with an image.

The specific image that appears on the screen depends on the instructions, or video signals, that the TV set receives from a broadcast network, cable box, satellite dish, or VCR/DVD player. A complete video signal consists of three separate parts representing picture, color, and synchronization (a signal that forces the television receiver to lock on in order to reproduce an image correctly). Every TV station is assigned a specific transmitting frequency and operating power. Stations can send their video signals through the air to television antennas (for broadcast networks), through cables to decoder boxes (for cable TV), or through satellites orbiting the earth to satellite dishes (for satellite TV).

The FCC established the first technical standards for scanning and transmitting television images in the United States in 1941, and these standards have been maintained ever since then. "Images are scanned in the television camera and reproduced in the television receiver or monitor 30 times each second," as the Museum of Broadcast Communications described in its publication "Television Technology." "Each full image, or frame, is scanned by dividing the image into 525 horizontal lines, and then sequentially scanning first all the even lines (every other line) from top to bottom creating one field, and then scanning the odd-numbered lines in the same manner creating a second field. The two fields, when combined (interlaced), create one frame. Therefore, 30 complete images or frames, each made up of two fields, are created each second."

In this way, television screens essentially display a series of still frames in rapid succession. In order to turn these still pictures into a moving image, television technology depends on a special ability of the human brain known as persistence of vision. Since the brain is not capable of processing visual images as quickly as 30 times per second, it perceives the succession of still frames on a TV screen as continuous motion.

TV was not yet sophisticated enough to record live events and broadcast them across long distances, so people turned to the radio for war news. Some TV stations tried to provide special wartime programming—such as training for air-raid drills and entertainment for wounded soldiers in Veterans Administration hospitals—but these efforts did not last long. Instead, television manufacturing and broadcasting mostly stopped during the war.

When the United States entered the conflict, the government placed a variety of restrictions on businesses in the interest of national defense. The U.S. military needed a large supply of electronic parts and communications equipment, for instance, so the government converted many TV and radio assembly plants to produce these materials for the war effort. Some RCA researchers began working on a secret military project to use high-frequency radio waves to locate and track moving objects. Their successful efforts became known as radar. The government also prohibited the construction of new radio and TV stations during the war years. U.S. leaders worried that spies might use these facilities to transmit information to the enemy.

Despite such restrictions, a few notable developments in the history of television occurred during the early 1940s. In April 1941, for example, the FCC adopted its first technical standard (a set of basic rules or guidelines for all manufacturers to follow) for commercial television. This standard specified that TV sets produced in the United States would divide images into 525 horizontal lines, each of which would be scanned by the TV camera and reproduced on the TV screen thirty times per second. Despite ongoing technological developments, this standard remained in place for more than fifty years.

The national television broadcasting network structure also began to take shape during the 1940s. Until 1943, NBC operated two separate radio networks, called Red and Blue. The U.S. government claimed that this arrangement unfairly limited competition and filed a lawsuit attempting to force NBC to sell one of its networks. The case went all the way to the U.S. Supreme Court, the highest court in the United States, which ruled against NBC. NBC then sold its Blue network, which became the American Broadcasting Company (ABC). When television started growing in popularity after World War II ended in 1945, the three major radio networks also became television networks. The so-called Big Three of ABC, CBS, and NBC controlled the American broadcasting industry until the rise of cable television in the 1980s.

For More Information

BOOKS

Barnouw, Erik. *Tube of Plenty: The Evolution of American Television.* New York: Oxford University Press, 1975.

Bilby, Kenneth. *The General: David Sarnoff and the Rise of the Communications Industry.* New York: Harper and Row, 1986.

Calabro, Marian. *Zap! A Brief History of TV.* New York: Four Winds Press, 1992.

Fisher, David E., and Marshall Jon Fisher. *Tube: The Invention of Television.* Washington, DC: Counterpoint, 1996.

Hilliard, Robert L., and Michael C. Keith. *The Broadcast Century: A Biography of American Broadcasting.* Boston: Focal Press, 1992.

Schwartz, Evan I. *The Last Lone Inventor: A Tale of Genius, Deceit, and the Birth of Television.* New York: HarperCollins, 2002.

Stashower, Daniel. *The Boy Genius and the Mogul: The Untold Story of Television.* New York: Broadway Books, 2002.

WEB SITES

Bellis, Mary. "Television History." http://inventors.about.com/library/inventors/bltelevision.htm (accessed on June 5, 2006).

Brain, Marshall. "How Television Works." *How Stuff Works.* http://www.howstuffworks.com/tv.htm (accessed on June 5, 2006).

Couzens, Michael. "United States: Networks." *Museum of Broadcast Communications.* http://www.museum.tv/archives/etv/U/htmlU/unitedstatesn/unitedstatesn.htm (accessed on June 5, 2006).

"The FCC History Project: Historical Periods in Television Technology." *Federal Communications Commission.* http://www.fcc.gov/omd/history/tv (accessed on June 5, 2006).

"50th Anniversary of the Wonderful World of Color," March 11, 2004. *U.S. Census Bureau.* http://www.census.gov (accessed on June 5, 2006).

"Pioneers of TV Technology." http://members.aol.com/aj2x/PIONRS.htm (accessed on June 5, 2006).

Runyon, Steve. "Television Technology." *Museum of Broadcast Communications.* http://www.museum.tv/archives/etv/T/htmlT/televisionte/televisionte.htm (accessed on June 5, 2006).

"Television History: The First 75 Years." http://www.tvhistory.tv/timeline2.htm (accessed on June 5, 2006).

2

Improvements in Television Technology

Although television sets first became available to the American people in the late 1930s, sales did not really begin to take off until after World War II ended in 1945. The following year, industry leader RCA (Radio Corporation of America) introduced the 630-TS set, a black-and-white model with a ten-inch screen. RCA sold ten thousand units in the first year, at a price of $385 each. In 1947 sales jumped to two hundred thousand units. In fact, the 630-TS became so popular that it was often referred to as the "Model T" of television (after the hugely successful early Ford automobile, which brought car ownership to many people).

The American television industry grew rapidly during the postwar years. TV ownership increased from 10 percent of American homes in 1950 to 67 percent in 1955, then reached 87 percent in 1960 and 94 percent in 1965. The number of commercial television stations grew rapidly as well—from nine immediately after the war ended in 1945 to five hundred by 1960. Continuing improvements in television technology—including the development of color TV, the use of satellite transmission systems, the invention of videotape technology, and the introduction of high-definition TV—helped fuel this remarkable growth.

Color TV makes its debut

After electronic systems overtook mechanical systems to become the television technology of choice, the next major technical challenge involved developing color TV sets. The Scottish inventor John Logie Baird (1888–1946) demonstrated the first color television as early as 1928. His mechanical system used a spinning disk with three colored filters on it. The disk rotated behind the TV screen, and the filters corresponded with special gas-filled cells that lit up to provide colors for viewers. The following year, Bell Laboratories, a communications research company, demonstrated the first color television system in the

United States. Like Baird's invention, it was a mechanical system that displayed a crude image on a screen the size of a postage stamp.

The first real breakthrough in color television technology took place shortly before the United States entered World War II (1939–45) in 1941. The main figure behind the development of color TV was Peter Goldmark (1906–1977), an engineer who worked for the Columbia Broadcasting System (CBS). CBS had been created in 1927 through the merger of two entertainment companies. Under the leadership of William S. Paley (1901–1990), CBS grew into a strong radio network by the mid-1930s. Around this time, Goldmark talked Paley into starting a small research department at CBS to focus on the emerging technology of television.

Goldmark first became interested in adding color to television in early 1940, when he saw the blockbuster movie *Gone with the Wind*. "For me it was a uniquely exhilarating experience, not because of the performers or the story, but because it was the first color movie I had seen, and the color was magnificent," he recalled in *Tube: The Invention of Television*. "I could hardly think of going back to the phosphor images of regular black-and-white television. All through the long, four-hour movie I was obsessed with the thought of applying color to television."

Upon returning to his lab at CBS, Goldmark spent the next six months working feverishly to develop a color television system. The method he came up with became known as a "field-sequential" color system. It involved two spinning wheels with red, blue, and green filters— one behind the lens of a TV camera and one in front of the cathode ray tube inside a TV set. The spinning wheel in the camera scanned the image in color, and the spinning wheel in the receiver reproduced the colors in sequence as they appeared in the original scene. In effect, the color TV set painted a black-and-white image in three colors in rapid succession. Goldmark's color system was a combination of mechanical and electronic TV systems because it used a mechanical spinning wheel to insert color into an electronic television system.

Goldmark had perfected his color television system by August 1940. That month, CBS sent him as a representative to the National Television System Committee (NTSC). This group of scientists and engineers studied television technology and made recommendations to help the Federal Communications Commission (FCC) establish national standards. (The FCC, a government agency, was created in 1934 to oversee and regulate all types of communications, including radio, television, telephone, and telegraph.) Since black-and-white electronic television systems had recently been perfected, the FCC was eager to set rules to guide manufacturers and broadcasters.

As the NTSC debated the benefits of various black-and-white systems, Goldmark got upset. He believed that his color television system was far superior to any existing black-and-white technology, so he felt it was pointless to spend a lot of time discussing black-and-white TV standards. He finally stood up and told the group that he had perfected color television broadcasting. "I calmly announced that we could transmit pictures in color, and I invited the assemblage to a demonstration in the CBS laboratory of a broadcast from the Chrysler Building [in New York City]," Goldmark remembered in his book *Maverick Inventor: My Turbulent Years at CBS*. NTSC attendees were eager to see Goldmark's technology.

Goldmark's demonstration impressed representatives of the FCC. According to *Tube: The Invention of Television,* seeing the CBS color system prompted FCC Chairman Lawrence Fly to rethink issuing black-and-white standards. "If we can start television off as a color proposition, instead of a black-and-white show, it will have a greater acceptance with the public," he declared. Although the FCC recognized the potential benefits of the CBS system, it ultimately decided that color television required further testing. When the FCC issued its first technical standards for commercial television broadcasting in April 1941, the rules only addressed black-and-white television systems. The FCC did allow CBS to begin experimental color broadcasts, but further development of the technology was suspended during World War II.

A "color war" pits RCA against CBS

David Sarnoff (1891–1971), the powerful president of RCA, had watched the development and testing of Goldmark's color television system with great interest. RCA had invested a great deal of time and money in developing black-and-white television systems and taking control of TV manufacturing. As soon as the ban on TV manufacturing was lifted following World War II, RCA emerged as the leading producer of black-and-white television sets in the United States. In fact, the company controlled 80 percent of the market. Sarnoff realized that his company stood to lose a fortune in sales if the FCC approved the CBS color system for commercial production.

In 1946 CBS invited FCC representatives to a formal demonstration of the Goldmark color system and once again asked for it to be adopted as a commercial standard. The new FCC chairman, Charles Denny,

CBS hosted many public demonstrations of color television in 1950, as shown here, in the hope of gaining positive feedback about the new technology. © BETTMANN/CORBIS.

initially seemed as impressed with the system as Lawrence Fly had been in 1940. But Sarnoff and RCA immediately began working to turn the FCC and the public against the CBS color television system. Sarnoff argued that Goldmark's system relied upon lesser quality mechanical technology that RCA and other TV manufacturers had discarded years earlier. According to Kenneth Bilby in *The General: David Sarnoff and the Rise of the Communications Industry*, Sarnoff claimed that adopting the CBS system as a technical standard would "set back the cause of our technology by a generation." He also declared that "RCA will never allow this counterfeit scheme [false plan] to be foisted on the American people." Sarnoff requested that the FCC wait until an all-electronic color TV system could be perfected before adopting a color standard.

As sales of RCA's black-and-white TV sets grew rapidly during the postwar years, Sarnoff added another argument against the CBS color system. He pointed out that it was incompatible, or did not work properly, with the growing number of black-and-white sets on the market. He meant that anyone who had already purchased a black-and-white set—and 250,000 people had done so by the end of 1947—would see nothing but static during color broadcasts. Goldmark tried to overcome this argument by creating a converter that could be attached to black-and-white sets to allow them to receive color signals. CBS also took out advertisements telling consumers to wait for color to become available before purchasing a television set.

Due in part to Sarnoff's objections, in 1947 the FCC once again decided to postpone the adoption of a color television standard. The FCC claimed that adopting an incompatible color standard would place an unfair burden on the growing number of consumers who had already purchased black-and-white TV sets. If they wanted to receive color broadcasts on their existing sets, they would have to pay for converter units or expensive modifications. The FCC also claimed that it was trying to protect broadcasters with its decision. If television networks chose to broadcast in color, the FCC commissioners argued, they would lose the portion of the viewing audience that had not yet converted to color receivers. Finally, the FCC noted that RCA and several other competitors were working on experimental electronic color TV systems that would be compatible with existing black-and-white systems.

Goldmark and CBS were understandably upset with the FCC's decision. After all, it allowed RCA to rush ahead with its production of black-and-white sets and thus limit the future market for color televisions. CBS executives became even angrier six months later, when Charles Denny resigned as chairman of the FCC to take a job as vice president and general counsel for NBC, the broadcasting arm of RCA. CBS claimed that Denny's job change indicated that RCA had bribed him in order to gain favorable FCC decisions. But Denny and RCA denied the charges.

CBS wins a temporary victory

In 1949 Goldmark used an American Medical Association conference to demonstrate his color television system to the public. CBS set up a number of TV sets at the convention center in Atlantic City, New Jersey, and broadcast live surgical procedures from a nearby hospital. An estimated fifteen thousand people witnessed the demonstration, and a fair number of them passed out at the sight of the bright red blood. "We began to measure the impact of our television shows by the number of faintings we could count," Goldmark noted in *Maverick Inventor.* The success of these broadcasts created a growing public demand for access to color television technology. Legislators heard the call and began pressuring the FCC to remove the barriers keeping color TV from the American people.

Later that year, CBS once again petitioned the FCC to adopt its color television system as the technical standard for the United States. To help make its case, CBS arranged for a side-by-side test against RCA's best electronic color system, which was still in development at that time. The CBS system clearly outperformed RCA's system in the test. As cited in *Tube: The Invention of Television,* even Sarnoff admitted that, with the experimental RCA system, "The monkeys were green, the bananas were blue, and everybody had a good laugh." But Sarnoff claimed that RCA's scientists were on the verge of perfecting electronic color television, and he argued that the mechanical CBS system was inferior technology. "You are being urged to build a highway to accommodate the horse and buggy when already the self-propelled vehicle is in existence," he warned the commission.

Thanks to the test results and the increasing political pressure, however, CBS finally managed to convince the FCC that adopting its color system was in the public interest. The FCC established Goldmark's system as the color standard in 1950 and authorized commercial production of color TV sets to begin immediately. RCA objected to the decision, and appealed it all the way to the U.S. Supreme Court, the highest court in the United States. When the Court upheld the FCC's decision in 1951, it marked an important victory for CBS. "We had taken on the great Sarnoff, the king of Radio City, and won," Goldmark stated in *Maverick Inventor.*

CBS launched a regular schedule of color broadcasts in June 1951. The first program, called *Premiere,* featured Ed Sullivan and several other well-known entertainers. Unfortunately for CBS, almost no one saw the show. Of the twelve million TV sets in American homes at that time, only about two dozen could receive color broadcasts. CBS soon found that there was very little it could do about the lack of color TV receivers. CBS had come to prominence as a radio network, and it did not have the capacity to manufacture television sets. To complicate matters, the United States was involved in the Korean War (1950–53) at this

TV executives gather for the first color TV broadcast by CBS, June 1951. From left to right are: Frank Stanton, president of CBS; Arthur Godfrey, media host; William S. Paley, CBS chairman; and Newton Minow, FCC chairman. © BETTMANN/CORBIS.

time, so most of the nation's manufacturing plants were dedicated to making military equipment. As a result, CBS faced a long and expensive battle to produce a profitable line of color television sets. In October 1951 CBS was forced to discontinue its color broadcasts due to the limited number of viewers who could watch them.

Color TV slowly gains acceptance

In the meantime, Sarnoff became committed to developing a workable electronic color television system. He ordered RCA's engineers to spend as much time and money as necessary to perfect the technology. In 1951, shortly after the Supreme Court ruled in favor of CBS, RCA unveiled the result of this effort: an all-electronic color television system

Electronic Color TV

Color television sets function in a very similar way to black-and-white sets, with a few important differences. Instead of a single electron beam within the cathode ray picture tube, for instance, a color TV set has three electron beams—one red, one green, and one blue. These beams move across the inside of the screen at the same time. Instead of a single sheet of phosphor that glows when struck by the electrons, the screen of a color TV set is coated with red, green, and blue phosphors arranged in a pattern of hundreds of thousands of tiny dots. As the three electron beams move across the screen and paint it with an image, the beam of each color strikes the phosphor dots of the same color, causing them to glow. If a portion of the picture was red, for example, then the red beam excites the red phosphor dots in that area of the screen.

The color TV camera also differs from a black-and-white one. When a color TV camera scans an image, it separates the light reflected off that image into its three color components before turning the information into electrical signals. A color TV signal is the same as a black-and-white signal except that it contains an additional element called chrominance. Black-and-white television sets simply ignore this part of the signal, while color TV sets use it to determine how to fire the three colored electron beams at the screen. This feature of electronic color television signals allows them to be viewed on older black-and-white sets, making the two systems compatible, or able to work together properly.

that was compatible with existing black-and-white broadcast standards (see sidebar "Electronic Color TV"). When RCA demonstrated the new system for the media, several reporters expressed the opinion that the FCC had made a terrible mistake by approving the CBS color system. As noted in *Tube: The Invention of Television*, Jack Gould of the *New York Times* wrote that RCA's successful development of electronic color TV "put the FCC on a spot which is certain to become controversial and embarrassing."

Both CBS and RCA put the development of color television on hold during the last two years of the Korean War. By the time the war ended in 1953, American consumers had purchased twenty-three million black-and-white TV sets. At this point, CBS gave up trying to manufacture its color system. CBS President William S. Paley decided that the large number of incompatible black-and-white sets in U.S. households would prevent Goldmark's mechanical color system from ever gaining a hold in the market. Later that year, the FCC reversed its earlier decision and established RCA's electronic color system as the commercial standard.

RCA began selling its all-electronic color TV sets to the public in 1954. Sarnoff predicted that sales would reach seventy-five thousand units in the first year, but only a few thousand of the sets actually sold. These figures prompted *Time* magazine to declare color television a "resounding industrial flop." American consumers were slow to accept color TV technology for a number of reasons. Prices of color sets were significantly higher than black-and-white sets, while the color screens were much smaller. Consumers often found it difficult to adjust the sets for proper color reception, and the sets required more maintenance than the time-tested black-and-white models. In addition, the public found little reason to buy color TV sets

The sales of color televisions were slow at first, but by 1967 most television broadcasts were in color, and by 1972 half of the TV sets in American homes were color. © H. ARMSTRONG ROBERTS/CORBIS.

because the major broadcast networks did not offer much color programming in the early years. For instance, CBS offered only eight hundred hours of color programming in all of 1965, while ABC provided only six hundred hours.

NBC offered more color programming than the other major networks because it wanted to help its parent company, RCA, sell color TV sets. One of the first hit programs to be broadcast in color was *Walt Disney's Wonderful World of Color,* which began airing on NBC in 1960. The show's success helped increase demand for color TV sets. After spending $130 million on product development and marketing, RCA announced that it had earned a profit on its color systems for the first time that year. By 1967 most television broadcasts were in color, and by 1972 half of the TV sets in American homes were color.

Improvements in TV transmission systems

Throughout the battle over the development of color television systems, scientists and engineers continued to improve upon broadcast technology. In 1945, for example, the Western Union telegraph company introduced the first experimental microwave relay system. This system consisted of a series of towers that relayed radio wave signals through the air between New York City and Philadelphia, Pennsylvania. Installing towers every few miles to carry broadcast signals cost considerably less than burying miles of coaxial cable to connect distant locations. (Coaxial cable—which consisted of copper wire surrounded by insulation, with an aluminum covering—could be used to transmit TV, telephone, and data signals.) As a result, microwave relay systems quickly grew in popularity, until by the 1970s they were used to carry most television broadcasts.

The birth of cable television In 1948, as the major broadcast networks were busy starting television stations in large cities across the country, some rural communities began testing cable television. Since the FCC limited the number of television stations it licensed, most stations were concentrated in cities with large populations. This strategy allowed the stations to reach more viewers with their broadcasts and thus attract more money for advertisers. One negative consequence, however, was that the residents of many rural areas did not enjoy good network TV reception. To address this problem the idea arose to run cables from the rural areas to television stations in nearby large cities.

Two of the first communities to test cable television transmission systems were the mountainous cities of Lansford, Pennsylvania, and Astoria, Oregon. Unlike the cable TV systems available in the 2000s, the pioneer cable providers did not offer a wide assortment of different channels. Instead, they mainly re-transmitted signals from the broadcast networks so that rural residents could get better reception. Cable television service grew slowly until the 1960s, when increasing numbers of local providers appeared. In 1960 there were 640 cable TV systems nationwide, with 650,000 subscribers. By 1970 these figures had increased to nearly 2,500 cable systems with 4.5 million subscribers.

The major broadcast networks began pushing the FCC to regulate, or make rules to control, cable television as early as the mid-1950s.

At first, however, the commissioners claimed that they did not have the authority to regulate cable systems since the technology did not use the air waves. In 1962, however, the FCC reconsidered and claimed jurisdiction (authority or command) over cable providers. The commissioners decided that they did have the authority to regulate cable TV because it had the capacity to affect broadcast networks.

Satellite broadcasting Another significant development in the transmission of television signals took place in 1962, with the world's first satellite broadcast of a TV program. Satellites are like giant antennas that orbit around Earth and can be used to relay communications signals. The development of satellite television capability grew out of an agreement between two American communications companies (AT&T and Bell Labs), the National Aeronautics and Space Administration (NASA), the British Post Office, and the French National Post Office. These institutions led an international effort to develop, launch, and transmit signals using telecommunications satellites. The first satellite, called TELSTAR, was launched into orbit around Earth from the Kennedy Space Center. The following day saw the first live television program ever transmitted across the Atlantic Ocean, between Andover, Maryland, and Pleumeur-Bodou, France.

The introduction of satellite technology marked a major development in television history. Satellite transmission made it possible for American TV viewers to see events elsewhere in the world as they occurred. Before this time, it could take days or even weeks for people in the United States to learn about events in distant countries. Some historians claim that satellite transmission of television signals helped increase Americans' understanding of other nations and cultures. It certainly enabled Americans to witness exciting and momentous events in their nation's history as they happened. In 1969, for example, an estimated 600 million people around the world watched live via satellite as American astronaut Neil Armstrong (1930–) became the first human being to set foot upon the Moon.

Fiber-optic cable Another major development in the delivery of television signals came in 1970, when a group of researchers for the Corning chemical company invented fiber-optic cable. This type of cable consists of clear rods of glass or plastic. They transmit TV signals or other types of information using rapid pulses of light. Fiber-optic cable can carry sixty-five thousand times more information than traditional copper wires.

The technology led to significant improvements in the delivery of television programming to American households.

Impact of videotape technology

Meanwhile, the process of creating television programs also changed technologically. In 1956 a company called Ampex introduced the videotape recorder (VTR). Up to this time, most television programs were broadcast live, as they happened. The only way to preserve video images for later viewing was through a process called kinescope recording, in which a special movie camera recorded what was displayed on a television monitor. Kinescopes were a kind of film, and they required several hours to develop. In contrast, the VTR captured live images directly from

TV cameras, converted them into electrical signals, and saved them onto reels of magnetic tape. The broadcast industry immediately recognized the VTR as vastly superior to the kinescope film system that had been used to record television programs. Videotape technology also provided much better visual and audio quality on home television sets.

The introduction of videotape also led to a shift in the relationship between broadcast networks and the advertisers who sponsored programs. Before the mid-1950s, the sponsor of a television program usually developed and produced that program. This gave advertisers a great deal of control over the content of TV programming. The sponsor could approve the script, select the actors, and even insert positive messages about its products into the stories.

When sponsors produced programs, they usually were broadcast live from network studios in New York City. Once videotape technology became available, however, television programs could be recorded almost anywhere. Within a few years, most of the artistic and technical parts of the TV industry moved to California in order to take advantage of the film talent and production expertise in Hollywood. The role of corporate sponsors gradually decreased, and the networks gained the power to develop their own programming.

VCRs make their debut

Nearly two decades later, videotape technology once again led to important changes in the television industry. In 1972, the Phillips Corporation introduced the first video cassette recorder (VCR) for TV viewers to use at home. VCRs allowed viewers to record television programs for later viewing. They used magnetic videotape enclosed in a plastic cassette. Competing companies soon offered similar machines that used cassettes of different shapes and sizes. In 1976, for instance, Sony introduced the Betamax format of home VCR. The following year, RCA released its VHS format VCR, which became the standard that is still used in the 2000s.

The earliest VCRs were large, expensive, and the subject of serious debate. In fact, shortly after home videotaping technology became available, several major Hollywood movie studios joined in a lawsuit, or court case, against the companies that manufactured the machines. The studios argued that VCRs should be outlawed because their main purpose was making illegal copies of television shows and movies. The studios felt that people who used home VCRs to tape movies were stealing

The VCR, shown here in between a cable box and a DVD player, allows the viewer to record a TV program for later viewing. PHOTO BY KELLY A. QUIN. REPRODUCED BY PERMISSION OF KELLY A. QUIN.

copyrighted material (a copyright is a form of legal protection for creative works—including books, pictures, music, films, and software—that prevents others from using the works without the creators' permission). The studios worried that widespread use of VCRs would reduce the income they earned from their movies.

The legal dispute over VCRs resulted in *Sony Corporation v. Universal City Studios* (more commonly known as the Betamax case), which went all the way to the U.S. Supreme Court. In 1984 the Court ruled in favor of Sony, the VCR manufacturer. The justices said that using a VCR to tape a television program or movie did not violate the studios' copyright protection, as long as the tape was intended for personal use at home rather than for commercial (moneymaking) purposes. As soon as it became clear that home VCR use was legal, sales of VCRs increased sharply.

As it turned out, VCRs did not cause harm to the movie industry. In fact, the popularity of home video actually led to an overall increase in income for the movie studios. "The studios have come to enjoy greater revenue from cassette sales and rentals than from theatrical exhibition, and must look back in wonder at their temporary insanity when the player-recorders first were sighted in North America," Michael Couzens explained in the Museum of Broadcast Communications publication *Networks*.

The impact of home VCR use on the broadcast TV networks has not been as positive as it has been on the movie industry. The most frequent use of the VCR draws viewers away from network television to watch movies that played in theaters. Many people also use their VCRs to record television programs for later viewing. When they watch these programs, however, they often use the VCR's fast-forward feature to skip the commercials. As of the early 2000s, the networks have been allowed to count the viewers who record programs in their audience totals. These figures are used to determine the rates networks can charge companies to advertise on certain programs. The larger the audience for a program, the higher the rates a network can charge for commercial time during that program. If studies continue to show that VCR users bypass commercials, however, advertisers may demand changes in the way audience numbers are calculated.

Improvements in picture and sound quality

By the turn of the twenty-first century, most television sets still worked on the same principles as the original sets that were invented in the 1930s. As described in *Tube,* both early and modern television systems "scan an image with a beam of electrons to create an electrical signal, and then re-create the image at the receiver by turning that signal back into an electron beam and bombarding a fluorescent screen." Despite using the same basic technology, however, television sets still underwent a number of technical improvements over the years. For instance, the first wireless TV remote control, a device that allows viewers to change channels from their seats, was introduced by Zenith in 1957. This futuristic technology, called the Space Commander, represented a vast improvement over earlier models, which were connected to the TV set by wires and did not function properly in direct sunlight.

The audio portion of television systems also improved over the years. The FCC authorized multichannel TV sound broadcasts for the first time in 1984. This meant that broadcasters could separate the sound portion of programs into different audio signals to create a more natural listening experience for people at home. Almost immediately afterward, new TV sets flooded into appliance stores offering stereophonic sound. Better known as stereo, this technology reproduced sound using two independent audio channels, which gave viewers the impression that the sounds on television programs came from various directions. The national television networks began broadcasting in stereo at this time, and within two years stereo TV broadcasts were available in all major U.S. population areas. In 1987, television sound improved further with the introduction of the Dolby noise reduction system for TV sets. This technology separated out high-frequency sounds, which could not be heard well over background noise on regular TV sets, and restored them to their proper balance with other parts of the audio signal. Again, viewers at home benefited from more pleasant and natural sound when watching television programs.

High-definition television Perhaps the most significant improvement in picture quality came with the development of high-definition television (HDTV). The first HDTV systems were introduced in Japan in the 1980s. These systems marked a major improvement in the visual quality available on a television screen. In order to be scanned by a TV camera and reproduced on a TV screen, an image is divided into horizontal lines. The American technical standard, which was established by the FCC in 1941, dictates that TV screens have 525 lines. The HDTV systems developed in Japan featured more than twice as many lines on a screen, allowing for a much sharper picture.

In 1987 the Japanese national broadcasting company, NHK, demonstrated a 1,125-line HDTV system in the United States. The remarkable picture quality impressed the FCC, which soon launched a competition to create an American HDTV system. A number of American electronics firms joined in the race to develop the new technology. The FCC expected all of the proposed HDTV systems to be compatible with the existing U.S. broadcasting system, which used an analog signal (continuous, measurable electronic impulses carried on radio waves). Under this system, every television channel was allowed a certain amount of space on the airwaves—6 megahertz (MHz) of frequency bandwidth—to broadcast its signal. A standard-definition TV picture fit into this space, or bandwidth, but the Japanese high-definition picture did not: it required 20 MHz of bandwidth. The FCC felt that the U.S. airwaves were too crowded to allow TV stations to expand their signals for high-definition broadcasting. Instead, the FCC wanted to find a way to squeeze more detailed pictures into the existing bandwidth.

The FCC received a number of proposals for adjusting HDTV to analog broadcasting. But then, in 1990, a California-based company called General Instrument (GI) announced that it had developed the world's first all-digital television broadcasting system. Unlike analog signals, which transmit information through continuous, measurable electronic impulses, digital signals turn data into a binary code consisting of long strings of the digits zero and one (for example, 1010100010111). This code can be understood by computers and all other types of digital devices. The main benefit of digital over analog transmission is that it allows a great deal more data to be sent over the same amount of bandwidth. For television signals, this means that digital technology can provide better picture and sound quality, as well as interactive features like program menus and on-demand movies and games.

The engineer who led the development of digital HDTV at General Instrument was Woo Paik, a Korean-born graduate of the Massachusetts Institute of Technology. His team found a way to compress 1,500 megabytes per second (mbps) of information into 6 MHz of bandwidth, which can usually carry only about 20 mbps of data. Their system compares each frame of a visual image and only transmits the parts that move or change. In other words, it provides just enough detail to make the human eye perceive a continuous picture with nothing missing. "Today's analog television system transmits a complete picture frame thirty times a second. But since most of the picture is unchanged from one frame to the next, a lot of redundant [repetitive] information is transmitted," *Tube* explained. "GI's digital system only transmits what changes in the picture, once it has presented a complete frame."

The FCC established technical standards for HDTV in 1994. It also rolled out a plan for the United States to make a gradual switch from analog to digital television broadcasting by 2006, although completion date for the transition was later moved back to 2009. Digital technology is expected to bring many changes to the television industry. It promises to allow networks to broadcast high-definition pictures over regular channels and allow stations to engage in multicasting, which means offering several different programs on a single channel. Digital television sets are also expected to be more interactive, giving viewers greater ability to select, respond to, and even change the content of programs.

For More Information

BOOKS

Barnouw, Erik. *Tube of Plenty: The Evolution of American Television.* New York: Oxford University Press, 1975.

Bilby, Kenneth. *The General: David Sarnoff and the Rise of the Communications Industry.* New York: Harper and Row, 1986.

Fisher, David E., and Marshall Jon Fisher. *Tube: The Invention of Television.* Washington, D.C.: Counterpoint, 1996.

Goldmark, Peter C. *Maverick Inventor: My Turbulent Years at CBS*. New York: Saturday Review Press, 1973.

Hilliard, Robert L., and Michael C. Keith. *The Broadcast Century: A Biography of American Broadcasting*. Boston: Focal Press, 1992.

WEB SITES

"The FCC History Project: Historical Periods in Television Technology." *Federal Communications Commission*. http://www.fcc.gov/omd/history/tv (accessed on June 5, 2006).

3

Growth of the Television Broadcasting Industry

Television signals, like other forms of wireless electronic communication, are carried by radio waves. Radio waves are a form of electromagnetic energy that travel through the air. The waves exist in a range of frequencies (repeating patterns) called the radio spectrum. Because only a limited number of frequencies can be used to carry communication signals, the U.S. government has regulated, or controlled, the use of radio waves since the early 1900s, when the age of electronic communication began.

From the time it was established in 1934, the Federal Communications Commission (FCC) has been the government agency responsible for regulating the broadcasting industry. One of the FCC's stated goals was to use the airwaves to serve the public interest. Although the term "public interest" was never fully defined by the U.S. government, it was generally taken to mean that the broadcast industry had a responsibility to benefit American society by providing informative and educational programming. The FCC also wanted to prevent any individual or corporation from gaining exclusive control of the public airwaves. Toward this end, the FCC established complicated rules for assigning frequencies to various forms of communication and giving out broadcast licenses to individual television stations. But some critics say that FCC regulations actually had the opposite effect, creating a system in which a small number of powerful networks (business organizations that create programs and distribute them to a group of connected local TV stations) controlled television broadcasting.

Early government regulation of broadcasting

The government's first effort to regulate electronic communication over the airwaves came with the Radio Act of 1912. This act allowed the secretary of commerce to issue licenses to people who wished to broadcast signals over radio waves. Telegraph operators were the only ones using the airwaves at this time, though, so the number of useful frequencies was large enough to provide for everyone who applied for a broadcasting license. (Introduced in 1835, the telegraph allowed people to exchange coded messages by transmitting a series of tapping sounds over electrical wires.)

By the 1920s, however, a new form of mass communication called radio was becoming very popular. Recognizing the trend, thousands of people applied for broadcast licenses in hopes of operating radio stations. The airwaves quickly became overcrowded, causing interference between stations broadcasting in the same geographic area. The U.S. Congress responded to this situation by passing the Radio Act of 1927. This act created the Federal Radio Commission (FRC) to regulate the issuing of broadcast licenses.

The act stated that the FRC should consider the "public interest, convenience, and necessity" when allocating, or giving out, frequencies to broadcasters. In the 1920s, large corporations had established complete control over a number of industries, like steel production and automobile manufacturing. The U.S. government wanted to prevent anyone from gaining similar control over the airwaves. In effect, the act granted ownership of the airwaves to the American people and gave broadcasters the right to use this public property through a system of licenses.

The invention of television prompted Congress to pass the Communications Act of 1934. This act updated the Radio Act of 1927 to include television and any other new communication technologies that might emerge. It created the Federal Communications Commission (FCC; see sidebar) and gave it responsibility for supervising all forms of electronic communication, including telephone, telegraph, radio, and television. Although the new agency did not attract a lot of public attention, it immediately assumed an important social role. "From the standpoint of the functioning of the American democracy, the FCC is probably the most important regulatory body in our government because of its impact on communications—the lifeline of democracy," Clark Mollenhoff declared in his introduction to *FCC: The Ups and Downs of Radio–TV Regulation*. The FCC took on the role of ensuring that electronic communications technologies were used to benefit the American people.

Growth of television broadcasting

The American television broadcasting industry officially started in 1941 when the FCC first recognized television as a new medium, or form of communication. The FCC established its first set of technical

The Federal Communications Commission

The Federal Communications Commission (FCC) is an independent government regulatory agency. In its original form, it consisted of seven commissioners, or members, but in 1983 the number was reduced to five. FCC commissioners are appointed by the president of the United States and confirmed, or approved, by the Senate. Each commissioner is appointed to a five-year term, with one serving as the chairman of the commission.

The main functions of the FCC are: making rules to control the broadcasting industry, issuing licenses to individual stations, and settling disputes among broadcasters. "Everyone who transmits any sound or image by radio or television must first obtain a license from the FCC," William B. Ray explained in his book *FCC: The*

Ups and Downs of Radio–TV Regulation. "It is responsible for regulating not only the broadcasting stations but all others as well, including citizens band, amateur, police and fire department, and cellular auto radios, plus many other forms of electronic communication, such as satellites, cable TV systems, and even the garage door opener down the street."

The FCC originally issued broadcast licenses for three-year terms but later extended the terms of radio and television licenses to eight years. Broadcasters who violate, or break, specific FCC regulations can be punished in several ways: they can receive a warning letter; they can be charged with fines; or they may be required to attend official hearings to determine whether their broadcasting licenses should be renewed.

standards for black-and-white television sets at this time, and it also approved the first commercial (profit-seeking) television stations. Television broadcasting was suspended, or stopped temporarily, in December 1941, when the United States entered World War II (1939–45). After the war ended in 1945, however, the television industry entered a period of rapid growth. Over the next three years, the number of commercial television stations on the air increased from 9 to 48, while the number of U.S. cities with TV service increased from 8 to 23.

By 1948 the FCC had issued broadcast licenses to more than one hundred TV stations across the country, and the applications continued to pour in. As many American people rushed to purchase TV sets, many entrepreneurs (people who start and run their own businesses) wanted to start TV stations in order to take advantage of the great new business opportunity television presented. Most of the early stations were concentrated in major cities, which provided a larger audience for programs. Since the airwaves had a limited capacity to carry television signals, however, many of these nearby stations overlapped in their coverage, creating interference (conflict between signals that creates static on TV screens).

A technician works the control panel in 1948 at KRSC.TV, one of the first TV stations to receive a broadcast license in the Seattle, Washington, area. © SEATTLE POST-INTELLIGENCER COLLECTION; MUSEUM OF HISTORY AND INDUSTRY/CORBIS.

Recognizing the problems that were developing, the FCC stopped processing applications for new broadcast licenses in September 1948. The commissioners wanted time to study the interference between stations and develop an orderly system for assigning broadcast licenses. The freeze lasted four years, until 1952. This period gave the FCC time to observe how television broadcasting was developing. New York City and Los Angeles each had seven television stations during this time, while most other major cities had one or two. Still, a number of large cities—including Austin, Texas; Portland, Oregon; Denver, Colorado; and Little Rock, Arkansas—did not yet have TV service.

The FCC and other interested parties all studied the cities where television service was available. They hoped to get an early idea about how television might affect American business and culture. The effects of TV began showing up immediately. For instance, a number of companies saw their sales increase dramatically after they began advertising on television. Hazel Bishop, a small lipstick manufacturer, increased its annual sales from $50,000 to $4.5 million through TV ads. Television also produced cultural changes. As the American people turned more of their attention toward the small screens in their living rooms, they went out less often for entertainment and pleasure. Attendance at movie theaters, sporting events, and nightclubs declined significantly in cities where people could watch television, while attendance remained the same or even increased in other parts of the country where television was not yet available. Restaurants emptied out shortly before prime-time programming (generally between the hours of 8 P.M. and 11 P.M.) came on television, while libraries noted a decline in circulation as people shifted from reading to television viewing.

The FCC establishes a framework

In 1952 the FCC established the basic framework for the American television broadcasting industry. It lifted the freeze on TV station licenses and set new regulations for assigning television channels. The rules allowed all of the entrepreneurs who had received licenses before the ban went into effect to keep them. Thus, immediately after the ban ended, there were 107 television stations broadcasting in 63 markets (see sidebar "The Nation's Largest TV Markets"). By this time, more than 15 million American households had television sets.

When the FCC resumed licensing commercial television stations, it set aside three sections of the airwaves, or bands of frequencies within the radio spectrum, for television channels. The bandwidth from 54 to 88 megahertz (MHZ, a measure of the frequency, or repeating pattern, of radio waves) was reserved for TV channels 2 to 6, and the bandwidth

The Nation's Largest Television Markets

The television broadcasting industry divides the United States into markets, or geographic areas that are served by distinct groups of TV stations. The national television networks are particularly concerned about creating programs that appeal to viewers in the country's largest markets. The size of a certain market is determined by the number of TV households, or homes with TV sets, that can receive broadcasts from the area's principal TV stations. Larger markets provide advertisers with more potential viewers per program than smaller markets.

As of 2000, the top ten television markets in the United States were: New York City (with 6.8 million TV households, or 7 percent of the national total); Los Angeles (with 5 million TV households); Chicago (with 3 million); Philadelphia (2.6 million); and San Francisco (2.6 million). Combined, these five markets account for one-fifth of all TV households in the United States. The next five largest markets, in order of size, are: Boston, Massachusetts; Washington, D.C.; Dallas-Fort Worth, Texas; Detroit, Michigan; and Atlanta, Georgia. Taken together, the top ten U.S. television markets include 29 million households, or one-third of the nation's total TV market.

from 174 to 216 MHZ was set aside for TV channels 7 to 13. FM radio was assigned the bandwidth from 88 to 108 MHZ, so it was carried on frequencies located between TV channels 6 and 7. These portions of the radio spectrum are known as very-high-frequency (VHF) channels. In contrast, the third part of the radio spectrum that was originally set aside for TV channels—from 470 to 890 MHZ for channels 14 through 83—is known as ultra-high-frequency (UHF). VHF channels were technically superior to UHF channels. They sent out a stronger signal that reached a wider area and could be received more clearly by early TV sets.

Every television station that received an operating license from the FCC was assigned a specific transmitting frequency and operating power. A typical television signal requires an amount of space on the airwaves equal to about 6 MHZ of frequency bandwidth. This fact, combined with the relatively small portion of the VHF radio spectrum that the FCC gave to television, limited the number of VHF channels that could be assigned to any geographic area without creating interference. To eliminate interference, as well as to provide television coverage to smaller markets, the FCC typically allowed a maximum of three VHF stations to operate in any large city. Each of these three stations received the 6 MHZ of bandwidth needed to broadcast a television signal.

The FCC soon encountered a problem with its process of allocating, or giving out, broadcast licenses. It turned out that many individuals and companies wanted to operate TV stations in large markets, or geographic areas with large populations, so that their programs would reach bigger audiences. This made it difficult for the FCC to choose which three stations would receive the highly desired VHF channels. The FCC rules established only enough VHF outlets to provide two TV channels to 90 percent of the U.S. population. The remaining 10 percent of the population could receive three VHF channels. After factoring in the 107 existing channels, which were located haphazardly throughout the country, this left few VHF outlets available for new stations.

The FCC attempted to make up for having so few available VHF outlets by allowing other stations to broadcast on UHF channels. This plan, however, presented some problems. "UHF television signals have always been technically inferior to VHF," Besen explained. "For this reason, UHF stations compete under a great handicap with their VHF counterparts [and] often cannot survive in intermixed markets [those with both VHF and UHF stations]." In addition, most of the television sets available during the 1950s were only capable of receiving VHF channels.

A TV antenna, examples of which are shown here, on the roof of a home or other building was necessary in order to better receive the weak signals transmitted by UHF channels. © BETTMANN/CORBIS.

Although UHF converters were available that allowed a TV to receive both UHF and VHF channels, they were expensive and difficult to adjust.

When the licensing freeze was lifted in 1952, the FCC licensed 80 new VHF and 162 UHF stations. The number of VHF channels increased rapidly over the next decade, reaching 458 by 1962. Yet the number of less-desirable UHF channels decreased dramatically during this time, reaching 83 in 1962. Most of the VHF channels were affiliated with powerful national networks, while most of the UHF channels were independent commercial stations (profit-seeking stations that were not related to one of the large networks) or nonprofit educational stations operated by colleges or other organizations.

Hoping to encourage more diversity in TV stations, the U.S. Congress passed the All-Channel Receiver Act in 1962. This act required all TV sets sold in the United States to be able to receive both UHF and VHF channels. It was intended to protect UHF broadcasters and improve their position relative to the networks. Although the three main national networks (ABC, CBS, and NBC) continued to dominate the American television industry for two more decades, the legislation did have a noticeable effect. It helped the number of UHF stations increase to 874 over the next thirty-five years.

Broadcasters form networks

From the beginning of commercial television in the 1950s, the broadcast industry has been dominated by a small number of powerful networks. Television networks are business organizations that create programs and distribute them to a group of affiliated, or connected, local stations. The local stations agree to broadcast the programs according to a uniform schedule designed by the network. Networks arose because radio waves can only carry television signals for a limited distance. Before satellite technology became available, the only way to achieve transmission of a television program across the United States was to turn a large number of local stations into a network.

Another advantage of the network arrangement is that it spreads the cost of creating programs over a large number of affiliated stations. It is significantly cheaper to produce one program and distribute it to many local stations than for every local station to produce its own programs. Networks also help advertisers to reach larger audiences by placing commercials on national broadcasts rather than local programs.

The number of national U.S. television networks that developed was largely determined by FCC regulations. In the early years of television broadcasting, only VHF channels could reach large audiences. Since FCC regulations effectively limited the number of VHF channels in any given market to two or three, that was the number of networks that could establish local affiliate stations in each market. This situation led to the development of three national television networks and made it virtually impossible for a fourth network to be able to compete.

The rise of the three main networks

Sometimes referred to as the Big Three, the main television networks—
ABC, CBS, and NBC—all started out as successful radio networks. In
fact, some of the first television programs were simply video broadcasts
of popular radio shows. One of the nation's largest radio manufacturers,
the Radio Corporation of America (RCA), started the National Broadcasting Corporation (NBC) as a radio network in 1926. NBC eventually
grew into two radio networks, called Red and Blue. RCA played a leading
role in the development of television technology, which put NBC in a
strong position for the start of television broadcasting. Under the leadership of David Sarnoff (1891–1971), NBC made its first experimental TV
broadcast in 1931 and its first regularly scheduled broadcasts in 1943.

The Columbia Broadcasting System (CBS) was formed in 1927
through the merger of United Independent Broadcasters (an organization
that promoted the work of classical musicians) and the Columbia Phono-
graph Company. During its first two years on the air, CBS struggled to
compete against Sarnoff's larger radio network. CBS executives approached one of the network's largest advertisers, Sam Paley, for help.
Paley was the millionaire founder of a Philadelphia cigar company. Although the elder Paley expressed doubts about investing in the network,
his son William S. Paley (1901–1990) talked him into buying CBS. At the
age of twenty-seven, the younger Paley became the president of the network. Over the next few years, William Paley built CBS into a respected
radio network that became nearly as successful as NBC.

In the early years of television, CBS spent a great deal of time and
money developing a color TV system that ultimately failed to sell. As a
result, the network was much slower to apply for broadcast licenses
than NBC. In fact, CBS owned just one TV station until the FCC lifted
its licensing freeze in 1952. Paley then began building a strong group of
local affiliate stations and luring popular radio performers to CBS
programs.

The last of the three major American television networks to form
was the American Broadcasting Corporation (ABC). It came into existence in 1943, after the FCC forced RCA to sell one of its two NBC
radio networks. Edward J. Noble, who made his fortune by creating
Life Savers candy, purchased the Blue network from RCA and renamed
it ABC. As the television age began, ABC struggled to catch up to NBC
and CBS in the number of local affiliates it could claim. Since FCC rules
only ensured that each market would have two VHF stations, ABC found

The DuMont Network—launched by Allen DuMont, pictured, in 1947— could not compete with the Big Three networks and went out of business in 1955. © BETTMANN/CORBIS.

itself shut out of many markets. It finally gained the financial resources it needed to compete in 1953, when the FCC allowed ABC to merge with United Paramount Theaters. The network gradually expanded its reach across the country and used its Hollywood connections to create break-through programming. Still, ABC remained in third place for many years. In fact, the network would not earn its first full-season ratings victory over its rivals until the 1970s.

A fourth network actually existed for the first few years of the television age. It was owned by Allen DuMont (1901–1965), an American engineer who developed some of the technology found in early television sets. DuMont formed his own TV manufacturing company in 1931. Although most TV screens were tiny in those days, he began selling a 14-inch model as early as 1938. DuMont eventually launched his own television network, with commercial broadcasts beginning in 1947. The 1952 FCC regulations that limited the number of VHF stations forced the DuMont Network to go out of business. DuMont tried to convince the FCC to assign a minimum of four VHF stations to each of the country's 140 largest TV markets, but his arguments were unsuccessful. Unable to sign up enough local stations to compete against the Big Three, the DuMont Network went out of business in 1955.

Public concerns about commercial television

From the beginning of commercial television broadcasting, the FCC left decisions about the subject matter of TV programs mostly up to the networks. The Radio Act of 1927 had given the American people control over the airwaves and licensed broadcasters to use airwaves in the public interest. But "public interest" was not fully explained in either the Radio Act of 1927 or the Communications Act of 1934. As a result, the FCC generally allowed broadcasters to establish their own rules to guide program content.

The National Association of Broadcasters (NAB), which included representatives from the three national television networks, adopted a set of guidelines called the Code of Practices for Television Broadcasters in 1951. The code established rules for the networks to follow regarding various issues, including the number of commercials aired per hour of programming. Stations that chose to follow the rules earned the right to display the NAB's Seal of Good Practice.

Over time, though, it became increasingly clear that the code was not effective in regulating the networks' behavior. Advertisers spent nearly a billion dollars per year purchasing commercial time on television programs during the 1950s. As a result, they had a lot of influence over the networks. The advertisers were willing to do whatever was necessary to attract large numbers of viewers to the programs they sponsored. In the mid-1950s, this situation resulted in a major television scandal.

Around this time, televised quiz shows (known today as game shows) were very popular. A number of shows—such as *The $64,000 Question* and *Twenty-One*—became popular by allowing successful contestants to continue appearing for several weeks in order to earn large cash

Charles Van Doren, right, testifies during the quiz show scandal investigation. Van Doren admitted to cheating on the quiz show Twenty-One. HANK WALKER/TIME LIFE PICTURES/GETTY IMAGES.

prizes. By 1957, five of the top ten television programs in the national audience ratings were quiz shows. The following year, however, the news was full of stories about quiz show contestants who claimed that the results of the quiz games were fixed. The charges eventually led to an investigation by the U.S. House of Representatives. In 1959, under questioning by members of Congress, several quiz show winners admitted that the shows' producers had supplied them with answers before they participated in the quiz game. The producers claimed that they did so under pressure from advertisers, who wanted to create drama and reward the contestants who were most popular with viewers.

The 1959 quiz show scandals caused many Americans to lower their opinions of the television networks. Some people openly questioned whether it was a good idea to entrust broadcasting to large corporations that were mainly interested in making money. All three national networks canceled their quiz shows and promised to be honest in the future, but advertisers continued to hold a great deal of influence over TV content. In fact, an FCC study found that 40 percent of all TV stations went over their own set limits on commercials shown per hour of programming. Yet the NAB largely ignored these code violations. It also let stations that were breaking rules continue to display the NAB Seal of Good Practice.

The Fairness Doctrine

Recognizing the growing concerns about commercial television, the U.S. government decided to take steps to ensure that broadcasters truly served the public interest. In 1959 Congress added an amendment to the Communications Act of 1934 that spelled out broadcasters' obligation "to operate in the public interest," and specifically "to afford reasonable opportunity for the discussion of conflicting views on issues of public importance." This law became known as the Fairness Doctrine.

In the case of news and informational programs, the FCC defined "serving the public interest" to mean presenting both sides of controversial issues fairly and accurately. The commissioners wanted to make sure that one point of view did not dominate the airwaves simply because its supporters held more financial or political power than the other side. They saw an important role for the FCC in making sure that less powerful groups, and less popular opinions, were able to gain access to the public airwaves. The Fairness Doctrine required broadcasters to devote a reasonable amount of time to coverage of controversial issues of public importance, and it also required licensees to make an effort to present different, opposing views on those issues. The FCC had the power to revoke the broadcasting license of any radio or television station that did not follow these rules.

The Fairness Doctrine received some criticism. The television networks argued that the government should not intrude into programming decisions. Broadcasters also claimed that they should be allowed to say what they wanted on their stations without the government forcing them to give equal time to opposing viewpoints. In contrast, supporters of the Fairness Doctrine said that the law actually promoted freedom of speech for members of the larger community who held opinions different from those of station owners.

TV advertisements for cigarettes, such as this 1950s commercial for Old Gold cigarettes, were banned from television in 1970. THE LIBRARY OF CONGRESS.

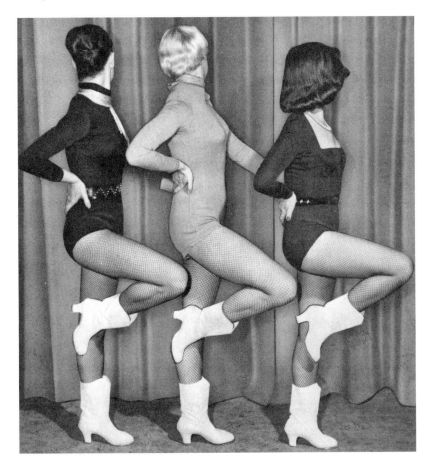

The most famous use of the Fairness Doctrine came in the mid-1960s. A young attorney, John Banzhaf III, sued CBS to force the network to air anti-smoking public service announcements (a type of message that provides viewers with information). Banzhaf argued that since CBS broadcast cigarette commercials, the Fairness Doctrine required it to also show evidence that tobacco use causes lung disease. The FCC agreed with Banzhaf's position and told the networks to begin airing anti-smoking ads. The case went all the way to the U.S. Supreme Court, which ruled in favor of Banzhaf in 1969. In explaining the decision, Justice Warren Burger (1907–1995) agreed that holders of TV station licenses had a responsibility to use their position to benefit the American people: "A broadcaster seeks and is granted the free and exclusive use of a limited and valuable part of the public domain; when he accepts that franchise it is burdened by enforceable public obligations."

The public service announcements proved to be very effective in reducing cigarette smoking. In fact, in 1970 tobacco manufacturers chose not to fight the passage of legislation banning cigarette advertisements from television. The companies decided that they would rather pull their commercials off of television than face an overall decline in cigarette use due to the anti-smoking ads that would have to be aired under the Fairness Doctrine.

Educational television

The effort to make television broadcasters serve the public interest gained strength in 1961, when President John F. Kennedy (1917–1963; served 1961–63) named Newton N. Minow (1926–) as chairman of the FCC. Just a few weeks after his appointment, Minow harshly criticized the poor quality of television programming in a famous speech before the NAB's annual convention. "I invite you to sit down in front of your television set when your station goes on the air and stay without a book, magazine, newspaper, profit-and-loss sheet, or rating book to distract you—and keep your eyes glued to that set until the station signs off," he told the broadcasters, as quoted by Robert L. Hilliard and Michael C. Keith in *The Broadcast Century*. "I can assure you that you will observe a vast wasteland." Minow also warned the broadcasters that their licenses would no longer be renewed without a review, noting that "There is nothing permanent or sacred about a broadcast license." He threatened to take away the broadcast license of any TV station that did not meet its obligation to serve the public interest.

In addition to enforcing FCC rules such as the Fairness Doctrine, Minow made an important contribution to improving the quality of television through his commitment to educational programming. When the FCC had first begun licensing commercial TV stations, it had kept some space on the airwaves for educational stations that did not accept commercial advertisements. Such stations appeared in most large television markets over the next decade. Yet the noncommercial stations struggled to find financial support until Minow took up the cause in the early 1960s. He encouraged the government to support non-commercial stations as a high-quality alternative to commercial network television.

In 1967 Congress passed the Public Broadcasting Act, which created the Corporation for Public Broadcasting to raise funds for educational television stations and programming. The corporation established the Public Broadcasting Service (PBS) to develop educational programs and distribute them to member stations. In this way, PBS functions like a commercial TV network, but member stations pay dues to help fund program development. PBS first appeared in 1970 with twelve hours of programming per week. Three years later, President Richard M. Nixon reduced government funding for the Corporation for Public Broadcasting because he felt that some PBS news programs were unfriendly toward his administration. Since then, most PBS funding has come from individual subscribers, state and local governments, charities, and businesses.

Deregulation of the broadcast industry

Both FCC regulation and network dominance started to decline during the 1980s. Under President Ronald Reagan (1911–2004; served 1981–89), the broadcast industry saw significant deregulation (a reduction in government rules). Reagan strongly believed in limiting the government's role in business. He felt that free competition between companies would provide consumers with more choices at a lower cost. Reagan appointed Mark Fowler as chairman of the FCC in 1981. Fowler immediately began dismantling the system of regulations that the FCC had long used to guide the television industry. He also tried to get rid of the whole idea that broadcasters had a responsibility to serve the public interest in exchange for being allowed to use the public airwaves.

The deregulation of the broadcast industry in the 1980s took a number of different forms. The Communications Act of 1934 set minimum standards to ensure that people who received broadcast licenses possessed good character qualifications. This rule enabled the FCC to reject applications from people who lied or allowed prejudice to cause them to treat others unfairly. In 1985, however, the FCC announced that it would limit its analysis of broadcasters' character to whether applicants had been convicted of a felony, a type of serious crime. This decision allowed people who had been charged with crimes, including fraud and bribery, to hold broadcast licenses as long as they did not have a felony conviction.

Another way that deregulation affected television broadcasting was to eliminate requirements for children's programming. In 1973, the FCC directed broadcasters to air children's programs with educational value as well as entertainment value. It also issued guidelines regarding the number of commercials that could appear per hour of children's programming. In 1985, however, the FCC eliminated these requirements. Although Congress passed a bill that would have reinstated the rules in 1988, Reagan vetoed the legislation. In 1989, the FCC abolished the Fairness Doctrine, which meant that broadcasters no longer had to present controversial issues in a balanced way.

Deregulation also had a significant effect on the ownership of television stations and networks. Faced with increasing competition, many companies in the television industry combined their operations or purchased other companies. In 1986, for instance, a large station group called Capital Cities purchased the ABC network for $3.5 billion. Later that year, RCA and its NBC network were sold to General Electric for $6.3 billion. Similarly, William S. Paley was forced to give up control of CBS to billionaire businessman Laurence Tisch (1923–2003). Within a year of the takeover, Tisch fired two hundred people from the CBS news division. In 1987 CBS dropped to third place in the full-season network ratings for the first time in its history.

The consolidation (merging or grouping together) of the broadcast industry continued in the 1990s, as Westinghouse acquired CBS and Walt Disney Studios purchased Capital Cities ABC. Critics claimed that these changes would create a situation in which a few large companies controlled most parts of the communications and entertainment industries.

Some people watched the effects of deregulation with disbelief. Critics claimed that the quality of programming decreased as the control of television networks passed from early industry leaders to large media corporations that focused primarily on making money. They argued that, without government rules in place, the networks no longer created TV programs with the goal of informing, educating, or inspiring the American people. Instead, they operated with the main goal of attracting large audiences and advertising dollars.

The decline of network power

From the late 1940s until the late 1970s, Big Three network programming dominated viewership. During the 1980s, however, the portion of the television market held by the networks began to decline. In fact, the share of prime-time audiences held by the Big Three decreased from 91 percent in 1978–79, to 75 percent in 1986–87, to 61 percent in 1993–94.

A number of factors contributed to the decline in network audiences. For instance, the introduction of home video cassette recorders (VCRs) and pay-per-view services allowed people to watch theatrical movies on their television sets. In addition, cable and satellite TV services grew

Rupert Murdoch launched the Fox broadcasting network in 1986. ALLAN TANNENBAUM/ TIME LIFE PICTURES/ GETTY IMAGES.

rapidly during this period, reaching more than 50 percent of American homes by 1990. These systems provided viewers with a wide variety of channels that suited their personal interests.

In 1986, the Big Three finally faced competition from a fourth national broadcast network. An Australian publisher named Rupert Murdoch (1931–) purchased a large U.S. station group called Metro Media and combined it with the Twentieth-Century Fox motion picture studio to create the Fox network. Fox started out offering only two nights of programming per week and gradually expanded to a full schedule. Thanks to hit programs such as *The Simpsons* and *The X Files*, Fox soon began defeating the Big Three in key ratings periods. The success of Fox encouraged three more Hollywood movie studios to enter television broadcasting in the 1990s. Warner Brothers launched the WB network, while Universal Studios and Paramount joined forces to form the United Paramount Network (UPN). (The WB network and UPN were scheduled to merge in the fall of 2006, forming a new network called The CW.)

Competition promised to grow even more fierce in the television broadcasting industry following the passage of the Telecommunications Act of 1996. This act marked the first successful government effort to update and improve the Communications Act of 1934. It reduced or eliminated many regulations that had separated various parts of the communications industry—including radio and television broadcasters, cable TV providers, and long-distance telephone companies—in order to increase competition and encourage the development of new services. As the FCC explained on its Web site, "The goal of this new law is to let anyone enter any communications business—to let any communications business compete in any market against any other."

The Telecommunications Act of 1996 reduced the limits on ownership of television stations, for instance, so that any individual or company could purchase multiple stations that, when combined, served up to 35 percent of the U.S. population. The act also extended the terms of radio and television broadcast licenses to eight years and made it easier for stations to renew their licenses. Finally, it allowed local stations to affiliate with more than one network, and it allowed networks to offer new program services.

Supporters of deregulation of the broadcast industry praised the legislation, predicting that it would lead to lower-cost telecommunication services for consumers. But critics claimed that the new rules would not decrease prices and instead would only give giant communications companies more power. In any case, many experts believe that the law will create widespread changes in the television broadcasting industry for many years to come.

For More Information

BOOKS

Baker, William F., and George Dessart. *Down the Tube: An Inside Account of the Failure of American Television*. New York: BasicBooks, 1998.

Barnouw, Erik. *Tube of Plenty: The Evolution of American Television*. New York: Oxford University Press, 1975.

Besen, Stanley, et al. *Misregulating Television: Network Dominance and the FCC*. Chicago: University of Chicago Press, 1984.

Bilby, Kenneth. *The General: David Sarnoff and the Rise of the Communications Industry*. New York: Harper and Row, 1986.

Blumenthal, Howard J., and Oliver R. Goodenough. *This Business of Television*, 2nd ed. New York: Billboard Books, 1998.

Gitlin, Todd. *Inside Prime Time*. New York: Pantheon, 1985.

Hilliard, Robert L., and Michael C. Keith. *The Broadcast Century: A Biography of American Broadcasting.* Boston: Focal Press, 1992.

Paper, Lewis J. *Empire: William S. Paley and the Making of CBS.* New York: St. Martin's Press, 1987.

Ray, William B. *FCC: The Ups and Downs of Radio-TV Regulation.* Ames: Iowa State University Press, 1998.

WEB SITES

Couzens, Michael. "United States: Networks." *Museum of Broadcast Communications.* http://www.museum.tv/archives/etv/U/htmlU/unitedstatesn/unitedstatesn.htm (accessed on June 14, 2006).

"The FCC History Project: Historical Periods in Television Technology." *Federal Communications Commission.* http://www.fcc.gov/omd/history/tv (accessed on June 14, 2006).

Messere, Fritz J. "U.S. Policy: Telecommunications Policy Act of 1996." *Museum of Broadcast Communications.* http://www.museum.tv/archives/etv/U/htmlU/uspolicyt/uspolicyt.htm (accessed on June 14, 2006).

4

The Rise of Cable Television

When television broadcasting got its start in the United States in the 1940s, the broadcast networks sent the electromagnetic signals that carried TV programs exclusively over the airwaves. They built tall towers that broadcast audio (sound) and video (picture) signals through the air to surrounding areas. Viewers used antennas on rooftops or attached to television sets to receive the signals. The main problem with this system of television transmission was that the signals grew weaker as they traveled farther from the towers. In addition, TV networks tended to concentrate their operations in heavily populated urban areas, where their signals would reach the largest number of viewers. As a result, millions of Americans living in rural areas found themselves with either poor TV reception or no access to broadcast television signals at all.

Within a few years of the start of TV broadcasting, creative citizens began experimenting with alternative ways to transmit television signals so that broadcasts would reach small towns and rural areas. The first successful alternative transmission method—originally known as Community Antenna Television (CATV) and later called cable TV—appeared around 1948. For the next thirty years, however, cable TV systems simply delivered existing broadcast network signals to communities that could not receive them over the airwaves. Unlike the extensive services cable TV companies provide in the 2000s, the first systems offered just a few channels and did not create their own programming. According to Ralph Lee Smith in "The Wired Nation," an influential 1970 article about the potential of cable TV, "The original purpose, and still the principal function, of CATV is to provide the viewer with better reception and a larger selection of existing TV stations than he can get from the air."

One of the people credited with inventing cable TV is Robert J. Tarlton. Born in Lansford, Pennsylvania, in 1914, Tarlton opened a radio sales and service shop after graduating from high school. He served overseas as a radio communications expert during World War II, then returned to

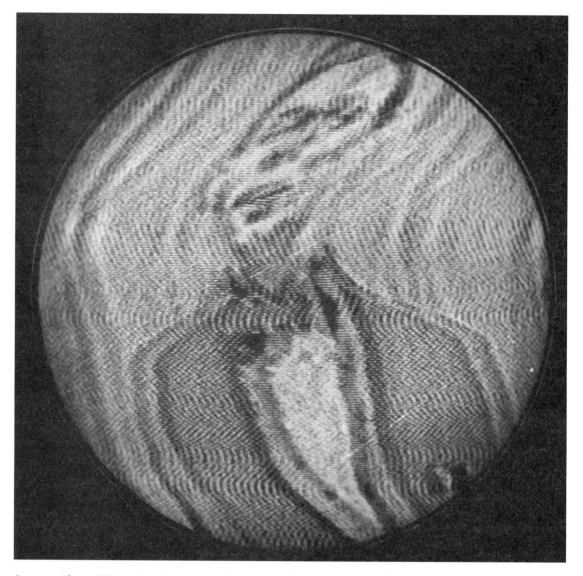

In areas with poor TV reception, pictures were often grainy and hard to see. TONY LINCK/TIME LIFE PICTURES/GETTY IMAGES.

his hometown and added the new technology of television to his business offerings. But Tarlton soon found that no one in Lansford was willing to invest in a TV set because the town had terrible reception. The closest TV stations were located 65 miles away in Philadelphia, and a mountain at the edge of town blocked the already weak signals before they reached residents' homes. Hoping to sell more TV sets, Tarlton convinced some investors to help him build a large antenna on top of the mountain in 1949. This antenna picked up signals from the Philadelphia TV stations,

fed them into an amplifier to return them to full strength, and carried them down into Lansford through coaxial cables. (Coaxial cable—which consisted of copper wire surrounded by insulation, with an aluminum covering—could be used to transmit TV, telephone, and data signals.) In exchange for a $125 installation charge and $3 monthly service fee, Lansford residents got the same quality reception for Philadelphia's three network television channels as residents of the big city.

Other independent businessmen developed similar CATV systems around the same time, including John Walson, a power-company lineman and appliance store owner who built an antenna in the Poconos to serve the residents of Mahanoy City, Pennsylvania; and L. E. (called Ed) Parsons, who erected an antenna on the roof of his apartment building in Astoria, Oregon, so that his wife could watch TV. Cable TV systems spread gradually across the rural United States during the 1950s and 1960s. In 1950 there were 70 systems providing service to 14,000 subscribers; by 1960 these totals had increased to 640 systems with 650,000 subscribers.

The FCC steps in

The growth of cable TV alarmed the main broadcast television networks— ABC, CBS, and NBC—which had almost totally controlled American TV audiences from the time television technology was first introduced in the 1940s. The networks expressed concerns about the impact of cable from the beginning. They argued that cable TV systems stole their programming by intercepting their signals and then charged subscribers a fee for delivering them. Network complaints got more extreme when various cable systems began using new technology to bring in television signals from distant cities. This development changed the nature of cable services from simply improving the reception of local TV stations to providing viewers with new program options from distant stations.

The three major networks urged the Federal Communications Commission (FCC) to impose rules and restrictions on cable operators. (The FCC, a government agency, was created in 1934 to oversee and regulate all types of communications, including radio, television, telephone, and telegraph.) For many years after the invention of cable TV, though, the FCC was unwilling to step in and make rules to control the technology. The Communication Act of 1934 only allowed the agency to regulate communication technologies that operated over the airwaves, such as radio. Cable, by contrast, was a hybrid (combination) communication system that used fixed cables to deliver over-the-air signals. In 1956 the FCC ruled that it did not have the authority to regulate cable since the technology did not use the airwaves. By 1962, however, the agency reconsidered this decision. The FCC asserted its authority over cable TV because cable had an impact on broadcast television—an industry that the agency was required to support and promote.

The FCC issued its first official guidelines regarding cable television in a 1965 document titled "First Cable Television Report and Order." The following year the agency issued its "Second Cable Television Report and Order." Taken together, these two sets of regulations successfully

limited cable TV systems to small, local markets that were not being served by the major broadcast networks. The regulations included "must carry" rules, which required cable operators to carry local broadcast signals, and "nonduplication" rules, which prohibited cable operators from bringing in programs from distant stations that were already available through local stations. The FCC commissioners believed that these rules were necessary in order to allow the broadcast networks to maintain their control over national TV audiences.

In 1969 the FCC issued new regulations that further limited the growth of cable TV. These rules prevented cable TV systems from entering urban markets, where they would compete directly with the broadcast networks. The rules also tied cable operators more closely to rural communities by requiring them to provide channels for local residents to air their own programming. Finally, the FCC placed limits on the content of cable programming in order to protect broadcasters. For instance, cable systems were forbidden to show movies that were less than ten years old or sporting events that had occurred within the past five years.

Despite the FCC's efforts, however, cable television continued to grow. By 1970 there were 2,500 cable TV systems in the United States serving 4.5 million subscribers. Around this time, various community groups and educational institutions began complaining about the limitations the government had placed on cable TV. They argued that cable had the potential to bring new social, educational, and entertainment services to the American people. They claimed that the FCC regulations, in protecting the interests of the powerful broadcast networks, actually harmed the public interest by preventing cable from reaching its potential.

Cable enters a growth phase

During the mid-1970s the FCC faced increasing public pressure to revise its rules limiting the growth of cable TV. This pressure came from cable customers who wanted access to appealing new channels and services that were then being developed. The FCC started loosening the restrictions on cable TV in 1972, when it issued another "Cable Television Report and Order" that allowed cable operators to bring in distant television signals. But the agency continued to restrict cable systems from providing service to the nation's top TV markets or airing recent programs.

Following the FCC's 1972 order, the information company Time Inc. launched a regional cable network called Home Box Office (HBO). HBO started out offering movies and special-event programming to markets on the East Coast on a pay-per-view basis. In 1975 the FCC issued a decision that allowed satellites (antennas that orbit Earth and relay communication signals over large areas) to be used for TV broadcasting. Under the leadership of Gerald Levin (1937–), HBO immediately took advantage of the ruling and began distributing its signal nationwide via satellite. HBO provided dozens of local cable operators across the country with dish-shaped antennas 30 feet (9 meters) wide in order to receive the signal. The local cable systems then delivered HBO programs to their subscribers through traditional cable lines. HBO demonstrated the power of satellite technology by broadcasting the 1975 world heavyweight boxing title match between Muhammad Ali (1942–) and Joe Frazier (1944–)

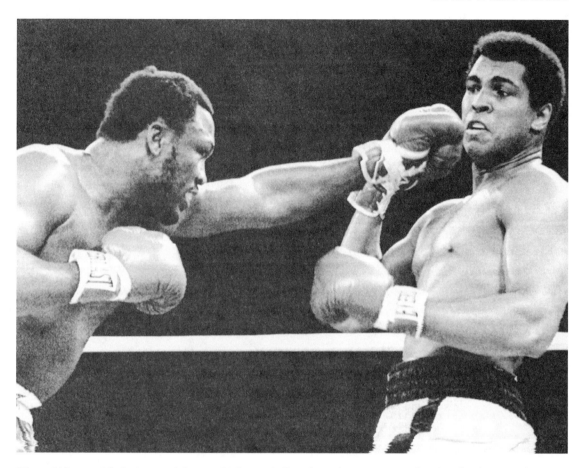

The world heavyweight boxing match between Muhammad Ali, right, and Joe Frazier was broadcast live from Manila, Philippines, to the United States using satellite technology. © BETTMANN/CORBIS.

live from Manila, in the Philippines. This event marked the first time that American television viewers were able to watch a major sporting event as it occurred halfway around the world.

With the success of the Ali–Frazier broadcast, HBO filed a lawsuit against the FCC in order to force the agency to give cable operators greater access to current programming. The federal district court in Washington, D.C., that heard the case of *HBO v. FCC* issued its decision in 1977. It ruled that the FCC was not justified in restricting cable TV in order to protect the broadcast networks. Following this first ruling, a whole series of court decisions overturned other FCC restrictions on cable TV. Cable operators gained the right to air current movies and sporting events, for instance, and to offer services in the nation's top television markets.

The rulings also freed the cable industry from FCC requirements to provide local communities with special channels to air their own programming.

New cable networks emerge

The sudden reduction in FCC regulations led to tremendous growth in cable TV systems from the mid-1970s to the mid-1980s. In 1975 there were 3,500 cable systems serving 10 million subscribers, and within a decade these numbers jumped to 6,600 systems serving nearly 40 million subscribers. The increase in cable TV subscribers encouraged a number of independent business people to begin new cable networks. As a result, the number of cable networks grew from 28 in 1980 to 79 in 1990. These new networks no longer simply delivered programs that aired on the broadcast networks. Instead, they came up with unique programs and services, often targeted toward specific, narrow audience groups. Several of the cable networks that emerged during this period affected the development of television specifically and American society and culture in general.

Ted Turner (1938–) was a pioneer in forming national cable TV networks and offering innovative cable programming. Turner started his career by working in his father's billboard advertising business. After purchasing several radio stations in the late 1960s, Turner bought his first television station in 1970. This station, WTCG in Atlanta, Georgia, was located at channel 17 on the inferior UHF portion of the broadcast spectrum. At that time, stations affiliated with the three main national broadcast networks occupied the scarce VHF channels in nearly every important television market. But Turner disliked network programming and believed that independent stations could succeed by providing more wholesome options. He began showing old movies, cartoons, and sporting events to give viewers an alternative to the network offerings.

In 1976 Turner turned his small, independent station into a national cable network. Like HBO had done the year before, Turner arranged to deliver his signal to cable systems across the country via satellite. He changed his call letters to WTBS (for Turner Broadcasting System) and referred to it as a "Superstation" because of its nationwide reach. He soon convinced a number of national advertisers to begin placing their commercials on his cable network.

Several other creative cable networks began sending their programs across the country via satellite shortly after HBO and TBS. The Christian

Broadcast Network launched CBN (which later became the Family Channel) in 1976, for instance, and the Showtime premium movie and sports service first appeared in 1978. A second Superstation, WGN from Chicago, achieved national satellite distribution that year as well.

Sports and music on cable

As cable television continued to grow into more areas of the United States, more and more specialized channels were launched.

ESPN One of the most successful of all the cable networks made its debut in 1979. Its founder, Bill Rasmussen, had recently lost his job as communications director for the Hartford Whalers, a professional hockey team. In thinking about a new career, Rasmussen came up with the idea of starting a sports network that would provide programming to regional cable TV systems. After doing some research, Rasmussen discovered that satellite transmission would cost the same whether he beamed a television signal over a small region or across the whole country, so he decided to form a national network. He gathered some investors, built a studio in Bristol, Connecticut, and made his initial broadcast on September 7, 1979. This new network was called the Entertainment and Sports Programming Network (ESPN).

For the first few years of its existence, ESPN had trouble convincing the broadcast television networks to share their coverage of major sporting events, such as pro football and basketball games. Instead, the new cable network often found itself broadcasting unusual sporting events, such as slow-pitch softball games, the World's Strongest Man Competition, and Australian Rules Football. ESPN soon connected with sports fans, however, with its technical innovations, story-like highlight reels, and lively on-air personalities. Over the next twenty-five years, ESPN became a multi-billion-dollar business and made a tremendous impact on American society and culture. "Two decades of round-the-clock coverage have changed the way we view sports, the way we talk about sports, even the way athletes play sports," Greg Guss wrote in *Sport*. For instance, the increased exposure provided by sports networks like ESPN helped turn athletes into celebrities who earned millions of dollars to endorse products for advertisers.

CNN In 1980 Turner launched the Cable News Network (CNN) to provide viewers with news and information twenty-four hours per day. When promoting the new network, he claimed that he wanted to provide the American people with a source of news that was independent of the powerful broadcast networks. Compared to the major broadcast networks, the new CNN had a small budget, and many people criticized its simple studio sets and low-cost production techniques. In fact, it appeared that CNN might be a short-lived experiment, as the network lost $20 million in its first year. But Turner's all-news format gradually attracted viewers and became profitable. It moved to the forefront of international news coverage during the 1991 Persian Gulf War, when CNN reporters provided live coverage of U.S.-led bombing raids from a hotel balcony in downtown Baghdad, Iraq.

CNN thus created a huge change in up-to-the-minute television news coverage. Its success led to the creation of numerous competing cable news channels, and it also prompted the broadcast networks to begin their own late-night news shows. "When the leaders of the world wanted to find out what was happening in the world—and, sometimes, in their own countries—they turned to CNN," L. J. Davis noted in *The Billionaire Shell Game.* Due to CNN news coverage, cable became Americans' top choice for information about breaking news events. By the time of the terrorist attacks on the United States of September 11, 2001, surveys showed that 45 percent of viewers went to cable news first for the latest information, while 22 percent turned to the three main broadcast networks and 20 percent to local newscasts.

Some critics, however, insisted that CNN's effects on American society were not entirely positive. For instance, they claimed that the need to provide round-the-clock news pushed the American media toward sensational journalism, which emphasized celebrity-centered stories instead of important, but more complex, national and international news events.

MTV Another influential early cable network was MTV—Music Television. Following its launch in 1981, MTV focused its programming on music. Record companies already produced short videos to accompany songs by the artists they wanted to promote, so MTV was able to keep its programming costs low by simply arranging to air these promotional videos. Even though there were a limited number of videos available at first, ratings for the network soared. It proved to be especially popular among teenagers and young adults. The music industry realized that MTV had the power to bring musical groups to their audiences, and music videos became essential tools for artists seeking to attract and connect with fans. MTV's influence could also be seen in broadcast network programming. Shows such as *Miami Vice* adopted the fast-paced, colorful style of music videos and were often accompanied by rock-music soundtracks. In the late 1980s MTV began offering original programming in addition to videos, and several of these programs launched new television trends. For instance, MTV's *Real World,* a show that brings seven strangers together to live in a house, is widely credited with launching the reality-TV craze—unscripted TV programming depicting people in real-life situations—that blossomed in the late 1990s and into the 2000s.

Within a few years of its 1981 launch, MTV had become a powerful force in the music and television industries. © JAN BUTCHOFSKY-HOUSER/CORBIS.

Cable becomes big business

After the FCC lost a series of court challenges in the late 1970s, the agency began loosening its regulations concerning cable TV. The move toward deregulation (removal of regulations) received a big boost when Mark S. Fowler (1943–) became chairman of the FCC in 1981. Fowler was appointed by President Ronald Reagan (1911–2004; served 1981–89), who believed that the federal government should limit its role in controlling private business. Upon taking office, Fowler made it clear that he intended to reduce FCC regulations governing television and allow direct competition between cable and broadcast networks.

Fowler achieved many of his goals with the passage of the Cable Communications Policy Act of 1984. This act effectively completed the deregulation of the cable TV industry and placed it on equal footing with broadcast TV. The act eliminated must-carry rules, so that cable systems were no longer required to carry local broadcast stations. The new law also removed FCC-imposed limits on the monthly rates that cable

How Cable TV Works

Cable television works on the same principles in the 2000s as it did fifty years earlier. Cable systems include a central facility where television signals are received, processed, and distributed to subscribers. Such facilities typically feature a large antenna that receives program signals and a vast system of cables that deliver the signals to customers. Television signals gradually lose strength as they pass through the cables, so the cable companies place amplifiers (devices that boost the strength of the signals) at regular intervals to return the signals to their original strength.

Vast networks of cables carry television signals to connected homes, where they are changed into images that can be viewed on a TV screen by either a cable box on top of the TV or a cable converter inside the TV set itself. Since the cables must be buried in the ground or strung along telephone or electric poles, cable providers have to make agreements with local communities to use this type of public property, known as a right of way. Communities usually grant cable operators access through a type of business arrangement known as a franchise. A cable operator pays the local city government a percentage of its revenues in exchange for the exclusive right to provide cable services for a certain period of time. Cable subscribers typically pay an initial installation fee to be connected to the cable company's network, and a monthly fee to receive programming. The monthly fee varies depending on the number and type of channels a viewer wishes to receive.

companies charged subscribers. Cable operators could now charge customers as much as they wanted, as long as they operated in a competitive market. The FCC defined this term to mean any television market in which viewers had access to at least three over-the-air broadcast signals, and 90 percent of American cities met this condition.

With the removal of the last few limitations on its growth and profitability, cable TV entered a period of rapid expansion. Cable networks started competing directly with the broadcast networks for the right to air major sporting events, and they also started showing reruns of popular network series. As the number of cable channels expanded and the quality of cable programming improved, cable systems increasingly moved into urban and suburban areas that had previously been off-limits. Davis wrote: "cable could offer its customers something that the networks didn't have, and the number of new choices could only grow."

Since TV cables had to be buried underground or strung along telephone or electrical poles, the cable companies needed to negotiate agreements with local communities to use this type of property, known as a right of way. Communities usually granted cable operators access through a type of business arrangement called a franchise. The cable companies agreed to pay a fee (usually 5 percent of their revenues) to the community in exchange for the exclusive (not shared with others) right to provide cable service for a certain period of time. In this way, most communities—and even entire regions—ended up being served by a single cable provider. A cable franchise thus allowed a company to operate as a monopoly (without competition), so operators competed fiercely for the right to provide service to the nation's top television markets. Some cable companies tried to convince city councils to select them for a franchise by offering to plant trees, build libraries, and provide new channels and services that did not even exist yet.

By the early 1990s, cable TV had become big business. The industry was dominated by a handful of large companies known as multi-system operators (MSOs). These companies purchased thousands of small, local cable providers in order to gain access to their valuable franchises. Tele-Communications Inc. (TCI), under the leadership of John Malone, became the largest MSO by gobbling up smaller competitors. TCI's reach eventually extended to forty-eight U.S. states, and in 1989 its cash flow was greater than the three broadcast networks combined. Malone also invested heavily in programming services; at one time, TCI's Liberty Media subsidiary held stakes in twenty-two of the top fifty cable channels in the United States. But TCI also became involved in questionable business deals and financial arrangements that gave the company billions of dollars of debt.

As part of the battle for profitable franchises, TCI and other major players in the cable industry spent more than $15 billion on infrastructure, or the basic tools and foundation needed to conduct business. Between 1984 and 1992, they launched communication satellites, built transmission towers, and laid cable in new areas. According to the *Encyclopedia of Emerging Industries,* this industry-wide effort was the largest private construction project in the United States since World War II (1939–45). But the cable companies passed much of the expense on to their customers, and rates for basic cable service grew rapidly. In fact, average cable rates increased by 25 to 30 percent between 1986 and 1988 alone.

The cable companies' rapid growth and massive spending did not please many people outside the industry. Some consumer groups began to complain about high cable rates and poor customer service, which they attributed to the cable companies' monopoly power over communities and regions. (A monopoly is where one company controls an entire industry or line of business.) Noticing the widespread problems with cable service, some lawmakers openly questioned whether deregulation had been a good idea.

Consumer concerns lead to re-regulation

By 1992 about 60 percent of American households subscribed to cable television service, yet the industry's unregulated growth had created widespread negative feelings. In addition to consumer complaints about high rates and poor customer service, the cable industry also faced a longstanding conflict with the broadcast networks. The three broadcast networks continued to claim that cable services profited from their programming illegally. The networks demanded that cable operators pay royalties (a fee for the use of material protected by copyright) in exchange for retransmitting their programs.

In 1992 the U.S. Congress responded to widespread concerns about the cable TV industry by passing the Cable Television Consumer Protection and Competition Act. This law gave local communities the power to regulate rates for basic cable television services. It also required the FCC to develop a plan to ensure that the broadcast networks would receive fair pay for their original programming.

In 1995 the number of cable TV subscribers declined for the first time. Industry observers attributed the drop to customer dissatisfaction with cable services, as well as increased competition from new technologies, such as Direct Broadcast Satellite (DBS). The following year the cable industry received some relief from government regulations with the passage of the Telecommunications Act of 1996. Although this legislation focused primarily on the telephone industry, it relaxed some of the 1992 rules affecting cable TV. For instance, it gradually eliminated all regulation of basic cable rates.

The main impact of the 1996 law, however, was to remove some of the restrictions that prevented companies from competing in multiple parts of the telecommunications industry. For example, it allowed telephone companies and broadcast television networks to own cable franchises. Following passage of the Telecommunications Act, the cable TV industry experienced a great deal of merger and acquisition activity (when one company buys another or two companies combine into one). In one of the largest deals in U.S. business history, the telephone company AT&T purchased TCI's cable services for $54 billion in 1999.

More than ever, the cable TV industry came to be dominated by large MSOs that were also involved in other communication businesses. As of 2001, 95 percent of all cable subscribers received services from the top twenty-five companies in the industry. Comcast, with 21.4 million subscribers, took over the top spot among cable providers in 2002 by purchasing TCI's cable operations from AT&T.

Satellite services provide new competition

Around 2000, cable providers began to face intense competition from satellite television systems. The transmission of TV signals using satellites orbiting the Earth was not a new technology at that time. In fact, a communications satellite was first used to transmit a broadcast television signal across the Atlantic Ocean in 1962. A decade later, the FCC authorized the use of communication satellites for transmitting signals within the United States. Cable TV systems such as HBO and TBS adopted satellite transmission in the mid-1970s, and the Public Broadcasting Service (PBS) became the first broadcast network to deliver all of its programming via satellite in 1978.

Almost as soon as satellite programming became available, a few enterprising people began setting up their own dish-shaped antennas to intercept the signals. But picking up a television signal from a conventional communication satellite required dish antennas that were very large and quite expensive. Even so, the early dishes did not work very well and often had to be adjusted by hand as satellites moved across the horizon. These problems prevented a solid market from developing for home satellite TV for many years. In 1990, however, Primestar became the first company to offer commercial satellite TV service direct to customers' homes. Subscribers had to lease a three-foot-wide dish antenna in order to receive Primestar signals.

A major change in satellite technology occurred in 1993, when Hughes Electronics launched the first direct broadcast satellite (DBS). In DBS systems, the service provider receives programs from broadcast and cable TV networks at a technologically advanced broadcast center. These signals are encrypted, digitally compressed, and transmitted to a direct-broadcast satellite orbiting 23,000 miles above Earth. The DBS beams a digital stream of audio and video data to small, individual reception dishes on the roofs of houses and buildings. These 18-inch dish antennas capture the signals and carry them to the television set, where they are decoded and decompressed by a box on top of the TV set.

A DirecTV satellite dish being installed at a California home. © KIM KULISH/CORBIS.

DBS suddenly made satellite TV available and affordable for American homes. Shortly after the Hughes DBS became available, DirecTV launched a home satellite TV service with an 18-inch dish antenna. Given the high level of dissatisfaction with cable TV providers at this time, DirecTV attracted 100,000 customers in its first year. But the cable TV industry, which had become more politically powerful as it had grown, recognized that DBS systems represented a threat to its business. The FCC soon took action to protect the interests of the cable industry, just as it had worked to support the broadcast industry in the early days of cable.

In 1994 the U.S. Congress passed the Satellite Home Viewer Act, which limited the ability of DBS systems to provide their subscribers with access to local TV channels. The law prohibited satellite services from offering programming from the three major broadcast networks— which consistently attracted more viewers than any cable network— except in certain cases. For instance, the satellite systems were allowed to provide broadcast stations to customers who could not receive good reception over the air and had not subscribed to cable TV in the previous six months. These restrictions limited the growth of DBS services and prevented satellite providers from competing against cable systems in most major markets.

Over the next few years, the FCC continued to hear complaints from consumers about problems with cable TV providers, including rate increases and poor customer service. As more people became aware of DBS services, they started demanding that the FCC allow satellite service to compete directly with cable. Congress responded in November 1999 by passing the Satellite Home Viewer Improvement Act, which allowed DBS services to rebroadcast local network signals just like cable providers. The law marked a major defeat for the cable companies and gave the two types of television delivery services equal rights for the first time.

Satellite TV services grew rapidly, especially after the 1999 law removed the restrictions against carrying broadcast network channels. The number of subscribers to DBS systems more than doubled from 8.2 million in 1998 to 17.4 million in 2001. Many new customers switched to DBS from cable because they were dissatisfied with their cable service. By 2003 DBS provided service to more than 20 million American households, to claim 15.6 percent of the market. Meanwhile, the number of cable subscribers declined to 66 million households, or 68.6 percent of the market. Like the cable industry, DBS is dominated by a few large companies. As a result of the high costs in leasing satellites, providing home reception equipment, and acquiring programming, there are only four competitors in the DBS industry. The two largest, DirecTV and EchoStar, control 95 percent of the market.

Cable's impact on American television

Cable television has come a long way since its origins in the late 1940s, when it was used exclusively as a way to expand the reach of traditional over-the-airwaves television broadcasts. In the Museum of Broadcast Communications article "Cable Television," Sharon Strover described cable as a "cultural force" that changed people's concept of television. Far from being a simple retransmission service, cable came to be considered an important form of communication in its own right, and its development led to profound changes in the overall television industry.

In the early 2000s, national cable networks created a huge variety of original programs. Although ABC, NBC, and CBS still produced popular shows, TV viewers could also choose from among hundreds of cable channels that offered news, sports, music, movies, and other forms of entertainment. The cable networks offered programming designed to appeal to specialized interests of small, distinct audiences. The variety of options available on cable also contributed to changes in television viewing habits, by encouraging Americans to surf, or move quickly, across the various channels.

As the quality of cable programming improved, cable channels began to draw more and more viewers away from the broadcast networks. Over the decade from 1983 to 1994, for example, the share of weekly television audiences held by the broadcast networks declined from 69 to 52 percent, while the share held by cable networks increased from 9 to 26 percent. By the 2000s, the cable networks actually earned higher ratings than the broadcast networks in some time periods. Cable channels earned particularly high audience ratings during the summer months, when the broadcast networks typically aired reruns (repeated episodes of programs that had aired earlier). The summer of 2005 marked the fifth year in a row that cable networks had triumphed in the ratings, nearly doubling the audience share earned by the broadcast networks, 60.9 to 32.4.

Despite such successes, however, cable TV continued to face significant challenges in the early twenty-first century. For instance, cable providers continued to face stiff competition from satellite services, which generally offered subscribers more channels and more interactive features than cable. In addition, an increasing number of telephone companies and Internet service providers were expected to enter the television market. Cable operators also experienced ongoing disputes about rates and content, as well as a continuing need to upgrade facilities and equipment.

As of the early 2000s cable TV showed potential for growth, especially in the area of digital services. Digital compression of television signals allows cable systems to offer more channels, superior picture quality, and new interactive services. As a result, the number of subscribers to digital cable services grew from 9.7 million in 2000 to 19.2 million in 2002. Cable companies also expanded their services to provide long-distance telephone calling and Internet access for their customers.

History shows the development of cable TV brought major changes to the television industry. As other players evolved to take advantage of these changes, however, cable companies unexpectedly found themselves struggling to keep up. "The cable industry remade the television world of the 'Big Three' networks, upsetting their hold on programming and viewers and initiating a 24-hour . . . domain," Strover noted. "As the larger video media industry changes, the cable industry's boundaries, roles, and influences will likewise be reshaped, but the historical legacy of its accomplishments will surely continue to be felt."

For More Information

BOOKS

Auletta, Ken. *Media Man: Ted Turner's Improbable Empire.* New York: W. W. Norton, 2004.

"Cable and Other Pay Television Services." *Encyclopedia of American Industries.* Farmington Hills, MI: Gale Group, 2004.

"Cable Television." *Encyclopedia of Emerging Industries,* 2nd ed. Farmington Hills, MI: Gale Group, 1999.

Davis, L. J. *The Billionaire Shell Game: How Cable Baron John Malone and Assorted Corporate Titans Invented a Future Nobody Wanted.* New York: Doubleday, 1998.

"Direct Broadcast Satellite Television." *Encyclopedia of Emerging Industries,* 2nd ed. Farmington Hills, MI: Gale Group, 1999.

Hirshberg, Charles. *ESPN 25.* New York: Hyperion, 2004.

PERIODICALS

Becker, Anne. "Cable's Summer Slam." *Broadcasting and Cable,* August 22, 2005, p. 10.

"Cable Television's Long March." *The Economist,* November 16, 1996, p. 63.

Guss, Greg. "Cult of Personalities." *Sport,* July 1998, p. 28.

Hill, Lee Alan. "Building a TV Sports Empire: How ESPN Created a Model for Cable Success." *Television Week,* September 6, 2004, p. 11.

Hoffer, Richard. "Bill Rasmussen." *Sports Illustrated,* September 19, 1994, p. 120.

Smith, Ralph Lee. "The Wired Nation." *The Nation* (special issue), May 18, 1970.

Taylor, Chris. "To Dish or Not to Dish." *Time,* October 28, 2002, p. 70.

WEB SITES

Couzens, Michael. "United States: Networks." *Museum of Broadcast Communications.* http://www.museum.tv/archives/etv/U/htmlU/unitedstatesn/unitedstatesn. htm (accessed on June 14, 2006).

Strover, Sharon. "United States: Cable Television." *Museum of Broadcast Communications.* http://www.museum.tv/archives/etv/U/htmlU/unitedstatesc/ unitedstatesc.htm (accessed on June 14, 2006).

"Wired, Zapped, and Beamed: 1960s through 1980s" and "Digitally Networked: 1990s through Today." *FCC History Project.* http://www.fcc.gov/omd/ history/tv/ (accessed on June 14, 2006).

5

Prime Time Network Programming, 1940s–1970s

From the beginning of commercial television in the 1940s, the broadcast networks have competed to produce programs that attract the largest number of viewers. Successful programs bring in advertising dollars, which allow the networks to remain in business and create more programs. The competition for viewers has always been particularly intense during "prime time," the evening hours—roughly between 8 P.M. and 11 P.M.—when American families have come home from work or school and are most likely to watch TV.

In order to attract viewers during this important period, the networks produced more than 5,000 prime-time series in the first fifty years of television. These programs ranged from serious dramas to silly comedies; from cowboy stories set in the Old West to futuristic adventures set in outer space; and from live music and variety shows to animated cartoon series. Many of these programs reflected current events and developments in American society, while others helped launch new cultural trends.

Through the years, television networks have often come under criticism for creating programs with the single goal of attracting mass audiences. Some critics claim that the networks often pay more attention to attracting wide audiences than to creating excellent programs. But some analysts of popular culture argue that television also has a number of positive effects on society. At its best, TV brings people together, gives them something to talk about, and makes them think about issues or relationships in a new way. "In such a diverse country as the United States, television has supplied everyone with common reference points and a shared culture," Steven D. Stark explained in *Glued to the Set*.

In any case, there is no disputing that television—and particularly prime-time network series—exerts a tremendous influence on American society. For instance, TV series encourages people to spend money on toys, clothing, and other products. Television news programs give viewers a close-up look at historic events taking place all over the world. Television coverage of politics influences the types of people who run for office, as well as the ways in which they appeal to voters. Finally, spending time watching television—instead of pursuing other activities like reading, exercising, or talking with other people—affects viewers' personal health and family life.

The 1940s: Americans gather around the TV

Television first became widely available in the United States in the late 1940s. Although the first television broadcasts had taken place years earlier, both the production of TV sets and TV broadcasting were stopped during World War II (1939–45). Once the war ended, however, the modern television industry began to take shape. In the 1940s, only 10 percent of American homes contained TV sets, so the new technology was quite a novelty. Since the networks only broadcast shows for a few hours in the evening, watching TV was a form of entertainment that people often shared with their friends and neighbors.

The earliest TV programs were filmed live in network studios in New York City. Most of the shows featured the same forms of entertainment that were popular before television came along. Playwrights and actors who had become famous through their work in the theater began staging dramas for TV. Radio comedies and adventure stories were also adapted for television. But perhaps the most popular early TV programs were variety shows—featuring comedy, music, dancing, and skits—based on the work of successful vaudeville entertainers. Vaudeville was a form of live entertainment featuring multiple acts that flourished around the turn of the twentieth century.

During the first few years of television, the most popular shows tended to take advantage of the visual element of television, or the fact that people could see performers instead of just hearing them on the radio. One prominent example was a variety show called *Texaco Star Theater,* which was hosted by Milton Berle (1908–2002) and ran on NBC from 1948 to 1953. Berle started out as a vaudeville comic, and he brought many aspects of his routine to his TV show. He wore ridiculous costumes, told bad jokes, and appeared with trained animals and jugglers. But he also managed to convince some of the biggest names in show business, such as the popular singer Frank Sinatra (1915–1998), to make guest appearances on his program.

TV Ratings

Television programs are rated based on the number of viewers who watch them. These ratings are used to determine the most popular shows for a particular week or year. Ratings are very important to the television networks. The more viewers that tune in to a given show, the more money the network can charge advertisers for commercials aired during that show. Advertising dollars provide a major source of funding for the networks, allowing them to stay in business and continue producing programs. For this reason, the networks use ratings to decide which shows to keep and which to cancel for each TV season. It is important to note that ratings do not measure the quality of TV programs. Instead, they measure the popularity of TV programs, or how many viewers watch them.

In the United States, national television ratings are compiled by a company called Nielsen Media Research. Since more than 110 million American homes have TV sets, Nielsen cannot possibly keep track of what everyone is watching at a particular time. Instead, the company uses a mathematical technique called statistical sampling to analyze the nation's viewing patterns.

Nielsen randomly selects about 5,000 American homes—containing about 13,000 individual viewers—to serve as a sample audience. In order to create a sample that is representative of the whole country, the company chooses homes in diverse geographic locations with viewers from various ethnic backgrounds and income levels. With the agreement of the homeowners, Nielsen installs special meters on the TV sets in these 5,000 homes. Whenever a TV set is turned on, the meter records which channel the viewer is watching. This data is collected and studied by the company's central computers every night.

Statistics, or numerical information, from the sample audience are used to estimate the total number of viewers that tune in to each program across the country. One point in the Nielsen ratings is equivalent to 1 percent of the national television households. Since there were about 110 million TV households in 2005, each ratings point represented 1.1 million households. For example, CSI: Crime Scene Investigation was the top-rated program for the last week of December 2005. It received a rating of 11.3, meaning that it was watched in 12.4 million U.S. households. Nielsen also reports its results in terms of audience share, or the percentage of all televisions in use at a particular time that were tuned to a specific program. CSI received an 18 share, meaning that the show is estimated to have appeared on 18 percent of all TV sets in the country at the time of its broadcast.

Nielsen also keeps track of statistics about various segments of the viewing audience. For example, the company finds out the age and gender of each member in its sample households. These individuals are asked to push a special button whenever they start or stop watching TV. Nielsen can use this data to determine which shows are the most popular among specific population groups, such as children or female viewers. The company collects and publicizes the most data about the nation's viewing habits during "sweeps" periods. These important ratings periods, which occur in February, May, and November each year, are when local TV stations establish their advertising rates. Accordingly, the networks typically choose these periods to air programs they expect to attract the largest audiences.

Milton Berle and Ethel Merman performing on **Texaco Star Theater.** © BETTMANN/CORBIS.

Within a year of its debut, Berle's *Texaco Star Theater* became a huge hit, attracting 75 percent of all TV audiences each week. In fact, the show was so popular that NBC delayed broadcasting the results of the 1948 presidential election until Berle's show went off the air. Berle thus emerged as the first superstar of the TV age and became popularly known as "Mr. Television."

The other networks soon introduced variety shows that imitated *Texaco Star Theater*. But Berle's popularity faded fairly quickly, and his show was canceled in 1953 after a five-year run. Television historians claim that Berle's brand of humor worked best in the era when groups of people gathered together to watch television. Once every family had a TV set that they could watch in the quiet of their own homes, his outrageous costumes and gags lost their appeal. In this new atmosphere, television programming of the 1950s became dominated by milder situation comedies, often focusing on family life.

The 1950s: Family hour

For most Americans, the 1950s was a very good decade. The U.S. economy was strong, creating an abundance of steady jobs that paid well. As a result, many people were able to buy homes and start families, creating a comfortable middle class. The situation was not as promising for African Americans, who were forced to use separate—and usually lesser quality—schools, transportation, and other public facilities during this era of segregation (the forced separation of people by race). Conflict began internationally, too, as the United States and the Soviet Union started competing to see which country would prove to be the dominant power in the post–World War II era. Nevertheless, many Americans in the 1950s seemed to feel positive about the future.

Television ownership expanded rapidly during the 1950s, from about 10 percent of U.S. households in 1950 to 86 percent in 1959. The networks gradually established regular broadcast schedules and made programming available for more hours each day. They also developed different types of programs—including situation comedies, adventure series, and game shows—to appeal to different parts of the viewing audience.

Situation comedies take shape

Probably the most popular type of program in the 1950s was the situation comedy, or sitcom. Most of these shows focused humorously on families and their everyday problems. Unlike *Texaco Star Theater* and other programs from the 1940s, many sitcoms from the 1950s remain popular into the early 2000s. Reruns, or repeat showings, of these programs attract new generations of audiences who enjoy the depictions of family life in an earlier, seemingly simpler time.

I Love Lucy Arguably the most successful television program of all time is the pioneering sitcom *I Love Lucy,* which aired on CBS from 1951 to 1957. It starred Lucille Ball (1911–1989), a well-known comedian and movie actress, and her real-life husband Desi Arnaz (1917–1986), a singer and bandleader from Cuba. They played a married couple, Lucy and Ricky Ricardo, who live in a New York apartment and are best friends with their older neighbors, Fred and Ethel Mertz.

When the network first approached Lucille Ball about appearing in a television series, she agreed—but only on the conditions that her husband would be her co-star and that the show would be filmed in Hollywood, California, rather than New York. Ball and Arnaz also introduced several technical innovations during the show's production. For instance, *I Love Lucy* was the first television program to be filmed live before a studio audience, and it was the first to use a three-camera technique that allowed the actors to play to the audience rather than to the cameras.

In addition to the differences in filming location and style, *I Love Lucy* introduced some new ideas to early TV audiences. Lucy Ricardo is a housewife and stay-at-home mother (like most married women in the 1950s), but she repeatedly tries to become more independent and add some excitement to her life. "Long before Betty Freidan [author of *The Feminine Mystique* (1963), an influential book in the women's rights movement] gave voice to the restless aspirations of a generation of housebound women, 'I Love Lucy' was doing something similar," Stark noted. Lucy's weekly struggles to launch her own career or make Ricky appreciate her were treated humorously, which made the show's underlying feminism, or focus on women's desire for equality with men, less threatening to audiences of the 1950s.

Thanks to the unique comic talents of its star, *I Love Lucy* became a huge hit. Reruns have aired in the United States and around the world ever since the series ended, and as of 2006 it is still considered a classic example of the sitcom format.

Leave It to Beaver Another 1950s sitcom with enduring popularity was *Leave It to Beaver,* which aired on CBS and ABC from 1957 to 1963. It followed the day-to-day activities of a middle-class white American family. The Cleavers live in a tidy house in the suburbs. Father Ward goes off to work each day, briefcase in hand, while mother June takes care of the house in her apron, pearls, and high heels. Most of the stories focus on the youngest son, Theodore "Beaver" Cleaver. Each week, Beaver faces the typical problems of childhood with the loving support of his parents and his older brother, Wally.

Leave It to Beaver was not a big success during its initial run. Some critics believe that it had limited appeal to 1950s audiences because adults were unaccustomed to shows that presented family life from a child's perspective. As American society changed over time, however, *Leave It to Beaver* became a huge hit. People who felt overwhelmed by modern problems took comfort in watching reruns of the show, because it portrayed an ideal family with two children cared for by both of their parents. "*Leave It to Beaver*—the sitcom that glorified the traditional, father-led, middle-class family of the 1950s—only began to gain mass popularity as that family model, and the era it represented, disappeared and the nation longed for both it and the stability it represented," Stark explained.

Leave It to Beaver remains popular in the 2000s. Some historians place the show at the beginning of a nostalgia movement, in which Americans are attracted to comforting images of a simpler time in the past. They claim that such feelings of longing for the past also explains the popularity of "oldies" and "classic rock" radio stations, which play songs from earlier decades, as well as the trend of turning old TV shows into movies.

Music rocks TV

While sitcoms became a major part of television programming in the 1950s, music and variety shows remained popular, too. The program that produced some of America's most memorable television moments was *The Ed Sullivan Show*, which aired more than one thousand episodes on CBS between 1948 and 1971. As host of the show, Ed Sullivan (1902–1974) had a permanent place on television for over twenty years. Although he had a somewhat wooden presence on stage—and mostly stood around with his hands in his pockets—Sullivan had a knack for recognizing talent. He invited many young artists on his show who went on to rank among the biggest names in American music. In this way, *The Ed Sullivan Show* had a major influence on popular culture.

Entertainers such as Bob Hope (1903–2003), Itzhak Perlman (1945–), and Liza Minnelli (1946–) made their first appearance on television on the program. Sullivan also featured a number of African American entertainers—such as Ella Fitzgerald (1917–1996), Lena Horne (1917–), and Richard Pryor (1940–2005)—at a time when it was rare for black performers to appear on TV. Sullivan is probably best known, however, for scheduling some of the earliest television performances by the young Elvis Presley (1935–1977), who became a tremendously popular rock-and-roll singer.

About 60 million people, or 82 percent of the total American viewing audience, tuned in to watch Elvis's first appearance on *The Ed Sullivan Show* in September 1956. Some of the more conservative viewers were shocked at the rock-and-roller's suggestive dance moves, which included

Millions of people tuned in to The Ed Sullivan Show *on February 9, 1964, to watch the American television debut of the* Beatles. AP IMAGES.

hip shakes and pelvic thrusts. When Elvis returned to the show in January 1957, Sullivan famously instructed his camera operators to only film the singer from the waist up. Seven years later, 70 million people tuned in to *The Ed Sullivan Show* to watch the American television debut, or first appearance, of a young British rock group called the Beatles.

Shortly after Elvis made his historic appearances on *The Ed Sullivan Show*, the other networks launched their own programs to try to take advantage of the growing interest in rock-and-roll music. The most successful of these programs was *American Bandstand,* hosted by Dick Clark (1929–), which aired on ABC for thirty years beginning in 1957. *Bandstand* started out as a daytime show on a local TV station in Philadelphia, Pennsylvania, but soon went national and moved into prime time. Although the featured bands played before a live audience, they often used recorded background tracks. The show also featured a regular cast of dancers and a segment in which audience members rated new records.

Over the years, *American Bandstand* often drew criticism for emphasizing music that was too commercial and mainstream. But some people gave the show credit for bridging the generation gap by presenting music that appealed to teenagers without putting off adults. *Bandstand* was particularly popular in the late 1950s and early 1960s. Its influence began to fade in the mid-1960s, when rock-and-roll took on more aggressive, protest themes that criticized the middle-class American lifestyle and lost the more romantic sound of much 1950s music.

Another hugely successful music program from the 1950s was *The Lawrence Welk Show*, which aired on ABC from 1955 to 1971. Lawrence Welk (1903–1992) was a North Dakota-born musician and bandleader who favored polkas over rock-and-roll. In contrast to Sullivan, Welk never tried to follow trends in American music. Instead, he gained a devoted following among older audiences by providing comfortable, familiar, wholesome entertainment.

Westerns ride into town

In terms of television drama, the 1950s is considered the age of the Western. Stories about cowboys and lawmen, such as *The Lone Ranger,* had been popular on radio and in the movies for many years. The genre, or type of program, started to take over television in the mid-1950s, when the United States and the Soviet Union entered a period of intense political and military rivalry known as the Cold War (1945–91). Westerns held appeal for TV viewers during this period because they emphasized traditional American values and offered a clear contrast between the good guys and the bad guys.

Gunsmoke, which aired on CBS from 1955 to 1975, is widely considered to be the original TV Western. It reached the number one spot in the annual television ratings for four years in a row, and it remained in the top ten for a total of twelve years. Its success in the 1950s created a trend in which many other Westerns were shown on television, including *Wagon Train, The Rifleman, Maverick, Rawhide,* and *The Big Valley.*

Gunsmoke starred James Arness (1923–) as Matt Dillon, the sheriff of the frontier town of Dodge City, Kansas. Each week, Dillon protected the townspeople from harm and helped them solve problems. The basic message of the show was that the forces of good always win out over the forces of evil. *Gunsmoke* and the other early TV Westerns did

TV Westerns, such as Gunsmoke, *the cast of which is pictured here, were very popular in the 1950s.* © BETTMANN/CORBIS.

not have much violence by the standards of the 2000s, but they did provide viewers with excitement and adventure.

Another tremendously popular Western, *Bonanza,* made its debut on NBC in 1959 and ran until 1973. It was different from *Gunsmoke* in two ways: it showed a family instead of a lone lawman; and it took place on a sprawling private ranch instead of in a frontier town. *Bonanza* focused on Ben Cartwright (played by Lorne Greene [1915–1987]), who operated a cattle ranch with the help of his three sons. Although the show reached the top spot in the annual ratings three times in the early 1960s, Westerns began to go out of style around this time. Some TV critics attribute the decline of the genre to the fact that there were too many Westerns on TV, while others claim that the cultural changes of the 1960s (including the African American civil rights movement and the women's rights movement) made Westerns seem old-fashioned, simplistic, and out of touch with the real world.

The quiz show scandal

Another television genre that became popular during the 1950s was the quiz show. During the mid-1950s, quiz shows were the most popular programs on prime-time TV. In fact, quiz shows occupied five of the top ten spots in the TV ratings for the 1957 season. Competing successfully on such programs as *Twenty-One* and *The $64,000 Question* turned ordinary Americans into instant celebrities. These question-and-answer shows rewarded well-informed, quick-thinking contestants with prizes and money.

The appeal of quiz shows started to fade in 1957, however, when rumors suggested that some of the programs were fixed to turn out a certain way. In some cases, popular contestants were allowed to win so that the program would receive higher ratings. Accusations by former contestants led to a formal investigation by the U.S. House of Representatives. Viewers tuned in to watch a parade of successful quiz show contestants testify before Congress about their television experiences. The biggest shock came when *Twenty-One* champion Charles Van Doren, the handsome son of a prominent family, admitted that the show's producers had provided him with answers in advance. Even though it was not illegal to fix game shows at that time, the nation's TV viewers were angry about what Van Doren reported. The networks responded by canceling most of the quiz shows.

The quiz show scandal affected the development of television in a number of ways. First, it led the broadcast networks to take control

Charles Van Doren thinks about his answer during an episode of the quiz show Twenty-One. AP IMAGES.

over programming. Before the scandal occurred, the networks had sold large blocks of air time to commercial sponsors. As part of a larger effort to promote their products, these companies had created the programs that the networks aired. But the scandal convinced the networks that this system did not work well and that they needed to take more control over program content. After 1957, the networks took charge of producing programs and began selling only brief commercial spots to advertisers. Second, the networks created formal news divisions in order to make a clear distinction between news and entertainment programs.

The quiz show scandal also affected American viewers' attitudes toward television. The scandal occurred in the 1950s, when most U.S. citizens, due to the prosperous post–World War II times, felt confident and optimistic and tended to trust the media. But the scandal reduced this level of trust and caused many Americans to question the honesty of television producers.

The 1960s: TV becomes an escape

The 1960s was a decade of great change and instability in the United States. African Americans fought for equality through the civil rights movement. Cold War tensions increased between the United States and Soviet Union, leading to widespread public concerns about Communist expansion and spying. The U.S. military began fighting a controversial war in the Southeast Asian nation of Vietnam, and antiwar protests rocked the nation. President John F. Kennedy (1917–1963) and civil rights leader Martin Luther King Jr. (1929–1968) were assassinated, and American astronaut Neil Armstrong (1930–) became the first person to set foot on the Moon.

Television news became increasingly sophisticated in the 1960s and provided extensive coverage of these important events. But most prime-time TV series did not address the serious issues facing American society that revolved around these and other events. Network executives were fearful of offending viewers, which could mean a drop in viewership and thus a drop in advertising dollars, by commenting on these issues. Instead, they took the opposite approach with entertainment programming, offering viewers an assortment of goofy comedies and lighthearted adventures. Many American audiences enjoyed the distraction this sort of programming offered.

One of the most popular programs of the decade, *The Beverly Hillbillies,* aired on CBS from 1962 to 1971. TV critics called the show tasteless and silly, but large numbers of viewers tuned in anyway. In fact, *The Beverly Hillbillies* rose to the top spot in the ratings within three weeks of its premiere, and it stayed there for two years. Even after the series ended its initial run, it remained popular in reruns.

The Beverly Hillbillies follows the comic adventures of the Clampetts, an unsophisticated family from the backwoods who unexpectedly strike oil on their property. They become instant millionaires and decide to buy a mansion in upscale Beverly Hills, California. Each episode contrasts the Clampett family's rural values with the shallow materialism of their wealthy neighbors.

The Beverly Hillbillies was one of the first TV comedies to deal with the subject of social class. It also launched the "fish out of water" type of sitcom storyline, in which the main characters are surrounded by, and must interact with, people who are very different from themselves. This type of storyline was used in later years by such programs as *Mork and Mindy* (featuring Robin Williams [1951–] as an alien), *Family Ties* (starring Michael J. Fox [1961–] as the sole conservative in a liberal family), and *The Fresh Prince of Bel Air* (featuring Will Smith [1968–] as an urban rapper in an upper-class suburban neighborhood).

In addition to *The Beverly Hillbillies,* viewers in the 1960s enjoyed *Mister Ed* (about a talking horse); *Gilligan's Island* (about a group of misfits

The Beverly Hillbillies, which aired on CBS from 1962 to 1971, was one of the first TV comedies to deal with the subject of social class. CBS/ GETTY IMAGES.

shipwrecked on a deserted island); and *The Munsters* and *The Addams Family* (about families of monsters living in suburban America). A few of these comedies reflected the changes taking place in U.S. society. But instead of referring to controversial subjects directly, they usually disguised the references in comic situations. "These sitcoms reflected their times more than it might at first seem," Stark wrote. "By packaging troubling cultural shifts in the guise [outward appearance] of comic fantasy, these shows made it easier for Americans to come to grips with rapid social change."

The sitcom *My Favorite Martian,* for example, was about a family trying to accept their strange uncle, who turned out to be a visitor from another planet. But some TV critics noted that the series suggested the civil rights struggle, when Americans of different races made new efforts to understand and accept each other. Similarly, the popular sitcoms *Bewitched* and *I Dream of Jeannie* featured female characters (a witch and a genie) who had magical powers. Some TV critics claimed that these series reflected the growing women's rights movement and helped prepare American society to accept greater empowerment of women.

Of course, not all sitcoms of the 1960s were strange, escapist comedies. In fact, two of the best shows of the era painted more realistic portraits of life in America at that time. *The Dick Van Dyke Show,* which appeared on CBS for five years beginning in 1961, captured the everyday experiences of America's growing middle class. Actor Dick Van Dyke (1925–) starred as Rob Petrie, a successful television writer. Mary Tyler Moore (1936–) played his wife, Laura, who stayed home to take care of their son Ritchie but did not always fit into the traditional housewife role. The show is not only about the relationship between Rob and Laura, but also about the relationship between Rob and his co-workers. The series creator, Carl Reiner (1922–), described it to Stark as "the first situation comedy where you saw where the man worked before he walked in and said, 'Hi, honey, I'm home!'" The well-written *Dick Van Dyke Show* won more than a dozen Emmy Awards. (Emmy Awards are given out annually by the Academy of Television Arts and Sciences for excellence in TV programming.)

Another popular sitcom of the era, *The Andy Griffith Show,* provided viewers with a sweet and funny chronicle of life in a small southern town. Andy Griffith's (1926–) character, Andy Taylor, is the easygoing, fair-minded sheriff of rural Mayberry, North Carolina. He is also a single father raising a young son, Opie, with the help of his elderly aunt. While the show had some silly characters and outrageous moments, its comfortable, down-home style made it seem more realistic than many other sitcoms. Originally airing on CBS from 1960 to 1968, it remains popular in reruns and is still mentioned among the best shows in its genre.

Dramas reflect the Cold War era

As the Western gradually lost its dominant place in prime-time TV schedules, the networks introduced several new kinds of drama series. Many dramas of the 1960s reflected the feelings of paranoia and suspicion

that gripped the United States during the Cold War. One of the most original series from this era was *The Twilight Zone,* which aired on CBS from 1959 to 1964. Created and hosted by playwright Rod Serling (1924–1975), this science-fiction show was so different from anything else on television that it failed to attract a large audience during its first run. In later years, however, *The Twilight Zone* developed a strong following in reruns and played an influential role in American popular culture.

Each episode of *The Twilight Zone* opened with Serling, dressed in a suit and tie, introducing the story to viewers. Other than that, however, no two episodes were alike or connected. Instead, each episode was a self-contained story that featured new characters and settings. In many cases, the situations appeared to be ordinary at first, but then turned strange or even frightening. Every episode ended with a surprising twist that was intended to make viewers rethink everything they had just seen.

In creating the show, Serling chose to include a science-fiction element because he felt that it gave him more freedom to comment on politics and current events. "*The Twilight Zone* presented an alternate universe which, as fantastic as it was, ultimately proved more authentic [real] than almost anything else [on TV]," Stark explained. Still, because the show touched on controversial issues, Serling continually battled with network executives and commercial sponsors, who were concerned about offending viewers.

As Cold War tensions escalated between the United States and Soviet Union, the news often contained stories about Communist expansion and international spies. The broadcast networks tried to take advantage of such concerns by introducing more than a dozen spy dramas during the 1960s, including *The Man from U.N.C.L.E., I Spy,* and *The Avengers.* One of the most original shows in this genre was *Mission: Impossible,* which aired on CBS from 1966 to 1973. It focused on a team of American secret agents led by Jim Phelps (played by Peter Graves [1926–]). Each week, the team received a tape-recorded message that informed members of their assignment, and then the tape would destroy itself.

Some TV critics argue that the 1960s spy dramas gave Americans a negative view of foreign countries and thus contributed to the fearful atmosphere that made the Cold War possible. Some also charged that these series led to an increase in the level of violence shown on television. Since many Americans worried about enemy spies, they seemed to find violence toward such characters more acceptable on TV shows. Other analysts attributed the rising levels of violence on some TV dramas to the violent Vietnam War imagery being broadcast into American homes each night via the evening news programs.

Police shows and legal dramas also replaced the Western in the 1960s. *Perry Mason,* which aired on CBS from 1957 to 1966, was the first show to present a lawyer as a hero. The title character (played by Raymond Burr [1917–1993]) was a brilliant defense attorney who always managed to uncover new evidence and find the real criminal so that his innocent clients could go free. Each episode featured a dramatic courtroom confrontation, in which Mason always prevailed. Some analysts of popular culture point out that *Perry Mason* and other legal dramas helped turn average Americans into amateur crime solvers. But while it taught viewers about some aspects of the criminal justice system, *Perry Mason* also gave viewers the misleading impression that most cases were neatly resolved.

Game and variety shows reflect changing times

New types of game and variety shows also reflected the cultural shifts and political controversies of the 1960s. As women began to break out of traditional roles and seek more sexual freedom, the most popular game shows began to focus on personal relationships rather than intellectual ability. In the hit show *The Dating Game,* for instance, an attractive single woman would interview three unseen male contestants and then decide which one she wanted to go out with. The question-and-answer sessions were often filled with sexual jokes and suggestions. Similarly, *The Newlywed Game* featured four recently married couples. The men and women would answer questions separately while their spouses waited backstage. When the couples were reunited to discuss their answers, they often revealed a great deal about their private lives, to the amusement of the viewing audience.

Both of these shows broke new ground on television by openly acknowledging sexuality. In contrast, most programs of the 1950s never talked about sex. They did not even show married characters getting into the same bed to sleep. Instead, a wife and husband usually slept in separate beds. The new wave of game shows also started a trend toward allowing contestants to humiliate or embarrass themselves on TV for the entertainment of the audience. The entertainment value of *The Dating Game* came from watching the woman's reaction—usually surprise or disappointment—as she met the man she had chosen to date. Likewise, viewers tuned in to *The Newlywed Game* mostly to watch the couples argue about their conflicting answers. In this way, the 1960s game shows were forerunners of later daytime tabloid talk shows such as *Jerry Springer* in the 1990s and prime-time reality series such as *The Bachelor* in the 2000s.

The 1960s also saw the return of comedy and variety shows to the prime-time lineup. All of these shows included some topical humor about political subjects and current events, but some handled controversial topics more carefully than others. The program that addressed such issues most directly was *The Smothers Brothers Comedy Hour,* which premiered on CBS in 1967.

Comedians Tom (1937–) and Dick (1939–) Smothers felt that the television networks were far too cautious about dealing with important subjects, such as American involvement in the Vietnam War (1954–75). They were determined to make their variety show reflect current public concerns and changing values. *The Smothers Brothers Comedy Hour* included mock political commentary, jokes and skits about current events, and performances by popular rock and folk artists. CBS executives worried that the brothers would go too far and anger or upset audiences and advertisers. In 1968 they demanded to see a videotape of the program each week before it went on the air, and in 1969 they canceled the show due to ongoing differences of opinion about its content.

Other variety shows of the period, including *The Carol Burnett Show* (1967–79) and *Rowan and Martin's Laugh-In* (1968–73), were more careful about covering their political commentary with humor. They thus managed to find a comfortable middle ground with viewers and advertising sponsors.

The 1970s: Serious comedy

During the 1970s, people in the United States witnessed social change in the form of the women's liberation movement, which encouraged American women to seek greater independence and freedom. As a result, women tended to remain single longer, and more married women began working outside the home. In the workplace, women demanded to be paid the same as men who did similar work. Divorce became more common, and a growing number of children found themselves living in nontraditional families. A family no longer consisted of two parents who were married, along with the children produced by that marriage.

The 1970s also saw political upheaval because the U.S. president was caught up in criminal activity. In the early part of the decade, Republican president Richard Nixon (1913–1994; served 1969–74) became involved in what was called Watergate scandal. It was named after the Watergate Hotel in Washington, D.C., where burglars with ties to the Republican Party broke into the offices of the Democratic National Committee. The crime led to an investigation that showed that White House officials, including President Nixon, knew about the break-in. In 1974 the Watergate investigations revealed convincing evidence against the president, and Nixon decided to resign in order to avoid impeachment, or prosecution. Nixon was the first U.S. president forced to resign from office. His disgrace led to widespread feelings of disillusionment and distrust about the government and other institutions.

In the meantime, people across the country continued to protest against U.S. involvement in the Vietnam War. Some young people who adopted the cause of peace developed their own culture and became known as "hippies." Thanks in part to public disapproval, the United States withdrew its troops from Vietnam in 1973. Three years later, the United States watched as North Vietnamese Communist forces defeated its South Vietnamese allies to take control of the battered Southeast Asian nation.

In the face of so much change and conflict, it is little wonder that sitcoms took over prime-time television in the 1970s. The viewing audience's preference for comedy lasted for the next twenty years, and only two dramas (*Dallas* and *Dynasty*) led the annual TV ratings between 1972 and 1995. Unlike the escapist comedies of the 1960s, however, the most popular and influential shows of the 1970s tended to present more realistic pictures of American working people and families. Many of them also featured a darker brand of humor that seemed to fit the troubled times.

The struggles of working people

One of the most critically acclaimed sitcoms of the era was *All in the Family*. It aired on CBS from 1971 to 1983 and was the top-rated show on television for five consecutive years. *All in the Family* broke new ground by focusing on the daily struggles of a working-class family, living in Queens, New York. Carroll O'Connor (1924–2001) starred as Archie Bunker, a loud, prejudiced, blue-collar worker who distrusted blacks, Jews, feminists, hippies, and other perceived threats to conservative American values. Archie shared a modest home with his gentle wife Edith, liberated adult daughter Gloria, and long-haired hippie and often unemployed son-in-law Mike Stivic. Their interactions consisted mainly of heated arguments, name-calling, and sarcastic comments. Much of the humor came from the difference between Archie's beliefs and actions and those of the other main characters.

CBS executives knew that some viewers might be shocked by *All in the Family*. Immediately before the series premiere, the network aired a message explaining that the show "seeks to throw a humorous spotlight on our frailties, prejudices, and concerns. By making them a source of laughter, we hope to show—in a mature fashion—just how absurd they are." CBS also set up a special telephone switchboard to field calls from viewers who found the program upsetting. As it turned out, though, the few people who called in offered mostly positive comments.

All in the Family influenced the development of TV comedy in a number of ways. First, it started a trend toward more realistic sitcoms that tackled a broader range of social and political subjects. For instance,

At the heart of All in the Family *was the Bunker family: (from left) daughter Gloria, son-in-law Mike, wife Edith, and husband Archie.* AP IMAGES.

the show addressed the so-called generation gap between older, more conservative people like Archie and younger, more liberal people like Mike. The arguments between the two characters probably reflected those taking place in many American homes at that time. Second, *All in the Family* focused on wordplay and verbal battles more than previous sitcoms. Many later TV shows adopted this approach, from sitcoms such as *Seinfeld* to news programs such as *Crossfire*.

Finally, *All in the Family* was one of the first programs to generate successful "spin-off" series with members of its cast. (Spin-off series are new programs built around a character that has appeared on another TV series.) Creator Norman Lear (1922–) built several new shows around characters from *All in the Family,* including *Maude* and *The Jeffersons*. Analysts of popular culture claim that spin-offs help viewers forge a closer connection to television, because they are able to watch familiar characters adjust to new situations and grow.

Another highly successful and influential sitcom, *The Mary Tyler Moore Show,* aired on CBS at the same time as *All in the Family.* Although both shows were realistic and dealt with social changes, in many ways they were complete opposites. *The Mary Tyler Moore Show* focused on a single career woman rather than a family, for instance, and emphasized the importance of getting along rather than confrontation. Like *All in the Family,* though, it did generate a number of successful spin-off series featuring supporting characters, including *Rhoda, Phyllis,* and *Lou Grant.*

The Mary Tyler Moore Show centered on Mary Richards, a single woman who worked as a news writer at a local TV station in Minneapolis, Minnesota. It struck a chord at a time when American women were becoming more independent, staying single longer, and building successful careers. The show also broke new ground by focusing on Mary's work life and interactions with her colleagues, rather than her personal life and romantic or family relationships. Some TV critics have credited the series with launching the genre of "workplace comedy," a type of program in which the majority of the show takes place in the main characters' place of work. Examples include such popular shows as *Taxi, Cheers, Murphy Brown,* and *The Office.*

The most-watched telecast of all time

Another 1970s sitcom remembered for its realism and dark humor was $M^*A^*S^*H,$ which aired on CBS from 1972 to 1983. It centered on a U.S. Army doctor, Benjamin Franklin "Hawkeye" Pierce (played by Alan Alda [1936–]), working in a field hospital near the front lines of the Korean War (1950–53). The staff of the hospital also included a number of supporting characters with widely differing backgrounds and viewpoints. More so than any previous sitcom, $M^*A^*S^*H$ combined comedy with serious and sad moments that often made it seem like a drama. Reviewers even coined a new term, "dramedy," to describe its unusually downbeat style of humor.

The series creator, Larry Gelbart (1928–), explained that he gave the series a dark side in order to comment on the senselessness of war. "We all felt very keenly that inasmuch as an actual war was going on [in Vietnam], we owed it to the sensibilities and the sensitivities of an audience to take cognizance of [recognize] the fact that Americans were really being killed every week," he told the *New York Times.* Stark claimed that the tone

The TV series M*A*S*H *used humor as well as sadness to show the working and living conditions during the Korean War.*
© BETTMANN/CORBIS.

of the series matched the mood of most Americans at that time. "All this darkness fit a post-Watergate, disillusioned nation," he wrote. "Looking back, one can detect a distinct sense that people expected to be depressed in the 1970s, and that $M^*A^*S^*H$ did not disappoint them."

$M^*A^*S^*H$ won fourteen Emmy Awards and enjoyed steady popularity during its decade-long run. Nevertheless, many critics were surprised by the phenomenal success of the series finale in 1983. This special episode was the length of a made-for-TV movie. In keeping with the dark tone of the series, it opened with Alda's character, Hawkeye, in a psychiatric ward after witnessing a tragic event and suffering a mental breakdown. It closed with the war coming to an end and Hawkeye returning to his life in the United States. More than 125 million viewers tuned in to watch the characters of $M^*A^*S^*H$ say a final farewell, making

The Most-Watched TV Telecasts of All Time

As of January 1, 2006, the following three telecasts (or single episodes) received the highest ratings in the history of network television broadcasting:

1. *M*A*S*H* series finale, 1983 (50 million households, 60.2 share)

2. *Dallas* episode "Who Shot J.R.?" 1980 (42 million households, 53.3 share)

3. *Roots* miniseries final episode, 1977 (36 million households, 51.1 share)

Five of the top ten most-watched telecasts of all time are sporting events (four NFL Super Bowl telecasts and one evening's coverage of the 1994 Winter Olympics). Rounding out the list are the two parts of the first television broadcast of *Gone with the Wind* in 1976.

It is interesting to note that—other than sporting events—the most recent telecast to rank among the most-watched telecasts of all time was the series finale of *Cheers* in 1993. Since then, cable TV has increased the number of channels available to viewers and thus made it more difficult for individual episodes to attract mass audiences.

the episode the most-watched single TV telecast of all time. Most experts predict that $M*A*S*H$ will never lose this distinction, thanks to changes in the television industry. Since the episode aired, the rise of cable TV has given viewers a vast array of channel options and made it virtually impossible for a single episode to attract such a large audience.

Taking comfort in TV families

Not all 1970s television series featured family conflicts and dark humor. In fact, a whole other vein of shows developed to provide young viewers with a safe, comfortable place to retreat from the disrupting changes taking place in other areas of American life. One of the shows from this era that has enjoyed enduring popularity is *The Brady Bunch*. The show did not attract a large audience during its initial run on ABC from 1969 to 1974. It developed a strong following in reruns, however, and remains popular into the 2000s.

The Brady Bunch concerns a nontraditional family that is formed when a widower (a husband whose wife has died) with three sons marries a widow (a wife whose husband has died) with three daughters. Sherwood Schwartz (1916–), the TV producer responsible for *Gilligan's Island*, came up with the idea for the series after reading an article about rising divorce rates and the creation of blended families, or new families that are created by combining previous families. He told Stark that he intended for the show to appeal to young audiences. "This was not a show for adults or their problems," he explained. "It's a show primarily for kids and their problems. A lot of those problems were relevant [important] 100 years before the show, and I'm sure that those same problems will be relevant 100 years after the show."

In fact, *The Brady Bunch* appealed to a broad range of kids—both boys and girls, of various ages—by giving them six different young characters with whom to identify. At a time when a growing number of young people had to deal with divorce and families created by second marriages, the Bradys provided a model of a highly functional blended family. It also appealed to kids of the 1980s and 1990s who enjoyed escaping into a more pleasant, innocent time. "While adult viewers began tuning in to more realistic and sophisticated shows, like *All in the Family* and *M*A*S*H,* a sizable young audience seemed to want, even need, an unthreatening, reassuring view of life," Joe Garner wrote in *Stay Tuned: Television's Unforgettable Moments.* "As societal problems and cultural gaps grew more intractable [impossible to change], *The Brady Bunch* appeared to provide a perfect way to restore childhood innocence once a week."

Another 1970s sitcom that appealed to this sense of nostalgia, or longing for the past, was *Happy Days.* It aired on ABC for a decade, beginning in 1974, and was the highest-rated program on TV for one season. Created by Garry Marshall (1934–), it followed the adventures of a high school student named Richie Cunningham (played by Ron Howard [1954–]), along with his loving family and group of friends. The key to its popularity was that it took place during the 1950s—a simpler era when social interactions centered on sock hops, soda fountains, and "going steady."

Another TV program that provided comfort to young viewers, *Little House on the Prairie,* aired on NBC from 1974 to 1983. Based on an autobiographical series of books by Laura Ingalls Wilder, the series followed the Ingalls family as they struggled to build a home on the prairie near Walnut Grove, Minnesota, in the 1800s. It starred Michael Landon (1936–1991) of *Bonanza* fame as Pa Ingalls and Melissa Gilbert (1964–) as his daughter Laura. Over time, the series tackled some difficult subjects, including blindness, alcohol addiction, and racism. But it always did so from a foundation of mutual love, respect, and sensitivity to others. *Little House on the Prairie* became popular with a whole new generation of fans in the twenty-first century, thanks to a growing interest in American history.

Expanding the boundaries of TV

Two hit shows from the 1970s were unlike anything that had come before, and both expanded the boundaries of television in their own ways. One of these shows was *Saturday Night Live* (*SNL* for short) a skit-comedy series which made its debut in 1975 and still played on NBC in the 2000s. From the beginning of its long run, *SNL* pushed the boundaries of language and subject matter considered acceptable on television. Although the quality and influence of the show varied over time, for many years it was a pop-culture phenomenon that young adults who wanted to be up-to-date could not afford to miss. Garner wrote: "The show was at its best and most influential with the original cast in the mid- to late 1970s, when it transformed television, societal mores [values], and America's social calendar for Saturday night."

The other show was *Roots,* which became the first successful TV miniseries (a program that includes more than one episode, but ends after a few episodes rather than continuing for an entire season) when it aired on ABC for eight consecutive nights in 1977. Based on a historical novel by Alex Haley, *Roots* followed four generations of an African American family descended from one African man who was brought to the United States and sold as a slave. To the surprise of the network, it became one of the most-watched television events of all time. All eight episodes ranked among the top twenty in total number of viewers up to that time, and the final episode held the top spot for several years.

Roots was broadcast six months after the nation's bicentennial (200th birthday) celebration, which had helped focus Americans' interest on history and the experiences of ancestors. Some people hoped that the miniseries would raise awareness of the hardships suffered by African Americans and thus lead to improved race relations in the United States. The success of *Roots* did change the history of television by giving rise to other successful miniseries—such as *Lonesome Dove* and *The Thorn Birds*—and multi-part serial dramas.

For More Information

BOOKS

Barnouw, Erik. *Tube of Plenty: The Evolution of American Television.* New York: Oxford University Press, 1975.

Calabro, Marian. *Zap! A Brief History of Television.* New York: Four Winds Press, 1992.

Castleman, Harry, and Walter Podrazik. *Watching TV: Four Decades of American Television.* New York: McGraw-Hill, 1982.

Engelhardt, Tom. *The End of Victory Culture: Cold War America and the Disillusioning of a Generation.* New York: Basic Books, 1995.

Garner, Joe. *Stay Tuned: Television's Unforgettable Moments.* Kansas City: Andrews McMeel Publishing, 2002.

Gitlin, Todd. *Inside Prime Time.* New York: Pantheon, 1983.

Jones, Gerard. *Honey, I'm Home: Sitcoms Selling the American Dream.* New York: St. Martin's Press, 1993.

MacDonald, J. Fred. *One Nation under Television: The Rise and Decline of Network TV.* New York: Pantheon, 1990.

Marc, David. *Comic Visions: Television Comedy and American Culture.* Boston: Unwin Hyman, 1989.

McNeil, Alex. *Total Television: The Comprehensive Guide to Programming from 1948 to the Present.* New York: Penguin Books, 1996.

Owen, Rob. *Gen X TV: "The Brady Bunch" to "Melrose Place."* New York: Syracuse University Press, 1997.

Spigel, Lynn. *Make Room for TV: Television and the Family Ideal in Postwar America.* Chicago: University of Chicago Press, 1992.

Stark, Steven D. *Glued to the Set: The 60 Television Shows and Events That Made Us Who We Are Today.* New York: The Free Press, 1997.

PERIODICALS

Gelbart, Larry. "Its Creator Says Hail and Farewell to 'M*A*S*H.'" *New York Times,* February 27, 1983.

WEB SITES

"How Do Television Ratings Work?" *HowStuffWorks.com.* http://entertainment/howstuffworks.com (accessed June 15, 2006).

"Top 10 Network Telecasts of All Time." *Nielsen Media Research.* http://www.nielsenmedia.com/ratings/topnetworktelecasts.htm (accessed June 15, 2006).

"The Top 100 Shows of All Time." *Classic TV Database.* http://www.classic-tv.com/top100 (accessed June 15, 2006).

TV Land. http://www.tvland.com/shows (accessed June 15, 2006).

"What TV Ratings Really Mean." *Nielsen Media Research.* http://www.nielsenmedia.com/whatratingsmean (accessed June 15, 2006).

6

Prime Time Audiences Gain More Choices, 1980s–2000s

The television broadcast networks controlled the evening hours known as "prime time" from the 1940s through the 1970s. They produced some memorable programs during those decades, many of which reflected the changes that were happening in American society at the time. In the 1980s, however, the networks began losing control of prime-time television and its audiences.

Cable television service spread rapidly during that decade, to reach 60 percent of American households by 1990. In addition, the 1980s saw the rise of national cable TV networks—such as CNN, ESPN, and MTV—that catered to the specific tastes of smaller segments of the viewing audience. Instead of the four or five broadcast channel options that were previously available, American viewers suddenly had up to fifty cable channels from which to choose.

The wide variety of new channels available on cable divided the mass audience that was once available to broadcasters into smaller, separate audiences. Videocassette recorder (VCR) technology also became more affordable in the 1980s, allowing people to watch theatrical movies at home or tape TV programs for later viewing. As a result of these developments, the networks' combined share of prime-time audiences declined from 90 percent to 70 percent over the course of the decade.

American viewers also gained a fourth broadcast network in 1987, when Fox moved into prime time. From the beginning, the new Fox network took a different approach from the Big Three networks (ABC, CBS, and NBC) that had dominated television for decades. These networks had tried to create programs that attracted the largest possible audiences. Such programs received high ratings (a measure of the percentage of viewers tuning into a particular program), which meant that the networks could charge advertisers more money to place commercials on the programs. Instead of trying to attract mass audiences, Fox narrowed its focus to target young, prosperous, trend-setting Americans. "We are going after the young-adult audience," Fox president

The Emmy Awards

The Emmy Awards are among the most prized honors in the television industry. Presented by the Academy of Television Arts and Sciences (ATAS) since 1949, the Emmys recognize excellence in various aspects of TV production and performance for a given year. There are separate Emmy Awards for prime-time programs, daytime shows, and news programs.

The ATAS consists of about 12,000 members, all of whom work in the television industry. The members of the academy are divided into twenty-six peer groups by area of specialty, such as performers, makeup artists, and camera operators. All members are allowed to suggest individuals or programs from within their category for consideration for Emmy Awards. All qualified entrants are placed on a ballot, and the members vote to narrow down the list of nominees to five per category. This final list of nominees is announced to the public.

A panel of judges reviews all of the nominated programs and votes to decide the winners. The judges' votes are tallied by the independent accounting firm Ernst and Young, which keeps the results secret until the day of the Emmy Award ceremony. No one knows the identity of the winners until the award presenters open sealed envelopes on stage.

Emmy Award winners receive a statue of a winged woman holding a model of an atom. According to the academy, the winged woman represents the arts, and the atom represents the sciences. The statue was designed by television engineer Louis McManus, who used his wife as a model. It was originally known as an Immy, after an early television camera part called the Image Orthicon tube, but the name was later changed to the more feminine Emmy. The statues are sixteen inches tall, weigh nearly five pounds, and are covered in 18-karat gold.

Receiving an Emmy Award can boost the career of an actor or director. Winning can also bring public attention to a show, leading to an increase in ratings and sometimes even saving a low-rated—but innovative or high-quality—show from cancellation. The TV networks also gain importance by claiming the highest total number of Emmys for a given year. In the 2005 Emmy Awards, CBS's veteran sitcom *Everybody Loves Raymond* was honored as the outstanding comedy series, and ABC's first-year thriller *Lost* received the award for best drama series. The cable network HBO claimed twenty-seven total awards to lead all networks for the third straight year.

Jamie Kellner declared in *Gen X TV.* "A large percentage of the network audience is over 50 and, in order to win the household ratings game and be no. 1, [the networks] must appeal to older viewers. Fox is not in that household ratings game. We believe that the future of television is going to be directed toward [specific audience groups]." By the mid-1990s, Fox had achieved its goal of attracting young viewers with such hit shows as *The Simpsons, The X-Files,* and *Melrose Place.* Its success led to the formation of two more broadcast networks in 1995, the Warner Brothers Network (WB) and the United Paramount Network (UPN).

Although it took a while for the new broadcast and cable networks to break into the national TV ratings, the availability of multiple channel options had an immediate impact on the Big Three. For instance, they increasingly imitated Fox and the cable networks in targeting smaller segments of the overall viewing audience. This change in focus led to more experimentation and greater diversity of programs. Even though the networks produced some hit shows, they saw their combined share of prime-time audiences decline to around 60 percent in the 1990s. By the 2000s, original cable programming was earning critical acclaim and even winning key ratings periods.

The 1980s: Wealth and power rule TV

The 1980s have often been characterized by critics as an era when Americans were obsessed with money, power, and importance. Former actor Ronald Reagan (1911–2004; served 1981–89) served as U.S. president for most of the decade. Reagan was known as "the great communicator," and his political fortunes were closely tied to his ability to use television to his advantage. Reagan initiated economic policies that reduced taxes, promoted business, and increased military spending. Supporters said that these policies helped create a prosperous economy and restore national pride. But opponents claimed that Reagan's policies ignored problems caused by poverty and at the same time glorified greed.

One popular television show that reflected the culture of the 1980s, *Dallas,* aired on CBS from 1978 to 1991. *Dallas* focused on the power struggle between two extremely wealthy Texas oil families, the Ewings and the Barneses. At the outset of the series, the two longtime enemies have recently been linked by the marriage of son Bobby Ewing (played by Patrick Duffy) and daughter Pamela Barnes (played by Victoria Principal). "*Dallas* was not among the most popular programs of the 1980s by accident," Joe Garner wrote in *Stay Tuned: Television's Unforgettable Moments*: "Its weekly displays of opulence [wealth] and excess fit the mood of the decade like a diamond-studded boot."

Dallas was essentially a soap opera, and it had a number of characteristics that had been developed in popular daytime dramas. The show featured far more characters than most prime-time programs, for instance, and used complex storylines that continued over multiple episodes. Like many soap operas, the action in *Dallas* often revolved around a villain—Bobby's scheming, ruthless, power-hungry older brother, J. R. Ewing (played by Larry Hagman [1931–]).

Television in American Society: Almanac

Dallas was a huge hit in the United States in the early 1980s, spending five years ranked either number one or number two in the annual TV ratings. It was also tremendously popular in other countries, making it one of the first American TV shows to reach a worldwide audience. In fact, the global audience for *Dallas* was estimated at 350 million viewers in fifty-seven different countries. Its popularity prompted some foreign governments to complain that the show was promoting superficial, materialistic American values.

In an era when sitcoms dominated television, *Dallas* proved that dramas could still connect with viewers. The show's success led to a number of spin-offs and copycat series, including *Knots Landing, Dynasty,* and *Falcon Crest.* (Spin-offs are new programs built around a character that has appeared on another TV series.) Later in the decade, other networks created prime-time soap operas aimed at teenaged viewers, such as *Beverly Hills, 90210* and *Melrose Place.* Though *Dallas* was influential in many ways, the show is probably best remembered for introducing the season-ending cliffhanger to prime time TV. (A cliffhanger is an episode that ends in suspense, which encourages viewers to tune in again to see how the problem is resolved.) The 1979–1980 season of *Dallas* ended with villain J. R. Ewing being shot by an unknown assailant. After a summer of suspense, 80 million viewers tuned in to the 1980 season premiere to find out "Who Shot J. R.?," making it the most-watched telecast up to that time.

New takes on the police drama

Several of the most popular television programs of the 1980s were police shows. While this type of drama had been around for many years, the 1980s versions featured new twists. One of the most critically acclaimed cop shows of the era, *Hill Street Blues,* aired on NBC from 1981 to 1987. It was created by Steven Bochco (1943–), a veteran TV writer who decided to experiment with the traditional police drama format. He ended up totally changing the genre by adding elements from the workplace comedy and the soap opera. *Hill Street Blues* was a gritty, intense, realistic police drama that featured well-developed characters and complex plots. It was also shot with a shaky, handheld camera, which gave it a distinctive, edgy look.

Each episode of *Hill Street Blues* presented a single day in the lives of the people who worked at an urban police station. It started with the officers assembling for a morning roll call, tracked developments in their cases and personal relationships throughout the day, and ended with a late-night discussion of the day's events. Although the show included more than a dozen regular characters, it revolved around Captain Frank Furillo (played by Daniel J. Travanti) and public defender Joyce Davenport (Veronica Hamel). Professionally, the two characters often found themselves on the opposite side of issues. Personally, however, they were involved in a secret affair that lasted three seasons and eventually resulted in marriage.

Hill Street Blues took a while to find an audience. In fact, it was among the lowest-rated shows on TV during its first season. But it earned widespread critical acclaim and six Emmy Awards, including one as the outstanding drama series of the year. NBC decided to renew it for another season based on the strength of the reviews, and it soon began attracting a solid audience of upscale, educated viewers who wanted TV to provide a source of engagement rather than escape. The innovative aspects of *Hill Street Blues* influenced a number of later dramas, including *Homicide, NYPD Blue, Law and Order,* and *ER.* In a review of the series for the Museum of Broadcast Communications, Thomas Schatz claimed that *Hill Street Blues* thus launched a "new golden age" of TV drama.

Another police show of the 1980s, *Cagney and Lacey,* has the distinction of being one of the most-discussed shows in TV history. The main characters, female police detectives Christine Cagney and Mary Beth Lacey, first appeared in a made-for-TV movie in 1981. The movie received strong ratings, so CBS expanded it into a series the following year. Actress Tyne Daly (1946–) repeated her role as Lacey in the series, while Sharon Gless (1943–) took on the role of Cagney. The show was surrounded by controversy even before it came on the air, as the original actress chosen for the Cagney role was removed because she had played a lesbian in an earlier television program. CBS executives decided that she was too "masculine" and wanted to avoid suggesting a homosexual relationship between the female characters.

The controversies continued once the show came on the air. Many storylines focused on Cagney and Lacey's struggles as women working in a male-dominated profession. The series also frequently dealt with issues of special concern to women, such as rape and abortion. But the unusual gender roles seemed to cause problems for network executives, who continually offered suggestions about the characters' clothing, hairstyles, body weight, and other appearance-oriented concerns that

Cagney and Lacey, *starring Sharon Gless (left) and Tyne Daly, was the first prime-time drama to star two women.* PICTORIAL PARADE/GETTY IMAGES.

would not have applied to male police officers. CBS actually canceled *Cagney and Lacey* in the spring of 1983, but fiercely loyal viewers launched a major letter-writing and public-relations campaign that ultimately convinced the network to renew it. The show lasted four more seasons and earned numerous awards.

A more popular but very different police show of the 1980s was *Miami Vice,* which aired from 1984 to 1989. Nicknamed "MTV Cops" because of its rock music soundtrack and film style resembling a music video, the show seemed representative of the flashy excess of the times. In fact, some critics claimed that it made police programs of the past seem dull and old-fashioned by comparison. Like most cop shows, *Miami Vice* revolved around a pair of police detectives, Sonny

Crockett (played by Don Johnson [1949–]) and Rico Tubbs (Philip Michael Thomas [1949–]). Working the vice division in glamorous, tropical Miami, Florida, they operated in the high-stakes world of drug dealers, gambling rings, and gun runners.

Miami Vice is probably best remembered for its visual style, which made it look different than anything else on TV up to that time. But the show also was a first because it stressed the moral problems that Crockett and Tubbs faced on a daily basis. As they worked undercover to infiltrate drug rings and other illegal—but highly profitable—activities, they were often tempted to cross the line and become criminals themselves. This type of moral uncertainty later became common in police shows. *Miami Vice* was also influential in its use of rock music and fast-paced, visually stylized film techniques. These soon became standard features in youth-oriented TV programs and movies.

Dramas target smaller audience segments

No history of American television would be complete without mentioning *Star Trek,* the TV series that attracted a more devoted following than any other. The original outer-space adventure series aired from 1966 to 1969 and did not receive much attention. Although it was popular among teenaged boys, it never rose above number 52 in the annual ratings. In an era when the networks defined a successful series as one that appealed to mass audiences, therefore, *Star Trek* could only be considered a failed experiment. This assessment of *Star Trek* began to change in the 1970s, when the original show became a tremendous success in syndication. (Syndication occurs when programs are sold to local TV stations for broadcast in their areas. Off-network syndication refers to programs, such as *Star Trek*, that originally ran on a network, but are sold to local stations as reruns. First-run syndication refers to shows that are broadcast for the first time as a syndicated show.) In fact, fans of the series developed a whole "Trekkie culture"—attending *Star Trek* conferences, buying merchandise, and reading books associated with the show.

The original *Star Trek* followed the crew of the twenty-third-century starship *Enterprise,* which was on a mission to explore the galaxy and build relationships with alien races. The ship's commander was Captain James T. Kirk (played by William Shatner [1931–]), a strong leader equally known for getting in fistfights and romancing attractive women. Although outrageous at times, the show often used science-fiction plot lines to comment upon current events and social issues.

The surge in popularity of the original *Star Trek* led its creators to release several theatrical movies based on the series in the late 1970s and early 1980s. When large, enthusiastic audiences turned out to see these beloved characters on the big screen, the creators decided that the *Star Trek* franchise should return to television. An updated version,

Star Trek: The Next Generation, made its debut in first-run syndication in 1987. It quickly became the highest-rated syndicated drama in the history of television.

Next Generation was set seventy-eight years into the future from the original series, and it featured an all-new cast. The captain this time was Jean-Luc Picard (played by Patrick Stewart [1930–]), who was a more cultured and intellectual leader than Kirk. The new series managed to establish new characters and a distinct story line and yet maintain the spirit of the original *Star Trek*. It was cancelled in 1994 so that the characters could be featured in theatrical movies. Two more series were launched in the 1990s to continue the franchise on TV: *Star Trek: Deep Space Nine,* which took place on board a space station orbiting a recently liberated planet; and *Star Trek: Voyager,* which followed the crew of a starship that was stranded in a distant part of the galaxy, 75 years' travel away from Earth. While these shows appealed mainly to fans of science fiction and followers of the original series, they showed an increased willingness among television networks to air programs that attracted small, but devoted, audiences.

Another show to target a specific group was *thirtysomething,* which aired on ABC from 1987 to 1991 and won an Emmy Award as outstanding drama series in 1988. It was one of the first programs to focus on young urban professionals (yuppies), a part of American society that had extra money to spend—and thus was of great interest to TV networks and advertisers. *thirtysomething* followed a group of friends in their thirties who lived in suburban Philadelphia. The group included two couples—advertising copywriter Michael Steadman and his wife Hope, and graphic artist Elliot Weston and his wife Nancy—and three single people. All of the characters were not quite ready to give up the freedom of youth and take on the responsibilities of adulthood.

thirtysomething attracted a devoted following among viewers who strongly identified with the characters and their struggles. It also received a great deal of media attention, much of it focusing on its portrayal of sensitive, family men who were not afraid to discuss their feelings. The series also turned off some viewers and critics, who found the characters self-indulgent and whiny. In any case, *thirtysomething* focused on a specific group in U.S. society and dealt with the transition from youth to adulthood. It influenced a number of later programs about groups of friends, including *Friends* and *Seinfeld.*

A new wave of sitcoms

Situation comedies, or sitcoms, had dominated prime-time TV in the 1970s. In those days, the most popular sitcoms—such as *All in the Family* and *M*A*S*H*—tended to present realistic or even dark views of life. Thanks to the success of *Dallas* and several innovative cop shows, however, dramas enjoyed renewed popularity that lasted through the first half of the 1980s. The popularity of dramas, combined with societal changes such as higher divorce rates, convinced some TV critics that the family sitcom could no longer capture large audiences. The program that proved the critics wrong was *The Cosby Show,* which aired from 1984 to 1992 on NBC and reached the top spot in the annual TV ratings for four seasons. The success of *The Cosby Show* gave new life to the sitcom format. In fact, within three years of its premiere, sitcoms accounted for seven of the top ten shows on television.

The Cosby Show was created by Bill Cosby (1937–), a successful African American comedian and actor. Tired of sitcoms featuring sassy, disrespectful children, he came up with an idea for a show about a professional, middle-class black family. Cosby played Dr. Cliff Huxtable, a successful physician and wise and loving father. The show's focus on a black family made it a bit unusual for its times, but the Huxtables appealed to viewers thirsty for a show about a stable, traditional family led by a strong father figure. In fact, *The Cosby Show* was sometimes criticized for being too bland and not addressing racial issues.

The tremendous popularity of *The Cosby Show* crossed racial, ethnic, and class boundaries. Many people hoped that its portrayal of a successful black family might help improve race relations in the United States. By the time the series went off the air in 1992, however, a number of racially charged events, including riots in Los Angeles and the highly publicized murder trial of African American football star O. J. Simpson (1947–), further divided American society. By the mid-1990s, new broadcast and cable networks—including the WB and Black Entertainment Television (BET)—were creating shows aimed specifically at black audiences. *The Cosby Show* turned out to be the last major network program with equal appeal to black and white viewers. After that, and into the 2000s, polls showed that black and white Americans tended to watch completely different sets of shows.

Another popular family sitcom of the era was *Roseanne,* which aired on ABC from 1988 to 1997. Like *The Cosby Show, Roseanne* starred a successful standup comedian and revolved around a family. In fact, the two

The popularity of The Cosby Show *crossed racial, ethnic, and class boundaries.* THE KOBAL COLLECTION.

shows were developed by the same team of producers. In every other way, though, the programs were complete opposites. *Roseanne* concerned a struggling, working-class family led by a strong mother figure. Comedian Roseanne Barr (1952–) played Roseanne Connor, a big, loud, sarcastic, working mother whose interactions with her family often took the form of wisecracks and insults. While some viewers found the character

brash and unappealing, many others found the Connor family more realistic and funny than the idealized Huxtables.

Roseanne was an immediate hit, reaching number two in the ratings in
its first season and grabbing the top spot the following year. It thus became the first number one show since *I Love Lucy* to feature a female
main character. The show often tested the boundaries of network standards by frankly discussing controversial issues, such as birth control
and homosexuality. Some critics felt that the controversies helped attract
viewers to the show.

An equally popular, though less controversial, sitcom of the era was
Cheers, which aired on NBC for a decade beginning in 1983. This workplace comedy centered on the staff and customers of a Boston pub called
Cheers. The owner of the bar, Sam Malone (played by Ted Danson
[1947–]), is a former pitcher for the Boston Red Sox and recovering alcoholic. The early years of the show chronicled the romantic tension between Sam and Diane Chambers, a prim and cultured waitress at Cheers.

Cheers took a while to find an audience and narrowly escaped cancellation after its first season. But once it caught on, the series spent seven
years in the top ten and one season as TV's top-rated show. It received a
record 111 Emmy nominations during its long run, and it won twenty-six
of the coveted awards. Many TV critics cite *Cheers* as one of the first programs to include soap opera elements in the sitcom format. In addition
to providing witty dialogue and comic situations each week, the show also
followed twists and turns in the personal lives of the characters over time.
Cheers also represented a change from the typical family sitcom. In a time
when fewer Americans belonged to a traditional family, *Cheers* showed
that friends and co-workers could serve as a support circle for each
other. The 1993 series finale attracted the second-highest ratings ever
for a sitcom episode (after the series finale of $M*A*S*H$). The following
year saw the launch of a very successful spin-off series, *Frasier* (starring
Kelsey Grammer), which ran until 2004.

The 1990s: Networks narrow their focus

The 1990s saw a number of major changes occur to the world order.
First, the Cold War (1945–91) ended with the fall of Communist governments throughout Eastern Europe. The Soviet Union, which had long
been America's main political and military rival, broke up into several
smaller, independent countries. This momentous event left the United
States as the world's lone remaining superpower. In 1991, the United

States led a group of other countries to victory over Iraq in the Persian Gulf War. Once the war ended, the United States entered a decade-long period of peace, prosperity, and economic growth.

In the television industry, the competition that had emerged during the 1980s became more intense. The new Fox broadcast network introduced several hit programs aimed at younger audiences, while cable networks continued to grow and draw more viewers away from broadcast offerings. Soon the Big Three networks followed Fox's lead and began focusing on smaller segments of the overall viewing audience. The breaking-up of the mass audience meant that a program could be considered a hit by reaching fewer viewers than ever before. For instance, the ratings that made *Seinfeld* the top show of 1995 would not even have placed it in the top 25 two decades earlier. This situation encouraged the networks to experiment and take more risks in order to create quality programs that would appeal to the upscale viewers favored by advertisers.

TV dramas target teens

The first major television trend of the 1990s was new programs aimed at teenagers. The Fox network was the first to specifically target young audiences, and the success of shows such as *Beverly Hills, 90210* convinced the other networks to begin aiming toward the youth market as well. *90210* was created by Aaron Spelling (1923–2006), who had produced a number of hit shows in the 1970s. The story followed a group of students at West Beverly Hills High School. It focused on twins Brandon and Brenda Walsh (played by Jason Priestly [1969–] and Shannen Doherty [1971–]), whose family had recently moved to southern California from Minnesota.

Although *90210* used some of the tricks of the prime-time soap opera, it treated the concerns of its youthful audience more seriously than most teen dramas. One of the main characters, Dylan, struggled with drug and alcohol abuse. Another member of the central group of friends, Donna, had to deal with a learning disability. Several other characters had to cope with the divorce and remarriage of their parents or faced the decision of whether or not to become sexually active. Although some critics complained that the show focused exclusively on upper-class white kids, many teenaged viewers recognized themselves and their problems in the characters. *90210* became a pop culture phenomenon, launching books and fan clubs and setting clothing and hairstyle trends across the country. It also started a trend in which the television industry increasingly targeted younger viewers.

Beverly Hills, 90210 *was a hit show for Fox from 1990 to 2000.* FOX BROADCASTING/GETTY IMAGES.

Following the success of *90210,* Fox introduced *Melrose Place* in 1992. Also set in southern California, this show featured a group of attractive people in their twenties. Most of the characters were concerned with starting careers or getting married. Compared to *90210, Melrose Place* tended to be less serious and more sensational, like a typical prime-time soap opera. The show's wild storylines and dark humor gained a huge following among college students, who enjoyed watching the show in large groups. *Melrose Place* also became one of the first programs to build a presence on the Internet, as fans gathered online to discuss plot developments and predict the fate of various characters.

Another youth-oriented drama that became very popular in the early 1990s was *Party of Five*. It focused on five siblings who live together after their parents are killed in an automobile accident. The formerly irresponsible oldest brother, Charlie Salinger (played by Matthew Fox [1966–]), ends up becoming the legal guardian of his younger brothers and sisters. He struggles to raise his siblings and help them with their problems while also trying to run his parents' restaurant. Executive producer Amy Lippman claimed that the show appealed to the increasing number of American kids who did not live in traditional families. "We found we were actually touching a nerve in people," she said in *Gen X TV*. "The definition of family these days is not two kids, mom and dad, and a dog in the suburbs . . . Kids are figuring out the value they have to each other without any parental presence enforcing them. They have to find their way to it themselves, and I think that really seemed to hit home for a lot of people."

Realistic dramas

The 1990s also saw the introduction of several high-quality, realistic drama series aimed at educated adult viewers. Facing increased competition from narrowly targeted cable programming, the broadcast networks made a conscious decision to create shows that would appeal to the upper-income groups that held the most value for advertisers. One program that was specifically designed to compete with cable was *NYPD Blue,* which premiered on ABC in 1993. The show marked the return of Steven Bochco, creator of *Hill Street Blues,* to the police drama format. This time, Bochco decided that in order to draw viewers away from cable, his show needed to include more adult content, such as nudity and strong language.

Even before the series debut, the content issues surrounding *NYPD Blue* generated a great deal of argument. In fact, the show became the target of a protest by the conservative American Family Association, which resulted in 25 percent of ABC's local affiliate stations refusing to air the program. But the publicity surrounding the protest only increased the audience size for the stations that did carry the show, and both audiences and critics liked what they saw. *NYPD Blue* was a gritty, urban cop show that featured compelling story lines and complex characters. It revolved around Andy Sipowitz (played by Dennis Franz [1944–]), a cynical, hot-tempered, but deeply dedicated veteran detective, and his relationship with his partners. The show provided new cases for the detectives to solve each week, but it also featured ongoing plot lines about their personal lives. *NYPD Blue* was perhaps most notable for its sensitive portrayal of male police officers. In addition to being tough, the detectives on the show also felt compassion for crime victims and often discussed their emotions.

Another popular series of the 1990s was *Law and Order,* an innovative combination of police and courtroom dramas. Each episode provided an inside look at the U.S. criminal justice system by following a crime from two perspectives. During the first half of the show, the action centered on the police detectives who investigated the crime and collected evidence. During the second half of the show, the action shifted to the district attorneys who used the evidence to prosecute the offenders. *Law and Order* was a tremendous success among both viewers and critics, and its popularity continued despite numerous cast changes over the years. It eventually became one of the longest-running drama series in TV history and created a number of successful spin-offs focusing on specific types of crimes.

ER, which premiered in 1994 and became the top-rated show on television three times in the second half of the 1990s, was another popular, realistic drama of the 1990s. *ER* took place in the emergency room of a Chicago hospital. Medical dramas had always been a favorite genre within the television industry. They were easy to film, since they took place within a controlled setting, and they also provided dramatic life-or-death situations. When *ER* came on the scene, however, some analysts of popular culture were predicting that shorter attention spans among viewers would spell the end of the hour-long drama in prime time.

To address this problem, the producers of *ER* divided each episode into shorter segments and increased the pace of the action so that it often approached chaos. As executive producer John Wells explained in *Gen X TV,* "The pace of the show [came about] because we wanted to be true to the real emergency room experience. . . . This is really what emergency rooms are like. You don't follow a patient through entire days like we saw in traditional medical shows." Many later programs adopted the fast pace and multiple story lines that helped make *ER* successful.

ER also differed from previous medical dramas by focusing on a group of young doctors. The series showed them dealing with their own problems as well as treating patients. In order to make *ER* seem more realistic, the characters used accurate medical terminology, and the story lines sometimes ended unhappily. Some critics pointed out that the show had special meaning for middle-aged Americans who were beginning to be concerned about illness and aging.

Sitcoms for singles

The situation comedies that aired on the broadcast networks in the 1990s also showed an increased focus on young, upscale viewers. For instance, a number of popular sitcoms centered on single people and their concerns. One of these shows, the workplace comedy *Murphy Brown,* focused on a high-powered career woman (played by Candice Bergen [1946–]). "Murphy Brown is one of the most original, distinctive female characters on television," Julie Prince wrote in a *Museum of Broadcast Communications* article about the show. "Her ambition and stubbornness frequently get her into trouble, and she often acts a little foolishly herself. But what sets Murphy apart from so many other female sitcom characters is that when she gets into a ridiculous mess, it is not because she is a woman. It's because she is Murphy."

Murphy Brown aired on CBS from 1988 to 1997—a time when women were taking on positions of increasing responsibility in corporate America. The series showed what took place behind the scenes of a fictional TV news program called "FYI." It explored the relationships between Murphy Brown and the reporters, producers, and other staff members.

In 1992, the show became part of a real news event. Then-Vice President Dan Quayle (1947–; served 1989–93) criticized the character of Murphy Brown for providing a poor example of family values (because Murphy had given birth to a child outside marriage). The show's producer, Diane English, defended the character's choice in the news media. The following season, the controversy became the focus of an episode of *Murphy Brown.*

Another landmark sitcom of the 1990s was *Seinfeld,* which debuted on NBC in 1990. Like many other popular sitcoms, it was based on the work of a well-known standup comedian, Jerry Seinfeld (1954–). The series followed the comic misadventures of Jerry and his self-absorbed, crazy friends in New York City. The most distinctive element of *Seinfeld* was its emphasis on the trivial, mundane aspects of life. Most episodes featured Jerry and his friends stuck in absurd, but still recognizable, situations. For instance, they spent one entire episode wandering around a parking garage looking for their car and another episode

Seinfeld was one of the most successful comedies in TV history. THE KOBAL COLLECTION.

scheming about how to make a fortune by exploiting bottle-return laws. Even though the show was admittedly about nothing, and in many ways the characters were stuck in adolescence, *Seinfeld* attracted a devoted following among viewers. Critics liked the show as well, praising it as an innovative update of the sitcom genre. It reached the top of the annual TV ratings in 1995 and 1998, and it is often mentioned among the best shows of all time.

Friends, which debuted in 1994 on NBC, was another popular and timely sitcom of the 1990s. *Friends* revolved around six close friends who live in New York City and hang out at a coffee shop near Central Park. The characters included Monica (Courteney Cox), an obsessively neat chef; Ross (David Schwimmer), her nerdy paleontologist brother; Rachel (Jennifer Aniston), her best friend from high school; Phoebe (Lisa Kudrow), an offbeat massage therapist and folk singer; Joey (Matt LeBlanc), a struggling actor and ladies' man; and Chandler (Matthew Perry), a witty but insecure office worker. Series co-creator Marta Kauffman noted that all of the characters are confused in some way. "They want love and commitment, they're afraid of love and commitment. Some of them have made career choices, some of them haven't. The most important thing is that their emotional situations are, we hope, universal," she said in *Gen X TV*.

Friends differed from most other sitcoms with its emphasis on dialogue and wordplay. In many scenes, the characters simply sit around and talk. Their discussions are often full of pop-culture references that have special meaning to media-savvy young audiences. In order to retain the interest of viewers with shorter attention spans, the show also featured three story lines per episode, rather than the two story lines in a typical sitcom. Finally, *Friends* was notable for following the personal development of the characters over time, as well as the continuing saga of their relationships with each other. By the end of the series in 2004, Monica and Chandler were married, and Ross and Rachel had a child together.

New family comedies

Not all sitcoms of the 1990s focused on single people and their concerns. In fact, three of the most popular comedies of the era focused on suburban families, and two of these shows represented a throwback to earlier times. *Home Improvement,* which debuted on ABC in 1991 and reached number one in the annual ratings in 1994, was set in suburban Detroit, Michigan. It starred comedian Tim Allen (1953–) as Tim "The Toolman" Taylor, host of a handyman show on cable TV. The main focus of the show was the relationship between Tim and his wife Jill, and their very different approaches to the everyday issues facing their family. Reviewers noted that *Home Improvement* demonstrated middle-class, Midwestern values while also exploring the challenges of being a man in the 1990s.

A very similar show, *Everybody Loves Raymond,* debuted on CBS in 1996. Based on the real-life experiences of comedian Ray Romano

(1957–), it focused on the relationship between Ray Barone, a magazine sportswriter, and his wife Debra. Much of the conflict and humor arose out of Debra's attempts to cope with Ray's interfering parents, who lived across the street. Like *Home Improvement, Everybody Loves Raymond* resembled family sitcoms of past eras, while also providing an updated portrait of a modern marriage. It ranked among the top five series for several years and won Emmy Awards as the outstanding comedy series of the year in 2003 and 2005.

Unlike these two programs, which provided viewers with a familiar look at suburban life, another popular family sitcom of the 1990s broke new ground in almost every conceivable way. *The Simpsons* cartoon family got their start on TV in a series of short clips on a Fox variety series, *The Tracey Ullman Show,* in 1987. Two years later they appeared in a Christmas special, and in 1990 Fox turned *The Simpsons* into a regular prime-time series. Created by comic strip artist and writer Matt Groening (1954–), the animated show presents a dysfunctional suburban family. The bumbling father, Homer Simpson, works as a safety inspector at a nuclear power plant and spends his spare time drinking beer. His sensible and loving wife, Marge, raises their three children: Bart, a troublemaking underachiever; Lisa, a highly intelligent, socially conscious saxophone player; and baby Maggie.

The Simpsons became an immediate hit, especially among younger viewers. It also garnered praise from TV critics for its sharp-edged social criticism and clever pop-culture references. *The Simpsons* pushed the boundaries of broadcast television with its cynical, sarcastic brand of humor and its constant jabs at American institutions—including politics, religion, family, and the media. "*The Simpsons* . . . was the single most influential program in establishing Fox as a legitimate broadcast television network," Matthew P. McAllister declared in a *Museum of Broadcast Communications* article about the show.

Television historians attribute the success of *The Simpsons* partly to conditions in the television industry in the early 1990s. The broadcast networks faced increased competition from cable at this time. Newcomer Fox, in particular, was under pressure to build an audience base and attract advertising dollars. This combination of factors encouraged Fox to take a chance on an unconventional and potentially controversial show like *The Simpsons.* The network's gamble paid off: *The Simpsons* became the first Fox program to move into the top ten in the annual ratings, and it even beat the tremendously popular *Cosby Show* among key viewing

Matt Groening, creator of The Simpsons, *pictured with his cartoon TV family.* © DOUGLAS KIRKLAND/CORBIS.

groups. *The Simpsons* made Fox seem innovative and edgy compared to other networks, and it thus opened the door to more experimental programming choices across the industry.

The 2000s: "Reality" conquers prime time

The turn of the twenty-first century saw a change in Americans' overall mood from optimism to fear and uncertainty. A long period of economic growth ended with the sudden collapse of Internet-related companies (known as dot.com companies, after the .com extension used for commercial Web sites) in the stock market, which wiped out millions of investors. The terrorist attacks against the United States that took place on September 11, 2001, created widespread fears about national security. In 2003 the United States invaded Iraq. Although the U.S. military succeeded in removing Iraqi dictator Saddam Hussein (1937–) from power, the United States became involved in a long, expensive, and uncertain military action in the Middle East.

Like the rest of the country, the American television industry faced tough economic times in the early 2000s. The networks continued to lose viewers to cable TV, while the Internet and other emerging technologies increasingly competed with television for Americans' time and attention. TV programs became more expensive to produce, while the basic genres started to seem uninteresting and predictable. The answer to these problems came in the form of reality television shows, which became very popular in the early 2000s.

In some ways, modern reality shows descended from the hidden-camera shows and game shows of earlier eras. They also grew out of the more recent success of *America's Funniest Home Videos* (1990–), in which viewers' home videos competed for a cash prize, and MTV's *The Real World* (1992–), in which the network filmed the interactions of a group of very different young people thrown together in one house. The networks liked reality shows because they cast regular people instead of stars, making them cheap to produce. They also required little development and were easier to launch than scripted series. Finally, reality shows held appeal for viewers who enjoyed watching real people, not actors, humiliate themselves on TV.

The show that introduced the reality-TV craze was *Survivor,* which debuted on CBS in 2000. In the series premiere, sixteen strangers from different backgrounds were taken by boat to the secluded island of Pulau Tiga, near Borneo in the South China Sea. They were given two minutes to pack as many supplies as they could carry on two small rafts, then they were forced to paddle to shore and set up makeshift camps. The TV cameras followed them for the next thirty-nine days, as they struggled to find food and shelter, competed in physical and mental challenges, and formed and dissolved alliances. Every three days they held a tribal council ceremony in which they voted to eliminate one contestant from the island. An amazing 51 million people watched the final episode of the season, in which scheming advertising executive Richard Hatch became the last "Survivor" and won one million dollars. The season finale thus became the second-highest rated show of the year after the Super Bowl. The popularity of *Survivor* continued the following season, when the second edition of the series became the highest-rated show of 2001.

The 2006 American Idol *winner Taylor Hicks, right, and runner-up Katharine McPhee at the highly rated May 2006 finale.* © FRED PROUSER/REUTERS/CORBIS.

The success of *Survivor* encouraged the other networks to begin their own reality series. Several of these shows enjoyed great popularity as well. In fact, by 2002 five of the top ten programs on television were reality shows. One of the most successful of these series was *American Idol,* which became the first show on the Fox network to win the annual ratings in 2004. *American Idol* was basically an extended audition, as a group of talented young singers competed for a recording contract. One contestant was eliminated each week, through a combination of judges' decisions and viewer call-in voting. Another popular series, *The Apprentice,* featured millionaire businessman Donald Trump (1946–) auditioning groups of business-savvy young people for a high-profile position in his corporation. Each episode ended with Trump informing one contestant, "You're fired!" In another twist on the same theme, *The Bachelor* featured a group of young women competing to win the heart of an attractive, eligible man, with one or more contestants being eliminated each week.

A common criticism of reality shows was that the intense competition—coupled with the desire to establish a TV personality that stood out from the crowd—caused the contestants to lie, cheat, and generally be mean to each other. While this sort of behavior made for entertaining television, many critics complained that it set a bad example, particularly for younger viewers. An exception to this rule was ABC's *Extreme Makeover: Home Edition*—a very different type of reality show that received high praise for promoting positive values. Each week, carpenter Ty Pennington and a collection of professional designers and building contractors performed a complete renovation of the home of a deserving family. Every episode ended with the family seeing their renovated home for the first time. The Parents Television Council named *Extreme Makeover: Home Edition* the best show for family viewing in 2004, calling it "an excellent example of a constructive and uplifting reality TV show. Unlike other reality series that emphasize and exploit contestants' worse qualities (greed, dishonesty, vanity, etc.), this inspiring program showcases charity and selflessness."

By the mid-2000s, the reality-TV craze seemed to be fading. A few of the big shows—such as *Survivor* and *American Idol*—remained popular, but many copycat series failed to attract viewers. In addition, the networks found that viewers tended to stop watching after one season. As of 2004, reality shows as a whole were performing worse than scripted shows and had lost 15 percent of their audience from the previous season.

Cable networks create prime-time hits

As reality shows dominated prime time on the broadcast networks, cable networks increasingly developed original programming with adult themes. One such show was *Sex and the City,* a comedy-drama that debuted on HBO in 1998. Based upon a memoir by Candace Bushnell, the show revolved around Carrie Bradshaw (played by Sarah Jessica Parker

The Best TV Shows of All Time

"What is the best television program of all time?" is a question guaranteed to start a lively discussion in any social gathering. Different series appeal to different viewers for different reasons, so every individual polled is likely to have a unique response. A number of TV critics, periodicals, and online sites have attempted to answer the question over the years, with predictably differing results. It can be interesting to compare the opinions of different sources. Here are two widely circulated lists of the top twenty shows of all time.

According to *TV Guide* in 2002, the top twenty are:

1. *Seinfeld*
2. *I Love Lucy*
3. *The Honeymooners*
4. *All in the Family*
5. *The Sopranos*
6. *60 Minutes*
7. *Late Show with David Letterman*
8. *The Simpsons*
9. *The Andy Griffith Show*
10. *Saturday Night Live*
11. *The Mary Tyler Moore Show*
12. *The Tonight Show Starring Johnny Carson*
13. *The Dick Van Dyke Show*
14. *Hill Street Blues*
15. *The Ed Sullivan Show*
16. *The Carol Burnett Show*
17. *Today*
18. *Cheers*
19. *thirtysomething*
20. *St. Elsewhere*

According to the *Classic TV Database* Web site in 2005, the top twenty are:

1. *I Love Lucy*
2. *M*A*S*H*
3. *Star Trek*
4. *The Andy Griffith Show*
5. *Cheers*
6. *The Dick Van Dyke Show*
7. *The Mary Tyler Moore Show*
8. *Bewitched*
9. *The Twilight Zone*
10. *All in the Family*
11. *The Carol Burnett Show*
12. *Happy Days*
13. *Mission: Impossible*
14. *The Cosby Show*
15. *The Simpsons*
16. *The Brady Bunch*
17. *The Avengers*
18. *ER*
19. *Seinfeld*
20. *The X-Files*

[1965–])—an attractive, single woman who lives an upscale lifestyle in New York City and writes a newspaper column about relationships and sex. Carrie often compares notes on the dating scene with her three female friends. While some viewers were shocked by the characters' frank discussions about their busy sex lives, many others tried to copy Carrie's fashion sense and trendy wardrobe.

Another hit series on HBO that pushed established limits on television content was *The Sopranos*. The show focused on Tony Soprano (James Gandolfini [1961–]), the boss of a modern-day organized crime family. Although Tony arranges murders and otherwise behaves like a typical gangster, he also attends regular sessions with a psychiatrist to manage his feelings of remorse and anxiety. *The Sopranos* included foul language and violence, but it also featured well-developed characters and interesting plot twists. As a result, from its debut in 1999 the series received critical acclaim, numerous Emmy nominations, and the highest ratings ever for an HBO original series.

Throughout the early 2000s, a number of cable networks introduced original prime-time programs during the summer months, when the broadcast networks typically aired reruns, or repeat showings of previous programs. Many of these series received praise from TV critics and attracted numerous viewers. In fact, this strategy helped the cable networks become the favorites of prime-time audiences during the summer season. The summer of 2005 marked the fifth straight year that cable networks had triumphed in the ratings, nearly doubling the audience share earned by the broadcast networks, 60.9 to 32.4. TNT ranked first among ad-supported cable networks in average prime-time viewers that year (with 2.58 million), followed by USA (2.13 million), Nick at Night (1.89 million), ESPN (1.79 million), and Fox News Channel (1.78 million), according to Aimee Deeken in *MediaWeek*.

Broadcast networks still generate buzz

Partly due to the success of original cable programs such as *The Sopranos,* the broadcast networks began including more blood, gore, and violence in their prime-time offerings. When the reality craze faded in the mid-2000s, many crime and mystery dramas filled network schedules. The networks favored these types of shows because the frightening elements and violence held viewers' attention. In addition, most of these shows featured self-contained episodes that still drew strong audiences in reruns. Compared to serialized dramas, where the stories continue to evolve over time, crime shows allowed people to watch one episode at a time without feeling like they were missing something, thus increasing the likelihood that they would tune in to the show again.

The CBS program *CSI: Crime Scene Investigation* led the annual TV ratings three times in the mid-2000s. It focused on a team of forensic scientists at the Las Vegas Crime Lab, who are called in to help the police process crime scenes and examine evidence in bizarre and often gruesome murder cases. The success of *CSI* led to two spin-off series which focused on forensic teams in New York and Miami, and it also prompted a wave of similar programs on other networks. By 2005, crime and mystery series accounted for 37 percent of the prime-time TV schedule, as well as eleven of the top twenty-five shows in the annual TV ratings.

The networks' crime wave generated some criticism about the increasing level of violence on television. In fact, an article in *The Americas Intelligence Wire* pointed out that sixty-three dead bodies were visible on prime-time network broadcasts during the last week of September 2005—more than twice as many as a year earlier. Some parents' groups expressed concern that exposure to TV violence might make children less sensitive to violent behavior in real life. But broadcasters argued that they were only trying to compete with cable shows, video games, and theatrical movies, in which the effects are usually more graphic.

In any case, a few broadcast networks showed a willingness to break out of the crowd and create innovative new shows, like those found on cable. This strategy worked particularly well for ABC, which scored big ratings and lots of media attention with its slate of new dramas in 2004. The network introduced *Lost,* a suspenseful drama about a group of plane crash survivors stranded on a spooky tropical island. It featured a large cast of characters whose background stories are gradually revealed in flashbacks, or scenes depicting memories of earlier events. The series also earned praise for its cinematography, which some critics said was worthy of a theatrical film. ABC also created a hit with *Grey's Anatomy,* a medical drama that focused on a group of young interns working at an urban hospital. The show climbed into the top five during the 2005 season, and the network recognized its popularity by awarding it the coveted spot following the 2006 Super Bowl.

Perhaps the most talked-about new show on ABC, however, was *Desperate Housewives.* Producer Marc Cherry (1962–) said that he wanted to create a show that ordinary viewers could identify with. He designed a smart, quirky, darkly funny soap opera about a group of middle-class, suburban wives and mothers. The story centers on four female neighbors who band together to figure out why a former member of their circle committed suicide. In an unusual twist, the dead woman narrates the tale. *Desperate Housewives* became an immediate hit with viewers and helped ABC vault from fourth to second place in the overall network ratings. Some critics hoped that ABC's success would encourage the other broadcast networks to focus on creating innovative, quality programming as well.

For More Information

BOOKS

Barnouw, Erik. *Tube of Plenty: The Evolution of American Television.* New York: Oxford University Press, 1975.

Calabro, Marian. *Zap! A Brief History of Television.* New York: Four Winds Press, 1992.

Castleman, Harry, and Walter Podrazik. *Watching TV: Four Decades of American Television.* New York: McGraw-Hill, 1982.

Garner, Joe. *Stay Tuned: Television's Unforgettable Moments.* Kansas City: Andrews McMeel Publishing, 2002.

Gitlin, Todd. *Inside Prime Time.* New York: Pantheon, 1983.

Lasswell, Mark. *TV Guide: Fifty Years of Television.* New York: Crown, 2002.

Lichter, S. Robert. *Prime Time: How TV Portrays American Culture.* Washington, DC: Regnery Publishers, 1994.

MacDonald, J. Fred. *One Nation under Television: The Rise and Decline of Network TV.* New York: Pantheon, 1990.

McNeil, Alex. *Total Television: The Comprehensive Guide to Programming from 1948 to the Present.* New York: Penguin Books, 1996.

Sackett, Susan. *Prime-Time Hits: Television's Most Popular Network Programs, 1950 to the Present.* New York: Billboard Books, 1993.

Stark, Steven D. *Glued to the Set: The 60 Television Shows and Events That Made Us Who We Are Today.* New York: The Free Press, 1997.

PERIODICALS

Bauder, David. "Almost Unnoticed, U.S. Prime-Time TV Becomes the Place for Blood and Guts." *The Americas Intelligence Wire,* November 21, 2005.

Boedeker, Hal. "Crime Dramas Dominate the Network TV Schedule." *Orlando Sentinel,* November 25, 2005.

Deeken, Amy. "TNT, USA Top Cable Ratings." *MediaWeek,* December 19, 2005.

Friedman, Wayne. "Stellar Programs Aside, Reality Losing Its Shine." *Television Week,* May 3, 2004.

Sellers, Patricia. "ABC's Desperate Measures Pay Off." *Fortune,* November 15, 2004.

Wallenstein, Andrew. "Emmy Still Loves Raymond." *Back Stage,* September 22, 2005.

WEB SITES

Academy of Television Arts and Sciences. http://www.emmys.tv/awards/index.php (accessed on June 15, 2006).

McAllister, Matthew P. "The Simpsons." *Museum of Broadcast Communications.* http:// www.museum.tv/archives/etv/S/htmlS/simpsonsthe/simpsonsthe.htm (accessed on June 15, 2006).

Nelson, Pamela. "How the Emmy Awards Work." *HowStuffWorks.com.* http:// entertainment.howstuffworks.com/emmy.htm (accessed on June 15, 2006).

Prince, Julie. "Murphy Brown." *Museum of Broadcast Communications.* http:// www.museum.tv/archives/etv/M/htmlM/murphybrown/murphybrown.htm (accessed on June 15, 2006).

Shapiro, Mitchell E. "Prime Time." *Museum of Broadcast Communications.* http:// www.museum.tv/archives/etv/P/htmlP/primetime/primetime.htm (accessed on June 15, 2006).

"Top 100 Shows." *Classic TV Database.* http://www.classic-tv.com/top100 (accessed on June 15, 2006).

"Top Ten Best and Worst Shows for Family Viewing." *Parents Television Council,* October 19, 2005. http://www.parentstv.org/PTC/familyguide/main.asp (accessed on June 15, 2006).

7

Children's and Daytime Programming

The television shows that air in the evening hours known as prime time attract the largest audiences and receive the most media attention. But television programming is not limited to the three-hour block between 8:00 and 11:00 P.M. In fact, most stations offer a variety of programs throughout the day, all designed to appeal to the viewers most likely to be watching at a particular time.

During the daytime hours, many Americans are away at work or school. Those who tend to be at home—and available to watch TV—during the day include small children, stay-at-home parents, retired senior citizens, and college students. Since daytime television programming is intended to appeal to these audiences, it is much different than the situation comedies and hour-long dramas that typically air in prime time. In the early 2000s, most daytime programming on the broadcast networks consisted of children's shows, soap operas, talk shows, and game shows.

Children's shows

According to the Federal Communications Commission (FCC), the government agency that regulates all types of communications, American children watched an average of three to four hours of television per day in 2005. Watching TV offers children some potential benefits. Educational programs can help prepare them to succeed in school, for example, by introducing such subjects as math, reading, and science. TV shows can also teach children important social skills, such as sharing, cooperating, and accepting differences.

However, television programs can also have a negative influence on kids. Many shows present racial and gender stereotypes (generalized, often negative ideas about a group of people), violent behavior, sexual situations, and strong language that are not appropriate for young viewers. Even programs specifically aimed at children feature commercials, and studies show that young people cannot always tell the difference

The Howdy Doody Show, *one of the first children's programs on TV, ran from 1947 to 1960.* HULTON ARCHIVE/GETTY IMAGES.

between entertainment and advertisements. Finally, many critics argue that kids could put the time spent watching television to better use— by reading, interacting with their families, doing homework, or engaging in physical activity.

Television has featured children's programming from its early days in the 1940s. Many of the earliest programs for children were half-hour action-adventure shows such as *The Lone Ranger* and *Lassie*. Another popular early kids' program was *The Howdy Doody Show,* which was broadcast on NBC from 1947 to 1960. It starred a cowboy, Buffalo Bob Smith (1915–1998), and his puppet partner, Howdy Doody. Like many of the popular variety shows of that time, *The Howdy Doody Show* featured jokes, songs, and skits. The episodes were filmed in front of a live studio audience filled with enthusiastic children and their parents.

While *The Howdy Doody Show* provided young viewers with entertainment, critics complained that it had no educational value. Conflicting opinions on the show's value began the longstanding debate about children's television. Some people claimed that the broadcast networks had an obligation to educate and inform viewers, but network executives preferred to concentrate on attracting large audiences, which brought the network more money from commercial sponsors.

The popularity of *The Howdy Doody Show* began to fade during the 1950s, when many children discovered Walt Disney's *Mickey Mouse Club*. This variety series ran on ABC on weekday afternoons from 1955 through 1959. It starred a group of talented young performers, called Mouseketeers, who sang, danced, and performed skits. A few of the Mouseketeers, such as Annette Funicello (1942–), went on to have successful careers in music and film.

The longest-running network children's series, *Captain Kangaroo*, also got its start in 1955. It starred Bob Keeshan (1927–2004), who had begun his acting career by playing Clarabell the Clown—a silent character who communicated by honking a horn—on *The Howdy Doody Show*. Keeshan felt that most TV shows aimed at kids were too loud and fast-paced. He wanted to tone down the action and focus on learning.

Captain Kangaroo included many of the same features as other children's programs of that time, including songs, skits, jokes, and puppets. But it was much quieter than other programs because it was not filmed in front of a studio audience. In each episode of *Captain Kangaroo*, Keeshan wandered through the Treasure House and talked with a variety of characters, such as Mr. Green Jeans, Dancing Bear, Bunny Rabbit, and Mr. Moose. Each show provided young viewers with a positive, educational message, but it was always delivered with gentle humor. *Captain Kangaroo* lasted for thirty years on CBS, then the program ran for six more years on PBS. During that time, Keeshan personally approved all of the commercials that aired during the program to ensure that the products were good for children.

The creation of PBS

During the 1960s, animated cartoons started to dominate children's programming on the major broadcast networks (ABC, NBC, and CBS), particularly on Saturday mornings. Some of the early shows featured

Captain Kangaroo, right, Mr. Green Jeans, middle, and a host of other characters brought their positive messages to generations of children on the show **Captain Kangaroo.** CBS/GETTY IMAGES.

such enduring characters as Bugs Bunny, Woody Woodpecker, Yogi Bear, and Huckleberry Hound. But the networks' emphasis on cartoons led to increased concerns about the quality of children's programming. Critics complained that cartoons had no educational value, and they pointed out that the cartoons often included violence, stereotyped characters, and commercial tie-ins (products for sale that are somehow connected to the program). Many people felt that the networks did not offer enough educational programming for children.

In 1967 the U.S. Congress responded to growing concerns about television quality by passing the Public Broadcasting Act, which provided

Public Broadcasting Service (PBS)

In the early days of television, many people believed that the new technology could become a valuable tool for informing and educating viewers. The first laws affecting the television industry tried to make sure that TV lived up to its potential. The Communications Act of 1934, for example, said that the airwaves which carry TV signals belong to the American people. Since television broadcasters use the public airwaves to distribute their programs, they have a duty to create programs that served the public interest.

When commercial broadcasting began in the late 1940s, though, a combination of factors allowed three powerful networks (ABC, CBS, and NBC) to take control of the limited number of Very High Frequency (VHF) channels available for TV broadcasting. The Big Three networks generally served their own interests rather than the public interest. That is, they broadcast whatever type of programs would attract mass audiences and generate advertising revenues. Only a few channels on the less desirable Ultra High Frequency (UHF) band were set aside for public service programming.

In 1967, the U.S. Congress tried to address the lack of educational and informational programs on television by passing the Public Broadcasting Act. This act created the Corporation for Public Broadcasting (CPB) to raise money to support public television and radio services. In 1969, the CPB established the Public Broadcasting Service (PBS), a national nonprofit organization designed to create and distribute TV programs that serve the public interest. While not a formal network, PBS eventually grew to include more than 350 member stations across the United States. Many of these stations operate out of colleges and universities. Instead of selling commercial time to make money, PBS stations receive funding from individual viewers, businesses, charities, and the federal government.

PBS started broadcasting in October 1970. From the beginning, PBS stations have aired the types of programs that do not attract large enough audiences to interest the commercial broadcast networks. Typical PBS shows include educational programs for preschoolers, how-to programs about cooking and home repair, cultural programs such as *Masterpiece Theater,* and news and documentaries. Over the years, PBS has broadcast many highly regarded children's shows, such as *Sesame Street, Zoom! Barney and Friends, Reading Rainbow, Arthur,* and the *Magic School Bus.*

While PBS has developed a number of award-winning programs, it has also created some controversy. Politicians occasionally try to discontinue government funding for PBS, claiming that it should be able to support itself through private donations rather than taxpayer money. However, some people argue that PBS should receive more government funding so that it does not have to depend on corporate sponsorships. They claim that corporate sponsors could influence programming choices, which would make PBS move away from educational shows and toward shows with more commercial (money-making) appeal.

government funding to create a national public broadcasting service. Unlike commercial broadcasting, in which networks sell advertising time to make money, public broadcasting receives funding from individual viewers, businesses, charities, and the federal government. The Public

The lovable Sesame Street *characters entertain children while teaching them letters, numbers, manners, and more.* CHILDREN'S TELEVISION WORKSHOP/GETTY IMAGES.

Broadcasting Service (PBS) focused on creating programs that would educate, inform, and enrich television viewers. One of the most popular shows on PBS was *Sesame Street,* which made its debut in 1969 and continued to air original episodes into the 2000s.

Sesame Street was created by Joan Ganz Cooney (1929–), an accomplished New York public TV producer. She conducted extensive studies on children's television viewing habits in order to develop a program for preschoolers that would be both educational and entertaining. Like earlier successful kids' shows, *Sesame Street* featured puppets, skits, and songs. Each episode was divided into short segments in order to keep young viewers' attention, and it also repeated key concepts in order to promote learning. The show became an immediate popular and critical success.

Within a year of its introduction, it was being watched by over half of the nation's children between the ages of three and five. In its thirty-five years on the air, *Sesame Street* won more Emmy Awards (annual honors presented for excellence in TV programming) than any other show in history.

Of course, not everyone liked *Sesame Street*. Some early critics complained that children who were used to the show's fast pace and short segments would have trouble paying attention to parents and teachers. Over the years, though, the pace of children's programs grew even more hectic, so that *Sesame Street* seemed slow by comparison. Other people worried that the show's success on PBS would discourage the broadcast networks from trying to create high-quality, educational programming for children. This prediction proved true, with a few exceptions, until the U.S. government stepped in and required the networks to provide educational programming in the 1990s.

Another popular PBS program was *Mister Rogers' Neighborhood*. This show was created by Fred Rogers (1928–2003), who believed that television programming could do more to educate, entertain, and support young children. "I got into television because I hated it so," he once told CNN, "and I thought there was some way of using this fabulous instrument to be of nurture to those who would watch and listen."

After spending a few years on local stations in Canada and Pennsylvania, *Mister Rogers' Neighborhood* made its debut on PBS in 1968. Each episode began with Rogers entering his house, taking off his coat and shoes, and putting on a comfortable sweater and sneakers. He reached out to young viewers by speaking directly to the camera in a kind, patient, and soothing manner. By the time the last original episode aired in 2001, *Mister Rogers' Neighborhood* had won many awards and earned widespread praise for providing children with a safe, calm place in which to learn about the importance of loving themselves and being kind to others.

An innovative network program designed to educate children was *Schoolhouse Rock,* which aired on ABC from 1973 to 1985. The show consisted of a series of three-minute segments that taught children about topics in math, science, grammar, and history. The series was created by New York advertising executive David McCall (1928–1999), who found that his young son struggled to learn his multiplication tables but had no trouble remembering the lyrics to rock songs. McCall and his colleagues set some educational information to music and added animated cartoons to illustrate the concepts. *Schoolhouse Rock* segments

Dora the Explorer, *a successful Nickelodeon program, teaches Spanish language while telling tales of friendship and fun.* NICKELODEON/ GETTY IMAGES.

such as "Conjunction Junction" and "I'm Just a Bill" proved so memorable that college students launched a successful campaign to bring the series back in the 1990s.

Cable television for children

In the 1980s the growth of cable TV and introduction of video cassette recorders (VCRs) began to change children's programming. Several cable networks emerged that featured only kids' shows, such as Nickelodeon, the Disney Channel, and the Cartoon Network. Other cable networks— such as Discovery, USA, the Learning Channel, and the Family Channel— carried a great deal of children's programming as well. The rise of cable thus led to more variety in television offerings for children.

The first all-children's cable channel, Nickelodeon, was launched in 1979. It offered reruns (repeats of episodes that had already appeared on the air) of older network series, as well as original programs that were both entertaining and educational. By the early 2000s Nickelodeon was the clear ratings leader in kids' programming, offering such success-ful shows as *Dora the Explorer, Blue's Clues, SpongeBob SquarePants,* and *Jimmy Neutron.* Nickelodeon also brought in $3 billion from sales of related products in 2004, demonstrating that merchandising (attaching products to TV shows or movies) can be a very profitable aspect of children's programming.

Concerns about quality

Over the years, many people have conducted studies about the effects of television on young people. One important issue that has grown out of this research concerns children's exposure to violence on television. The U.S. Congress held hearings about the level of violence in TV programs as early as 1952. Following additional hearings in 1964, Congress pub-lished a report that recognized television's role in children's development and criticized the quality of television programming. In 1972 the U.S. government released the results of a large-scale study about the effects of TV violence on children. This research showed that viewing violent programs on television tended to increase children's aggressive behavior, make them less sensitive to the pain and suffering of others, and cause them to become more fearful of the world around them.

Many later studies confirmed these effects of children's exposure to TV violence. Nevertheless, the TV networks continued to air program-ming with violent content because it grabbed viewers' attention and received high ratings. According to Mary L. Gavin in the 2005 online article "How TV Affects Your Child," an average American child can expect to see two hundred thousand violent acts on TV by the age of eighteen. In response to growing concerns about children's exposure to TV violence, in 1992 the broadcast networks adopted a ratings system that would provide on-screen advisories for all programs with violent content. The Telecommunications Policy Act of 1996 took the effort

TV Content Ratings

In the 1990s the major producers of children's television programming worked together to create a ratings system. Modeled after the ratings system used for theatrical films, it was intended to inform parents about program content that might be inappropriate for younger viewers. The ratings appear in newspaper TV listings, in cable and satellite program descriptions, and on the screen during the first fifteen seconds of shows. Here are the various ratings and what they mean:

- **TV-Y:** Suitable for all children.
- **TV-Y7:** Directed toward kids seven and older, who are able to distinguish between pretend and reality; may contain mild fantasy or comedic violence.
- **TV-Y7-FV:** Directed toward children seven and older; may contain more intense fantasy violence than TV-Y7.
- **TV-G:** Suitable for a general audience, but not directed specifically at children; contains little or no violence, sexual content, or strong language.
- **TV-PG:** Parental guidance suggested; may contain inappropriate themes for younger children, and contains one or more of the following: moderate violence (V), some sexual situations (S), occasional strong language (L), or suggestive dialogue (D).
- **TV-14:** Parents strongly cautioned, suitable only for children over age fourteen; contains one or more of the following: intense violence, intense sexual situations, strong language, or intensely suggestive dialogue.
- **TV-MA:** Directed at mature adults and not suitable for children under seventeen; contains graphic violence, strong sexual activity, or crude language.

The TV content ratings can be a valuable tool for parents to use in evaluating whether shows are appropriate for their children to watch. But the system has a number of shortcomings. For one thing, many types of programs are not rated, including news broadcasts, sporting events, and commercials. Some of these programs may include material that is not suitable for younger viewers. In addition, research has shown that some young viewers—particularly teenaged boys—are actually more interested in programs rated TV-MA than TV-PG. In general, experts say that it is important for parents to monitor what their children watch on TV, rather than relying exclusively on program ratings.

to protect children from violence on television a step further by requiring all new TV sets to be equipped with a V-chip—a device that can detect program ratings and be set to block programs that contain an unacceptable level of violence.

Children's television programming has also come under criticism for featuring too much advertising and not enough educational content. According to Gavin, American children see an average of 40,000 television commercials each year. Studies show that many children, particularly those under the age of six, are unable to tell the difference between program content and commercials. In 1974 the FCC issued its Children's TV Report and Policy Statement, which set guidelines for the amount of commercial time allowed during children's programs. But the networks mostly ignored these rules during the 1980s.

In 1990, the U.S. Congress passed the Children's Television Act (CTA). This law required all television networks to broadcast at least three hours of educational/informational (E/I) programming per week. It also limited the amount of advertising allowed during children's programs to 10.5 minutes per hour on weekends and 12 minutes per hour on weekdays. Finally, the CTA prohibited host selling—a practice in which the main character of a children's TV program promotes products—and required clear separation between shows and commercials.

The CTA rules, combined with the growth of cable networks dedicated to children's programming, led to the introduction of many new kids' shows in the 1990s. Some of these programs clearly had educational value. But the law did not include specific guidelines for determining whether a show could be considered E/I. Some critics claimed that the networks counted programs that were not necessarily educational, such as *The Flintstones* cartoon show, toward meeting the three-hour E/I requirement.

In 2004 the FCC extended the CTA rules to digital multicasters (companies that use digital compression technology to squeeze multiple channels of programming into the frequency space that once carried a single broadcast channel). The FCC also placed limits on the types of Web addresses that could appear on the TV screen in order to protect children from seeing certain advertising on the Internet. The new rules were scheduled to take effect in 2006, but they were put on hold after several major entertainment companies challenged them in court.

Soap operas

Another popular type of daytime television program is the serial drama, more commonly known as a soap opera. Soap operas have been around since the earliest days of TV. They got their name because the original shows were sponsored by detergent manufacturers (soap companies) hoping to sell their products to housewives. Soap operas tell complicated, sometimes outlandish, ongoing stories that continue over weeks, months, or even years. Each episode is open-ended, with some loose ends remaining to be resolved in future episodes. Soap operas feature large casts of characters whose lives typically revolve around a central location, such as a hospital or a family home. The characters in a soap opera change over time, get older, and sometimes die. They also face many problems and crises as the show's writers try to advance the story and keep it interesting.

Soap operas attract the most loyal audiences of any type of television program. Since the stories are so complex, viewers must watch regularly in order to keep up with new developments. In addition, watching their favorite characters grow and change helps fans form strong attachments to the shows. Many viewers record their favorite programs when they are away from home and seek additional information about the shows in soap-opera magazines and Web sites. Fans claim that the programs can add excitement to their lives and help them put their own problems in perspective. But critics argue that soap operas are unrealistic and silly and can give viewers false ideas about life and relationships.

Serial dramas were a popular form of entertainment on the radio beginning in the 1920s. In the late 1940s and early 1950s, sponsors adapted these programs to the new form of home entertainment, television. The early TV soap operas were aimed at women, who were generally assumed to be home during the day taking care of the house and children. Most of the shows were sponsored by the makers of household cleaning products, packaged foods, and cosmetic items.

A small broadcasting company called the DuMont Network aired the first continuing TV drama, *Faraway Hill,* beginning in 1946. The Big Three broadcast networks—ABC, CBS, and NBC—began their own successful soaps in the early 1950s. *Guiding Light,* which originated in 1937 as a radio drama, came to television in 1952. The show remained on the air into the 2000s, making it the longest continuing story ever told. TV soap operas started out being broadcast in fifteen-minute segments. They were expanded to thirty minutes in 1956, beginning with *As the World Turns,* and became an hour long in the 1970s.

A number of new daytime dramas got their start in the late 1960s and 1970s. As African Americans fought for equality in the civil rights movement, and many people took part in protests against U.S. involvement in the Vietnam War (1955–1975), some TV producers decided to update soap operas to include more social conflict. Writer and producer Agnes Nixon (1927–), who is widely considered the queen of the modern soap opera, began *One Life to Live* in 1968. This program focused on the differences in ethnic background and social class among the residents of a fictional town. The story revolved around Victor Lord, a wealthy newspaper owner. It followed the ever-changing relationships between his family and working-class families of Irish, Polish, and Jewish descent. In 1970 Nixon launched another successful soap, *All My Children*. This show became the first fictional TV series to deal with the effects of the Vietnam War when a major character reacted to news that her son had been killed in the conflict.

The introduction of new soap operas created intense competition. Some producers began experimenting with the traditional soap opera form in hopes of attracting younger viewers. When *General Hospital* started airing on ABC in 1963, for instance, the action had revolved around the hospital, and the main characters were all doctors and nurses. In 1978 executive producer Gloria Monty moved the show's focus outside the hospital and introduced a number of appealing young characters. Monty also added action and suspense to the program, while maintaining the usual element of romance. Her changes led to a dramatic increase in ratings for *General Hospital*. In fact, the show attracted 30 million viewers—the largest daytime audience ever—for the November 1981 episode that presented the wedding of two main characters, Luke Spencer and Laura Webber.

During the 1980s many soap operas tried to imitate *General Hospital* by offering viewers more action and adventure. By the 1990s, however, most of the programs changed direction once again and started featuring more realistic, issue-oriented plots. The daytime dramas tackled a number of much-debated topics that received limited coverage in prime-time programming, including abortion, drug abuse, homosexuality, AIDS, and mental illness.

Despite such changes, the number of soap opera viewers declined toward the end of the twentieth century. There are several possible explanations for the smaller audiences. More women work outside the home, for example, so they are less likely to be around during the daytime to watch TV. Soap operas also face new competition from cable networks, including some that are targeted specifically at women. Another factor is the growing popularity of talk shows, which cover some of the same interesting subjects as soaps but are much less expensive for the networks to produce. Finally, some fans of serial dramas switched to prime-time programs that include soap-opera elements, such as *Desperate Housewives* and *The O.C.*

Still, daytime dramas have played an important role in the development of television. Soap operas influenced many other types of programs, including prime-time dramas, news coverage, and even sports.

For instance, producers of the Olympics often feature personal background stories about the athletes in order to create drama and attract female viewers.

Talk shows

Another popular type of program on television during the daytime is the talk show. Most talk shows feature a host, whose name often appears in the title, and include some discussion of current events in the fields of news and entertainment. Television talk shows grew out of similar programs on the radio. In fact, talk shows were so popular that they accounted for one-fourth of all radio programming between 1927 and 1956. The earliest TV versions starred successful radio personalities such as Arthur Godfrey (1903–1983), Edward R. Murrow (1908–1965), and Jack Paar (1918–2004). The talk show format also enjoyed great popularity on TV and accounted for half of all daytime programming on network television between 1949 and 1973. In many cases, talk shows provided a forum in which people could discuss important social and cultural issues that were not necessarily being addressed on popular prime-time TV shows.

The morning talk show, which typically features a mixture of information and entertainment, originated in the 1950s. The pioneer of this format was NBC's *Today* show, originally hosted by Dave Garroway (1913–1982). Following the success of the *Today* show, the other networks began competing morning talk shows, including *Good Morning, America* on ABC. Most of these types of shows took place within a TV studio, with the hosts providing light news coverage and visiting with celebrity guests.

There are also late-night talk shows, which typically contain more comedy and entertainment than news. The best-known program of this type is *The Tonight Show,* which made its debut in 1954 with comedian Steve Allen (1921–2000) as host. Johnny Carson (1925–2005) assumed the hosting duties in 1962 and defined late-night talk for the next thirty years. He started each episode of *The Tonight Show* with a monologue (speech), in which he made jokes about politics and current events. The rest of each show was like a variety series, with skits, musical performances, and interviews with celebrity guests.

The modern issue-centered daytime talk show originated in the late 1960s. Journalist Phil Donahue (1935–) felt that the talk shows of that time did not do a good job of covering the serious issues facing the American people, such as the civil rights movement and the Vietnam

Phil Donahue, holding microphone, pioneered the issue-centered talk show format, bringing topics of interest to viewers and encouraging discussion between the audience and guests. AP IMAGES.

War. He believed that American women would be interested in watching a show that provided information and discussion about such important topics. "The average housewife is bright and inquisitive [curious]," he stated in *Donahue: My Own Story*, "but television treats her like a mental midget."

Donahue also changed the usual talk-show format to include a studio audience, and he encouraged audience members to ask questions and react to guests. *Donahue* never avoided hotly debated topics. In fact, the first guest on the program was Madalyn Murray O'Hair, an outspoken atheist (someone who does not believe in God) whom *Life* magazine named "the most hated woman in America." *Donahue* remained on the air for thirty years. At its peak in the 1970s and early 1980s, nine million viewers tuned in every day.

The daytime talk show underwent another revolution in the 1980s, when journalist Oprah Winfrey (1954–) began her hugely successful program. Winfrey followed Donahue's lead and tackled some tough topics on *The Oprah Winfrey Show*, but she used a more intimate and sympathetic approach. She openly discussed her own personal struggles and hardships, for instance, which helped her form a deeper connection with guests and viewers alike. Her reassuring style also encouraged guests and audience members to share their experiences and feelings. By the mid-1990s *Oprah* was attracting ten million viewers daily. The show's success made its host one of the wealthiest and most influential women in the world.

A number of other talk shows tried to copy the successful formula of *The Oprah Winfrey Show* during the 1990s, but no other host was able to duplicate Winfrey's connection with her audience. Then competing shows began trying to use shocking subject matter to draw viewers away from *Oprah*. Many talk shows set up surprise confrontations between guests in order to create drama and attract viewers. This approach often led to crying, shouting, and fighting between guests— sometimes with disastrous results. Geraldo Rivera (1943–), the host of a talk show called *Geraldo*, suffered a broken nose when a fight broke out between two groups of guests. An episode of the *Jenny Jones* program— which invited a male guest to meet his secret admirer, only to find out that the person was another man—resulted in tragedy when the guest later murdered his admirer.

The Jerry Springer Show started out as another in a long line of sensational talk shows when it launched in 1991. Six years later, however, a new production company took control of the program. Fights had often erupted between guests on the show before, but the old producer had edited them out. The new producer decided to highlight the fights, which resulted in a ratings increase of 183 percent from 1997 to 1998. Jerry Springer (1944–) became the king of offensive and rude TV, and his show became the first in a decade to top *Oprah* in the daytime ratings.

Producers and hosts of these types of talk shows claim that they provide a service by openly discussing tough topics—like family conflicts and race relations—that ordinary TV programs often ignore. They also claim that the sensational talk shows make viewers feel normal and help them gain a better outlook on their own problems. But critics argue that shows such as *Jerry Springer* showcase the worst parts of human nature, make bad behavior seem acceptable, and create a negative view of American society.

Syndication of TV Programs

Most of the programs seen on daytime television arrive there through a process called syndication. Syndication involves selling the legal rights to a television program to customers other than the major broadcast networks, such as independent stations and cable channels. The program's producer, or a program distributor known as a syndicator, tries to sell the broadcast rights to the show to at least one station in each major television market across the United States. These stations can broadcast the show whenever it fits best into their schedules. In contrast, when a program is picked up by one of the major broadcast networks, it automatically appears on the same day and time on all of the stations nationwide that are affiliated (linked through formal agreements) with that network.

Syndication first became a part of the television industry in the late 1950s, when videotape technology allowed producers to record and keep a copy of programs. Before this time, all television shows were broadcast live from network studios. As soon as TV production shifted to videotape, network executives began selling the rights to programs for rebroadcast. In the early days, independent stations and even network affiliates did not offer a full day's worth of programming. They often used syndicated programs to help fill out their broadcast schedules.

Syndication received a big boost in 1970 as a result of two different decisions by the Federal Communications Commission (FCC). The first decision, called the Financial Interest and Syndication Rule (Fin-Syn), gave independent producers of television programs more control over their creations. It stated that the broadcast networks only owned the rights to shows during their first run on TV. Then the rights passed back to the original creators of the program, who

were free to sell them to other customers through syndication. The second FCC decision, called the Prime Time Access Rule, allowed local stations to choose their own programs to fill the time slot between 7:00 and 7:30 P.M. Before this rule took effect, local stations were required to air network programming during this vital time period, which came immediately before prime time. Afterward, many local stations decided to air popular syndicated programs instead.

There are two main types of syndication. First-run syndication describes programs that are created especially for independent distribution. In other words, the programs are syndicated when they appear on the air for the first time. Many daytime programs are seen in first-run syndication, including talk shows such as *The Oprah Winfrey Show*, game shows such as *Wheel of Fortune*, and cartoons. Many programs that are distributed in this manner appear on the air as strips—at the same time every weekday. One of the most-watched syndicated shows of all time, *Star Trek: The Next Generation*, made its debut in first-run syndication in 1987.

The second type of syndication is off-network syndication. This occurs when programs that originally ran as network series are sold for a second time in syndication. Reruns of popular shows are often handled through off-network syndication. In addition, some series that fail to find a large enough audience to satisfy the demands of a major network can continue in syndication. For instance, ABC cancelled *The Lawrence Welk Show* in 1971, but it continued to air for another decade in syndication. The popular sitcom *Seinfeld* entered off-network syndication in 1994 and became the most successful rerun ever.

Game shows

Game shows have been a popular type of program since the early years of television. Viewers enjoy game shows because it is fun to watch ordinary people, like themselves, compete and win prizes. In addition, many people find game shows easy to follow while they are doing other things, such as cleaning the house, cooking dinner, or doing homework. TV networks like game shows because they are relatively cheap and easy to produce, while advertisers like the fact that the shows give them a way, other than commercials, to promote their products.

The first game shows on television usually focused on contestants' intellectual abilities. Many of the programs used a question-and-answer format to test players' knowledge of facts and offered large cash prizes to the winners. These types of quiz shows were tremendously popular in prime time during the 1950s. In 1957, however, an investigation by the U.S. Congress revealed that some of the TV quiz shows were set up to ensure that the most popular players won. Several former contestants admitted that the shows' producers had given them answers in advance. The scandal caused the TV networks to cancel most of their quiz shows.

The quiz show scandal caused a change in the history of game shows. Afterward, the majority of these types of programs started to shift their focus away from factual knowledge. Instead, the newer game shows tended to feature more gambling, physical contests, and tests of everyday knowledge. In addition, most of the game shows that remained on the air following the scandal—such as *The Price Is Right* and *Name That Tune*—offered only modest prizes.

The quiz show scandal also led to the creation of the second-most successful game show of all time. It planted an idea in the mind of successful TV producer and talk show host Merv Griffin (1925–). He wondered what would happen if a game show provided players with the answers and asked them to come up with the right questions. This idea led to the creation of *Jeopardy!,* which made its debut in 1964 and remained popular into the 2000s. Although *Jeopardy!* tested factual knowledge, like the early quiz shows, it offered relatively small prizes.

In 1975, Griffin came up with the idea for the most successful game show of all time, *Wheel of Fortune.* Based on the children's guess-the-letter game "Hangman," the show had contestants spin a giant wheel for a chance to fill in the blanks of a word puzzle.

A contestant competes in an episode of the 1950s game show Beat the Clock. CBS/GETTY IMAGES.

Wheel of Fortune arrived at a time when an increasing number of game shows were appearing on TV. This change occurred after the FCC issued its Prime Time Access Rule in 1970. The ruling gave local stations control over the important time period from 7:00 to 7:30 PM, which fell just before the start of prime-time programming (local stations eventually gained control of the period from 7:30 to 8:00 PM as well). TV producers

TV producer Merv Griffin created the game shows Jeopardy! *and* Wheel of Fortune, *pictured.* DOUG BENC/GETTY IMAGES.

introduced a number of new game shows to help local stations fill the opening. In fact, more than four hundred different game shows came on the air between 1970 and 2000.

During the 1980s and 1990s, an increasing number of cable networks began airing game shows as well. The Game Show Network was created especially to feature that type of program. Other cable channels introduced game shows aimed at their primary audiences. For instance, Lifetime featured a speed-shopping show called *Supermarket Sweep* that was aimed at women. The continuing success of game shows even led to the return of this type of program to prime time, through such hit shows as *Who Wants to Be a Millionaire, The Weakest Link,* and *Deal or No Deal.* Even reality shows such as *Survivor, Fear Factor,* and *The Amazing Race* grew out of the enormous, long-lasting popularity of game shows.

For More Information

BOOKS

Allen, Robert C. *To Be Continued: Soap Operas around the World.* London: Routledge, 1995.

Calabro, Marian. *Zap! A Brief History of Television.* New York: Four Winds Press, 1992.

Cantor, Muriel G., and Suzanne Pingree. *The Soap Opera.* Beverly Hills, CA: Sage, 1983.

Donahue, Phil. *Donahue: My Own Story.* New York: Simon and Schuster, 1979.

Livingstone, Sonia, and Peter Lunt. *Talk on Television: Audience Participation and Public Debate.* London: Routledge, 1994.

Munson, Wayne. *All Talk: The Talk Show in Media Culture.* Philadelphia: Temple University Press, 1993.

Owen, Rob. *Gen X TV: "The Brady Bunch" to "Melrose Place."* New York: Syracuse University Press, 1997.

Priest, Patricia Joyner. *Public Intimacies: Talk Show Participants and Tell-All TV.* Creskill, N.J.: Hampton, 1995.

Stark, Steven D. *Glued to the Set: The 60 Television Shows and Events That Made Us Who We Are Today.* New York: The Free Press, 1997.

PERIODICALS

Ault, Susanne. "Who Watches Daytime?" *Broadcasting and Cable,* January 22, 2001.

Collins, James. "Talking Trash." *Time,* March 30, 1998.

"Days of Our Lives." *American Demographics,* May 1, 2001.

Flamm, Matthew. "The Oprah Factor." *Crain's New York Business,* April 25, 2005.

Jacobs, Karre. "A Soapy Slide in the Ratings." *Broadcasting and Cable,* February 14, 2005.

McGraw, Dan. "Is PBS Too Commercial?" *U.S. News and World Report,* June 15, 1998.

Meyers, Kate. "Donahue Dawns on Daytime." *Entertainment Weekly,* November 8, 1996.

Shaw, Jessica. "Hospital Birth." *Entertainment Weekly,* April 1, 1994.

Shields, Todd. "FCC, Kids' Networks Playing for Keeps." *Brandweek,* October 10, 2005.

"Too Much of a Good Thing? Children's Television." *Economist,* December 18, 2004.

WEB SITES

Alexander, Allison. "Children and Television." *Museum of Broadcast Communications.* http://www.museum.tv/archives/etv/C/htmlC/childrenand/childrenand.htm (accessed on June 15, 2006).

Allen, Robert C. "Soap Opera." *Museum of Broadcast Communications.* http://www.museum.tv/archives/etv/S/htmlS/soapopera/soapopera.htm (accessed on June 15, 2006).

Aufderheide, Patricia. "Public Television." *Museum of Broadcast Communications.* http://www.museum.tv/archives/etv/P/htmlP/publictelevi/publictelevi.htm (accessed on June 15, 2006).

"Children's Educational Television," September 28, 2005. *Federal Communications Commission.* http://www.fcc.gov/cgb/consumerfacts/childtv.html (accessed on June 15, 2006).

Fletcher, James. "Syndication." *Museum of Broadcast Communications.* http://www.museum.tv/archives/etv/S/htmlS/syndication/syndication.htm (accessed on June 15, 2006).

Gavin, Mary L. "How TV Affects Your Child." *KidsHealth,* 2005. http://www.kidshealth.org/parent/positive/family/tv_affects_child.html (accessed on June 15, 2006).

Hoerschelmann, Olaf. "Quiz and Game Shows." *Museum of Broadcast Communications.* http://www.museum.tv/archives/etv/Q/htmlQ/quizandgame/quizandgame.htm (accessed on June 15, 2006).

Jenkins, Henry. "Bob Keeshan." *Museum of Broadcast Communications.* http://www.museum.tv/archives/etv/K/htmlK/keeshanbob/keeshanbob.htm (accessed on June 15, 2006).

"Mister Rogers Dies at Age 74." *CNN.* http://www.cnn.com/2003/SHOWBIZ/TV/02/27/rogers.obit (accessed on June 15, 2006).

"Television Syndication." *Answers.com.* http://www.answers.com (accessed on June 15, 2006).

Timberg, Bernard M. "Talk Shows." *Museum of Broadcast Communications.* http://www.museum.tv/archives/etv/T/htmlT/talkshows/talkshows.htm (accessed on June 15, 2006).

"Violence on Television." *American Psychological Association.* http://www.apa.org/topics/topicviolence.html (accessed on June 15, 2006).

8

Sports on Television

Americans watched and competed in a wide variety of sporting events long before the invention of television. From the time the new medium arrived in the 1940s, however, it completely transformed sports. "Television has changed the sports landscape—changing everything from the salaries, number of teams, and color of uniforms, to the way that fans conceive of sports and athletes alike," Steven D. Stark wrote in *Glued to the Set*. In fact, many Americans in the twenty-first century might find it difficult to imagine what sports would be like without the influence of television.

In many ways, sports and television are a perfect fit. TV cameras put viewers in the middle of the action, giving them a much closer view than they could get by sitting in the stands. Televised sports also feature live action, high drama, real heroes and villains, and unpredictable endings. "People like to watch people in dramatic situations; they like the unpredictable, the unknown," said Roone Arledge (1931–), the legendary head of ABC Sports, in *Sports Illustrated*. "They want to watch something that has the quality of an event."

The natural appeal of sports on television has created large, enthusiastic audiences for many different types of athletic contests. In fact, TV was responsible for introducing a number of lesser-known sports to American viewers, including ice hockey, soccer, golf, tennis, and auto racing. TV profits, in turn, have made many professional sports leagues, teams, and players very wealthy. A number of top athletes have taken advantage of the broad reach of television to become celebrities and entertainers, known as much for the products they promote as for their athletic ability.

Some critics claim that television has corrupted sports in the United States. For instance, some say that the high-stakes competition for TV money has caused an overall decline in sportsmanship, as many athletes have shifted their focus from teamwork and winning to attracting media attention and winning endorsement contracts. (Endorsement contracts pay an athlete to be associated in advertising with a given product. For example, an athlete may appear in television commercials for the product or use the product in competition.) Moreover, several major sports have changed their rules to accommodate the demands of television. Basketball implemented the shot clock (a rule that gives the offensive team only a certain number of seconds to shoot the ball) to speed up play, for example, and baseball introduced the designated hitter (a player who is allowed to bat in place of another player, usually the pitcher) to increase scoring. Games are often moved to inconvenient times just to fit broadcast schedules, and seasons are often extended in order to increase opportunities for TV coverage.

Television has also changed the way that sports leagues operate. All of the major professional sports have expanded their number of teams in order to reach more TV markets. The National Hockey League (NHL), for instance, has grown from its original six teams to thirty. Arguments between leagues and player organizations over TV revenues have resulted in player strikes (protests in which players refuse to practice or compete) and management lockouts (protests in which team owners refuse to allow players to practice or compete) in all of the major professional sports. The big money available from television contracts has also caused the breakup of several longtime college sports conferences, as top teams left in search of higher-profile competition and increased TV ratings.

While the relationship between sports and television has both positive and negative aspects, there is little doubt that televised sports are big business. TV contracts brought the National Football League (NFL) a whopping $3.7 billion in 2005, accounting for more than half of the league's total revenues. The popularity of sports on TV has also led to the success of cable networks dedicated to sports-related programming. Viewers in the 2000s can literally tune in at any time of day or night and find some sort of athletic competition to watch on television.

Sports drive the growth of TV

While television has had a huge impact on sports, sports also played an important role in the development and growth of television. During the early days of commercial broadcasting in the 1940s, the networks relied upon telecasts of sporting events to increase demand for TV sets. "Television got off the ground because of sports," early network sports director Harry Coyle told Stanley J. Baran in the Museum of Broadcast

Communications publication "Sports and Television." "Today, maybe, sports need television to survive, but it was just the opposite when it first started. When we put on the World Series in 1947, heavyweight fights, the Army-Navy football game, the sales of television sets just spurted." In fact, sports programming helped the number of households with TV sets increase from 200,000 in 1948 to more than 10 million in 1950.

In many ways, sports provided an ideal form of programming for the early TV networks. For one thing, sports programs were less expensive to produce than many types of entertainment programs. Since sporting events were happening with or without TV coverage, the networks only needed to show up with cameras and crews to film the games. In contrast, producing an entertainment program required the networks to build sets and hire writers, directors, costume designers, and actors. Another factor in the appeal of sports for the early networks was the primitive nature of television cameras in the 1940s and 1950s. The cameras of that time required bright light in order to produce a clear picture, and sporting events tended to be well lit. Finally, sporting events featured natural breaks in the action that the networks could fill with advertising messages.

Of course, some sports adapted to the television era better than others. The size of the ball used was one factor in selecting sports programming for the early broadcast networks. When TV screens were small and pictures fuzzy, sports such as golf and hockey were difficult for viewers to follow. Some sports also provided better TV viewing because of the way the action unfolded, with the potential for something exciting to happen at any moment. The most popular sports in the early years of television broadcasting were baseball, boxing, and wrestling. The action in these events tended to be concentrated in a small space, making it easier for TV cameras to follow.

The first sporting event to be televised was a 1939 college baseball game between Columbia and Princeton universities. It was filmed using a single TV camera—situated in the stands along the third base line—and the broadcast was received by about two hundred TV sets. The first Major League Baseball (MLB) telecast took place a few months later, during a demonstration of television technology at the 1939 World's Fair. The game was a doubleheader between the Brooklyn Dodgers and the Cincinnati Reds. Dodgers' announcer Red Barber (1908–1992) introduced many of the elements of modern sportscasts during this event. He provided play-by-play announcing, conducted between-game interviews with players and managers, and finished with a post-game summary or wrap-up.

The first regularly scheduled network sports broadcast was *Friday Night Fights,* which aired on NBC beginning in 1944. The premiere telecast featured a featherweight championship boxing match. Within a few years the program was expanded and renamed *Gillette Cavalcade of Sports* after its sponsor, a shaving razor manufacturer. The show remained on the air for two decades, until televised sports grew so popular that it became too expensive for individual advertisers to pay to televise major events. Once that occurred, the networks began purchasing the broadcast rights to various sporting events and sold small blocks of commercial time to advertisers.

During the early years of television, sporting events were often broadcast in the evening hours known as prime time. In fact, sports programming once accounted for up to one-third of the networks' prime-time schedule. But this situation began to change in the mid-1950s, when the networks found that situation comedies and variety shows drew more female viewers. The networks then moved their primary sports telecasts to weekends, where they have drawn consistently strong ratings ever since. In fact, watching sports on TV became a regular weekend activity for millions of Americans.

At first, many people worried that showing sports on television would reduce attendance at live sporting events. Television did have a negative impact on attendance at some types of events, such as boxing matches. Fights at New York's Madison Square Garden drew an average of 12,000 fans in 1947, for instance, but the popularity of programs such as *Friday Night Fights* contributed to a decline in average attendance to 1,200 a decade later. Such statistics convinced a number of sports leagues to institute TV blackouts. These measures prohibited the television networks from broadcasting home games in local markets, so that fans would have to go to the stadium to watch the games.

MLB commissioner Ford Frick (1894–1974) was so concerned about television's effect on attendance at baseball games that he took steps to limit the quality of telecasts. As sports writer Charles Hirshberg noted in *ESPN 25,* Frick issued a rule stating that "the view a fan gets at home should not be any better than that of the fan in the worst seat of the ballpark." For many years, television cameras were kept so far away from the action that there was little reason for casual fans to watch baseball on TV. Rather than causing fans to flock to the ballpark, though, Frick's rule only encouraged viewers to watch other sports on TV instead. Over time, it became clear that when television coverage was done well, it could actually increase fan interest in sports.

Sports telecasts gain entertainment value

In the 1960s, sports programming underwent a major change. Rather than simply providing viewers with film footage of the event itself, the networks started offering special features that turned sports into high-quality television entertainment. The man most responsible for this transition was Roone Arledge, a visionary programmer who joined ABC Sports in 1960. At that time, ABC was the smallest and least influential of the so-called Big Three broadcast TV networks. Its competitors, CBS and NBC, controlled the television rights to America's most popular sporting events. But ABC did manage to win the contract to broadcast college football games. In preparing for the start of the season, Arledge began thinking of ways that ABC Sports could make its football telecasts stand out from the competition.

Arledge came up with a plan to make the game more interesting and exciting by giving viewers an inside look at the action. He described his ideas to his colleagues in a memo that has earned a spot in TV sports history, according to Hirshberg. In the famous memo, Arledge encouraged the operators of ABC's six fixed cameras to "cover all the other interesting facets of the game when [they are] not actually engaged in covering a game situation." He also proposed using portable cameras "to get the impact shots that we cannot get from a fixed camera—a coach's face as a man drops a pass in the clear—a pretty cheerleader after her hero has scored a touchdown—a coed who brings her infant baby to the game—the referee as he calls a particularly difficult play—two romantic students sharing a blanket late in the game on a cold day—the beaming face of a substitute halfback as he comes off the field after running seventy yards for a touchdown. . . . In short—WE ARE GOING TO ADD SHOW BUSINESS TO SPORTS!" Most of Arledge's suggestions became a standard part of sports on television, as other networks followed ABC's example and increased the entertainment value of their sports broadcasts.

In 1961 Arledge used the ideas he expressed in his memo as the basis for an innovative new sports program, *ABC's Wide World of Sports*. This show grew out of the fact that ABC's competitors held the rights to televise all the major U.S. sporting events. Arledge decided that ABC Sports should take a different approach and focus on the wide variety of sports available in the rest of the world. He believed that these lesser-known sports might attract a solid audience, as long as the events were presented in an entertaining way. The show's well-known introduction,

read by host Jim McKay (1921–), explained its mission: "Spanning the globe to bring you the constant variety of sport. The thrill of victory, and the agony of defeat. The human drama of athletic competition. This is ABC's *Wide World of Sports.*"

ABC Sports sent camera crews all over the world to provide coverage of such little-known events as table tennis, badminton, curling, cliff

"Battle of the Sexes"

One of the most culturally significant American sporting events was a 1973 tennis match known as the "Battle of the Sexes." It pitted the 29-year-old reigning women's tennis champion, Billie Jean King (1943–), against a 55-year-old former men's champion, Bobby Riggs (1918–1995). The highly publicized match took place during the women's liberation movement, a period stretching from the 1960s into the early 1970s, when American women fought to break out of traditional gender roles and gain equal rights and opportunities in society.

King is an important figure in the history of women's sports. She had an outstanding pro-fessional tennis career that included five years ranked number one in the world, six Wimbledon singles championships, and four U.S. Open titles. King's influence continued off the court, where she helped launch the women's professional tennis tour, fought for equal prize money for male and female players, and started the Women's Sports Foundation to increase athletic opportunities for women. Her success helped make it socially acceptable for American women to be athletic and work up a sweat.

Riggs had been a solid player in his day, but by 1973 he was past his tennis prime. Nevertheless, the outspoken hustler challenged a number of top female players to compete against him. Riggs claimed that men were naturally superior to women in terms of athletic skills, and he insisted that no woman could ever defeat him in a tennis match. King turned down several invi-tations to play against Riggs, but she changed her mind and accepted the challenge after Riggs beat Australian women's champion Margaret Court (1942–) in a match known as the "Mother's Day Massacre."

During the hype leading up to the "Battle of the Sexes" match, King realized that millions of American women were pinning their hopes on her. "I thought it would set us back 50 years if I didn't win that match," she recalled to Larry Schwartz of ESPN SportsCentury. "It would hurt the women's tour and affect all women's self-esteem."

King faced Riggs on September 20, 1973, at the Houston Astrodome in front of 30,000 specta-tors—the largest crowd in tennis history. ABC paid $750,000 for the right to televise the event, and the network broadcast the match to 50 million people in 36 countries. Riggs tried to fluster his opponent with an array of trick shots, while King applied a simple strategy of running her older opponent all over the court. King pulled out a convincing victory in straight sets, 6–4, 6–3, 6–3. Her win inspired countless American women to continue fighting for equality and also led to increased interest in women's sports.

diving, and drag racing. It also showed international gymnastics and ice-skating competitions at a time when these sports received minimal cov-erage. The most notable aspect of *Wide World of Sports* was that it pre-sented sporting events as entertainment. It was the first show to provide "up close and personal" profiles of athletes, for example, and to use technical innovations such as instant replay and slow motion,

A German camera crew captures the action at the 1936 Summer Olympics in Berlin, Germany. The Olympics were not broadcast in the United States until 1960. TIME LIFE PICTURES/GETTY IMAGES.

which allowed viewers to see the action over again and in detail. *Wide World of Sports* earned forty-seven Emmy Awards during its four-decade run on ABC. In the early 2000s, its influence can be seen in many aspects of sports broadcasting, especially in the coverage of multi-event athletic contests like the Olympic Games.

The world watches the Olympic Games

The Olympic Games have supplied some of the most memorable moments in the history of televised sports. These international competitions feature the best athletes in the world, all representing their home countries and trying to defend national pride. Both the Summer Games and the Winter Games only take place every four years, which gives the events added meaning. Every Olympic telecast has treated viewers to intense competition, with dramatic, once-in-a-lifetime triumphs as well as crushing defeats.

The first TV coverage took place at the 1936 Summer Olympics in Berlin, Germany. The German government used American technology to broadcast the competition to a dozen TV sets located in public areas throughout the city. The Olympics were not broadcast in the United States until 1960, when CBS paid $50,000 for the right to air fifteen hours of coverage from the Winter Games in Squaw Valley, California.

Since then, the special nature of Olympic competition has turned the broadcast rights to the Games into the most coveted and expensive property in TV sports. In 1980, for instance, NBC paid $87 million for the right to broadcast the Summer Olympics in Moscow. Four years later, the price increased to $225 million for ABC to telecast the Summer Games in Los Angeles. Then NBC paid more than double that amount, $456 million, to gain the TV rights to the 1996 Summer Olympics in Atlanta, Georgia.

The broadcast networks are willing to pay such astronomical fees because their Olympic coverage typically attracts 50 percent of the U.S. viewing audience, as well as an estimated one billion viewers around the world. As a result, broadcasting the Games can increase a network's prestige and give a boost to its other programs. Of course, a network also faces a great deal of public and industry scrutiny for its Olympic coverage. Some critics claim that the networks tend to overproduce the Games—providing an array of background stories and interviews with the athletes—in an attempt to attract female viewers. They contend that the networks devote too much air time to these special features and do not provide enough coverage of the actual sports.

Just as television has affected other sports, TV coverage has changed the Olympic Games in a number of ways. Beginning in 1994, for instance, the schedule of Summer and Winter Olympics was staggered so that one set of Games occurs every two years, rather than both sets taking place every four years. The desire to attract large TV audiences also convinced Olympic organizers to abandon the long tradition of allowing only amateur athletes to compete. Today, professional athletes routinely represent their countries in basketball, hockey, tennis, and other sports.

Finally, the opportunity to gain international television exposure has led some countries and groups to use the Olympics as a stage to draw attention to world political issues. The most frightening incident took place at the 1972 Summer Games in Munich, Germany. Arab terrorists, upset about developments in the Middle East conflict, took eleven Israeli athletes hostage and murdered the captives when their ransom demands were not met. TV cameras captured footage of a hooded gunman in the Olympic village. In the 1980s national governments used the Olympics as a tool in foreign relations. The United States refused to participate in the 1980 Summer Games in Moscow to protest the Soviet Union's invasion of Afghanistan, and in return the Soviet Union declined to compete in the 1984 Summer Games in Los Angeles.

TV cameras catch a member of the terrorist group that took eleven Israeli athletes hostage during the 1972 Summer Olympics.
AP IMAGES.

Football takes over TV

Of all the major American sports, professional football has developed the most successful relationship with television. TV coverage has helped make pro football the nation's most popular sport, with 33 percent of Americans naming it as their favorite in a 2005 poll cited by John Gallagher in the *Detroit Free Press*. By comparison, only 14 percent named baseball, which was long considered to be America's national pastime. The NFL, in turn, has contributed a great deal to the success of television. The Super Bowl is always one of the most-watched programs of the year, attracting an audience of about 100 million viewers in the United States alone. It is also the most financially rewarding program of the year for the television network that handles the broadcast. ABC charged advertisers $2.5 million for each 30-second commercial that aired during Super Bowl XL in 2006.

In many ways, football seems ideally suited for television. Games are played only once per week, which gives the networks plenty of time to publicize upcoming contests. Moreover, the nature of the game makes it easy to film. "The shape of the field corresponds to that of the screen. The action, although spread out, starts with a predictable portion of the field," Arledge explained in *Sports Illustrated*. Football games also have natural breaks in the action that the networks can use to provide information or analysis. "The reason football is easier to cover is because every play is a separate story," CBS Sports director Sandy Grossman told Baran. "There's a beginning, a middle, and an end, and then there's 20 or 30 seconds to retell it or react to it." As a result of all these factors, TV coverage can bring viewers closer to the action and enhance their understanding of the game.

Pro football began its rise to the top of televised sports in the 1960s, with the first telecast of the Super Bowl. The sport of football had existed for nearly a century before the potential for TV revenues convinced the NFL to organize its first championship game at the end of the 1966 season. Super Bowl I was played in January 1967 at Memorial Coliseum in Los Angeles. This game, between the Green Bay Packers and the Kansas City Chiefs, drew a national TV audience estimated at 60 million people.

The Super Bowl soon became one of the biggest television events of each year. Various Super Bowl telecasts account for half of the twenty highest-rated TV programs of all time in the United States. The big game also attracts an estimated one billion viewers in other countries around the world. Over the years, the networks expanded coverage to last all day, providing viewers with extensive pre-game background, analysis, and predictions. For millions of Americans, Super Bowl Sunday became a national holiday to celebrate by eating snack foods in front of the television set. In 1990 the NFL agreed to extend its season and add more playoff games in order to push the Super Bowl into the key ratings period known as February sweeps, when the networks set their advertising rates.

Football's Notorious "Heidi Game"

In 1968, when professional football was just starting to climb to its current position as the most popular sport on TV, NBC received a clear message about fans' interest in the game. Due to a combination of technical considerations and contract obligations, the network interrupted the final moments of a close contest between the Oakland Raiders and New York Jets to broadcast the children's movie *Heidi*. This decision outraged football fans across the country and generated thousands of angry telephone calls. In fact, the high volume of calls caused the network's switchboard to blow twenty-six fuses in an hour. NBC issued an apology to viewers later that night and replayed the final minute of the football game on a network news program. As Joe Garner wrote in *Stay Tuned: Television's Unforgettable Moments*, the uproar surrounding the *Heidi* incident "ensured that no television executive would ever again question the appeal of pro football on television."

Green Bay Packers quarterback Bart Starr led his team to victory at the first Super Bowl in January 1967. FOCUS ON SPORT/ GETTY IMAGES.

For many years, NFL games (including the Super Bowl) were broadcast on Sunday afternoons. Television industry experts assumed that women controlled the TV set during the evening hours and that female viewers did not watch football. But Roone Arledge did not agree with these assumptions; he believed that football could do well in the weekly prime-time schedule. When ABC won the broadcast rights to NFL games in 1970, Arledge introduced a new sports program called *Monday Night Football.* Building on the success of *Wide World of Sports,* he continued to offer viewers a combination of sports and entertainment. As the program's original producer, Dennis Lewin, told Joe Garner in *Stay Tuned: Television's Unforgettable Moments*: "It was a form that would appeal to an entertainment audience, not just a sports audience."

Monday Night Football incorporated state-of-the-art TV technology. ABC filmed the games using nine cameras, instead of the usual four or five, including some handheld models that roamed the sidelines. Arledge also put together an unusual team in the broadcast booth in order to increase viewer interest in the games. He combined Howard Cosell (1918–1995)—a hard-driving, opinionated journalist who tended to stir up strong feelings (both positive and negative) in TV audiences—with Don Meredith (1938–)—a funny, laid-back former quarterback for the Dallas Cowboys. The team also included an experienced play-by-play announcer, first Keith Jackson (1928–) and later Frank Gifford (1930–). "The three created, for want of a better phrase, 'watercooler' talk [a type of discussion that takes place in the break area of a workplace]," Lewin noted. "Every Tuesday morning people all over the country would say, 'Hey, did you hear what Howard said to Don, or what Don said to Howard, what was said about this coach, what was said about that player?' It created a whole different atmosphere."

Before long, *Monday Night Football* became so popular that restaurants and sports bars across the country started hosting parties around it. For many years, the program was also a trendy spot for prominent athletes, entertainers, and politicians to show up, chat with the hosts, and promote their projects. *Monday Night Football* remained a winner in the ratings for 35 years, despite numerous changes in the broadcast booth. Both Cosell and Meredith left the show in the mid-1980s. Al Michaels (1944–) joined the broadcast team in 1986 and was a permanent member of it over the next two decades. In 2000 ABC tried to recapture the chemistry of the Cosell-Meredith era by adding comedian Dennis Miller (1953–) to the telecasts, but the experiment was a flop with viewers. Nevertheless, *Monday Night Football* helped the NFL emerge as the king of televised sports.

In addition to making regular appearances in prime time, NFL games eventually were broadcast on holidays such as Thanksgiving and Christmas.

Cable transforms sports coverage

In the 1980s, the increasing popularity of football and other sports on television led to the creation of cable networks devoted entirely to sports programming. The best-known of these networks, ESPN, made its debut in 1979. From the beginning, ESPN's sports coverage had a look and feel that set it apart from the broadcast networks. The anchors of its signature show, *SportsCenter,* tended to be young, fashionable, and funny. They appealed to younger viewers by bestowing silly nicknames on athletes and showing humorous, story-like highlight film footage.

ESPN also set itself apart from the competition by introducing a number of technical innovations to sports programming. In 1980, for instance, the cable network used the first electronic cut-in at the National Collegiate Athletic Association (NCAA) basketball tournament. This innovation allowed ESPN to cut away from one game in order to join another one in progress. In 1983 the network offered the first sports broadcast with stereo sound, and two years later it became the first to provide scores and news in graphic form across the bottom of the screen. Ticker-style on-screen graphics later became a standard part of all kinds of broadcasts. In 1995 ESPN introduced the in-game box score to sports telecasts. Over the next decade, viewers came to expect this constant graphical reminder of the score and time remaining when watching any type of game. In 2001 ESPN won a sports Emmy Award for creating the K Zone—the first graphical picture of the strike zone (the imaginary box, defined by baseball rules, in which a pitcher must throw the ball in order for the umpire to call the pitch a strike) in a baseball telecast.

These innovations helped ESPN become the fastest-growing cable channel in the United States in the 1990s. By 2005 the network was available to more than 75 million subscribers across the country. ESPN helped shift the focus of American sports coverage from local to national. Before the introduction of 24-hour sportscasts on cable, most viewers only saw scores and highlights featuring their local teams. By bringing superstars to widespread attention, the network contributed to the trend toward athletes becoming celebrities. Finally, some analysts argue that ESPN has led to an overall increase in the level of interest in sports.

TV sports become big business

The rise of dedicated cable sports networks like ESPN provided TV viewers with more coverage of athletic contests than was ever available before. The broadcast and cable networks began competing for the television rights to major sports leagues and events. As demand for TV sports contracts increased, the prices the networks paid rose dramatically. In 1970, for instance, the networks paid $50 million for a contract to televise pro football, $18 million for Major League Baseball, and $2 million for pro basketball. By 1985, the prices had increased to $450 million for the NFL, $160 million for MLB, and $45 million for the NBA.

Around this time, however, the TV ratings for individual sports programs began to decline. The nation's biggest sporting events—such as the NCAA Basketball Tournament, the NBA Championships, college football bowl games, and the NFL Super Bowl—continued to draw large audiences, and sports programming in general remained very popular. But the competing broadcast and cable networks offered American viewers so many choices of sports on TV that the audience became fragmented among the various options. As a result, the broadcast networks that signed huge TV contracts with pro sports leagues often lost money on the deals. Over time, the low ratings for individual sports programs made the national broadcast networks less willing to air regular-season sporting events. These games mostly moved to cable networks and independent stations, while the national networks increasingly concentrated on broadcasting league playoffs and big events like the Olympic Games.

For More Information

BOOKS

Arledge, Roone. *Roone: A Memoir*. New York: HarperCollins, 2003.

Barnouw, Erik. *Tube of Plenty: The Evolution of American Television*. New York: Oxford University Press, 1975.

Calabro, Marian. *Zap! A Brief History of Television*. New York: Four Winds Press, 1992.

Garner, Joe. *Stay Tuned: Television's Unforgettable Moments*. Kansas City: Andrews McMeel Publishing, 2002.

Hirshberg, Charles. *ESPN 25: 25 Mind-Bending, Eye-Popping, Culture-Morphing Years of Highlights*. New York: Hyperion, 2004.

O'Neil, Terry. *The Game behind the Game: High Pressure, High Stakes in Television Sports*. New York: Harper and Row, 1989.

Powers, Ron. *Supertube: The Rise of Television Sports*. New York: Coward-McCann, 1984.

Rader, Benjamin G. *In Its Own Image: How Television Has Transformed Sports*. New York: Free Press, 1984.

Spence, Jim. *Up Close and Personal: The Inside Story of Network Television Sports*. New York: Atheneum, 1988.

Stark, Steven D. *Glued to the Set: The 60 Television Shows and Events That Made Us Who We Are Today*. New York: The Free Press, 1997.

PERIODICALS

Arledge, Roone. "It's Sport . . . It's Money . . . It's TV." *Sports Illustrated,* April 25, 1966.

Gallagher, John. "The NFL Means (Big) Business." *Detroit Free Press,* January 28, 2006.

Hill, Lee Alan. "Building a TV Sports Empire: How ESPN Created a Model for Cable Success." *Television Week,* September 6, 2004.

Sandoval, Emiliana. "Five Things about Super Origins." *Detroit Free Press,* January 23, 2006.

Schuster, Rachel. "Tune into the History of Sports TV." *USA Today,* December 3, 1991.

WEB SITES

Baran, Stanley J. "Sports and Television." *Museum of Broadcast Communications.* http://www.museum.tv/archives/etv/S/htmlS/sportsandte/sportsandte. htm (accessed on June 19, 2006).

Schwartz, Larry. "Billie Jean Won for All Women." *ESPN SportsCentury.* http://espn.go.com/sportscentury/features/00016060.html (accessed on June 19, 2006).

9

Television Coverage of News and Politics

Between 1945 and 2005, television became the first place most Americans turned for information about political issues and breaking news events. The amount of news available on TV expanded greatly through the history of the medium—from a daily fifteen-minute network update in the 1940s to the twenty-four-hour news coverage offered by many cable channels in the early 2000s. Advances in technology also helped TV newscasts grow more sophisticated and effective in the final decades of the twentieth century. Satellites orbiting the Earth allowed television news programs to show viewers live footage of events taking place around the world, for instance, while computerized graphics scrolled across the screen to provide continuous updates on other stories.

Although TV news programs are more numerous and up to date than ever, many critics claim that the quality of information they provide to viewers has declined over time. In order to attract and hold viewers' attention, TV news tends to focus on stories that can be presented in short segments and feature a dramatic visual element—such as natural disasters and violent crime. Critics argue that this focus often prevents TV news from covering stories that may be more complex and less exciting, yet also hold greater importance in viewers' lives. As the major broadcast networks have faced increasing competition from cable news channels, critics complain that TV news has also become more like tabloid magazines, full of celebrity gossip and sex scandals. In addition, many people feel that TV news coverage has become less balanced and more opinionated over time. Finally, critics claim that television news overwhelms Americans with stories that do not necessarily help them become more informed and productive citizens.

The development of TV news programming

From the time TV technology was invented, many people believed that television broadcasting had tremendous potential as a resource for news

John Cameron Swayze reporting for Camel Newsreel Theater, *NBC's first network news program.* © BETTMANN/CORBIS.

and information. In fact, some of the earliest experimental TV broadcasts in the 1930s were news bulletins. When commercial television got its start following World War II (1939–45), all of the broadcast networks provided news updates. These early news telecasts usually featured a male journalist, known as an anchor, reading news reports from a script.

NBC's first network news program, *Camel Newsreel Theater,* made its debut in 1948. It aired for ten minutes every weekday, and it featured radio commentator John Cameron Swayze (1906–1995) reading news stories while images from movie newsreels (short news reports that were shown in movie theaters through the 1940s) appeared on screen. CBS launched a competing program, *CBS-TV News,* later that year. It ran for fifteen minutes each evening, with Douglas Edwards (1917–1990) serving as the anchor.

Until the 1960s, TV technology was not advanced enough to provide good coverage of breaking news, or events that took place immediately

A group of politicians prepares to appear on the news program Meet the Press *in 1972.* © BETTMANN/CORBIS.

before or during the newscast. Television cameras were big and bulky, so they were not easily transported to distant locations. The cameras also recorded images on film, which had to be physically carried to a network studio and then developed for several hours before it could be shown. As a result, any news reports that came in from the field were outdated by the time they appeared on the air.

Most early newscasts were filmed live in network studios. The images behind the anchor usually consisted of still photographs on easels or short film clips from the newsreels that were shown in movie theaters at that time. Despite the primitive nature of early newscasts, though, the TV networks felt that their daily news updates provided a valuable public service.

Television featured many public affairs programs early in its history. One of the longest-running shows on TV is *Meet the Press,* which made its debut in 1947 and was still on the air as of 2006. *Meet the Press* used an interview format, in which a well-known politician or public figure answered questions posed by a panel of news reporters. Discussions on the program tended to have a more open style, and featured a wider range of topics, than the political talk shows that aired on the radio. Some people criticized the program for being too showy and elevating journalists to the level of celebrities. But others praised it for giving the American people a more personal, close-up look at their leaders than they had ever before.

Another pioneering early news show was *See It Now*, which aired on CBS from 1951 to 1958. This show consisted of a series of documentaries (fact-based films) that investigated serious issues affecting U.S. society, like the relationship between cigarette smoking and lung cancer or the unfair treatment of migrant farm workers. The host of the program was Edward R. Murrow (1908–1965), who had become famous as a CBS radio correspondent during World War II. Murrow pushed the network to use the power of television to expose problems and fight injustice.

See It Now is probably best known for a 1954 program about Joseph McCarthy (1908–1957), a U.S. senator from Wisconsin who had ruined the careers of many U.S. politicians and entertainers by falsely accusing them of being Communists. McCarthy used the tensions of the Cold War (1945–91; a period of intense military and political rivalry between the United States and its democratic system of government and the Soviet Union and its Communist system of government) to hurt his enemies and advance his own career. Murrow's show helped turn public opinion against McCarthy, and the senator soon fell from power. Before the episode went on the air, however, CBS executives felt so nervous about the subject matter that they did not promote it. Murrow and his producer, Fred W. Friendly (1915–1998), were forced to use their own money to purchase a full-page advertisement in the *New York Times*.

Another news-oriented program launched in the early years of TV was *Today*. When it made its debut on NBC in 1952, it marked one of the earliest network efforts to provide programming in the morning hours. From the beginning, *Today* provided a mixture of news and elements of the variety shows that were popular on radio at that time, including celebrity interviews, light comedy, and music. The show's producers believed that viewers would not be interested in watching straightforward newscasts first thing in the morning. They added entertainment in order to appeal to all members of TV households. In fact, during its early years, the show even featured a chimpanzee to appeal to children.

The producers also organized *Today* as a series of brief segments, so that viewers could watch bits and pieces of it while they got ready for work or school.

Today became very popular, and it remained on the air as of 2006. Many of its hosts became big stars, including Barbara Walters (1931–), Tom Brokaw (1940–), Jane Pauley (1950–), Bryant Gumbel (1948–), and Katie Couric (1957–). The success of *Today* helped prove that television could attract viewers all day long, rather than only in the evening hours. TV critics even coined a new term, "infotainment," to describe the combination of news and entertainment in shows like *Today*.

TV becomes a force in American politics

Politicians recognized the power of television almost as soon as the new medium was introduced. When it came time to nominate candidates for the 1948 presidential election, for instance, both the Democratic and Republican political parties decided to hold their nominating conventions in Philadelphia, because the city's TV broadcasts could be seen on fourteen stations along the East Coast.

As early as 1952, it became clear that television could make or break political candidates. The Democratic candidate for president that year, Adlai Stevenson (1900–1965), bought half an hour of network air time to broadcast a campaign speech. Unfortunately for Stevenson, his speech upset many viewers because it replaced the most popular prime-time program of the era, *I Love Lucy*. In the meantime, Republican candidate Dwight D. Eisenhower (1890–1969) aired a series of thirty-second campaign commercials that helped turn the election in his favor.

The American political figure whose fortunes were most affected by television was Richard M. Nixon (1913–1994). In 1952 Eisenhower chose Nixon—then a U.S. senator from California—to be his vice presidential running mate. During the campaign, Nixon was surrounded by rumors that he had improperly taken money and gifts from wealthy donors for his personal use. When Eisenhower considered dropping him from the ticket, Nixon decided to address the rumors in a televised speech. In an emotional appeal that was watched by 60 million Americans, Nixon denied that he had used campaign funds improperly. He insisted that the only gift he had ever accepted was a black-and-white cocker spaniel dog, which his young daughters had named Checkers. Nixon's "Checkers Speech" saved his political career, generating three million letters and two million telegrams in support of his campaign.

Richard Nixon, delivering his 1952 "Checkers Speech," used the power of television to save his political career. AP IMAGES.

After serving two terms as vice president under Eisenhower (1890–1969; served 1953–61), Nixon ran for president in 1960. This time, however, television hurt rather than helped his chances in the election. With a comfortable lead in the polls over his relatively unknown opponent, Democratic U.S. senator John F. Kennedy (1917–1963) of Massachusetts, Nixon agreed to take part in the first-ever televised presidential debates. On the day of the first debate, Nixon was not feeling well and appeared pale and tired. Kennedy, by contrast, looked suntanned and healthy. As the two candidates answered questions on stage, Kennedy seemed calm and confident, while Nixon sweated visibly and appeared uncomfortable.

The quality of Nixon's verbal responses measured up to his opponent's, and the majority of people who listened to the debate on the radio felt that Nixon had won. But television viewers gave the victory to Kennedy by a wide margin. The debates helped Kennedy convince the American people that he had the experience and maturity to be president, and he ended up winning the election a few months later. "That night I learned TV was a very dangerous medium," the debate's producer, Don Hewitt of CBS News, recalled in *Zap! A Brief History of Television*. "We elected a president that night and we didn't have to wait to vote."

The Kennedy–Nixon debates not only affected the result of the 1960 election, but also changed the way that the United States selected presidents from that time forward. "Politics would never again be the same," Robert L. Hilliard and Michael C. Keith wrote in *The Broadcast Century*. "Image would replace issues in reaching the public through television, and most of the public would thereafter vote on the basis of personality rather than policy." Some critics blamed the media for this change. They claimed that TV news coverage of political campaigns focused on the candidates' personalities and strategies rather than informing voters about their positions on important issues.

TV news expands its influence

Television news coverage expanded its influence during the 1960s. Several factors contributed to its growth, including increased attention from the federal government, new technological developments, innovations in program format, and coverage of a series of major news events. Upon taking office, President Kennedy (1917–1963; served 1961–63) appointed Newton N. Minow (1926–) as chairman of the Federal Communications Commission (FCC), the government agency charged with regulating television. In 1961 Minow made a famous speech before the National Association of Broadcasters (NAB). He criticized the content of TV programming as a "vast wasteland" and encouraged the networks to make a greater effort to serve the public interest. With Minow applying pressure through the FCC, the broadcast networks placed an increased emphasis on news and information programming.

At the same time, a series of technological developments helped modernize TV news coverage. In 1956 the Ampex Corporation introduced the first videotape recorder. Within a few years, videotape had replaced film in the production of television news programs. This technology reduced the delay between the time a news story was filmed and the time it appeared on the air. Videotape allowed the networks to check and play news footage quickly, without spending valuable time transporting and developing film. It also gave news programs the ability to record interviews in the studio for later broadcast, and to delay broadcasts until a more convenient time for viewers on the West Coast (where there is a three-hour time difference from the East Coast).

Also during the early 1960s, communication satellites in orbit around the Earth allowed the networks to show viewers live events from around the world. Newscasts started placing live, moving images on display screens behind the anchor, and they also added more sophisticated graphics. These changes increased viewer interest in the news and convinced the networks to expand their nightly newscasts from fifteen to thirty minutes. One of the first programs to take advantage of these changes was the *CBS Evening News,* which made its debut in 1963 with Walter Cronkite (1916–) as anchor.

60 Minutes is another influential news program that was introduced in the 1960s. Created by CBS News producer Don Hewitt (1922–), who had worked on Edward R. Murrow's show *See It Now, 60 Minutes* adapted the documentary style to tell viewers engaging stories. Each episode of the long-running show features several different segments, like the articles in a print magazine. Some segments report on the results of detailed investigations, while others feature celebrity interviews. *60 Minutes* took a while to find an audience, but by the mid-1970s it had become the highest-rated and most profitable news show in TV history. It spent twenty years among the top ten prime-time series, and as of 2006 it was the only show to hold the number one position in the annual TV ratings in three different decades.

TV news covers the biggest stories of the 1960s

TV news also expanded its influence during the 1960s by providing the American people with coverage of several momentous events in U.S. history. One of these events took place on November 22, 1963, when President John F. Kennedy was shot and killed as he rode through Dallas, Texas, in the back seat of an open car. All of the TV networks suspended regular programming to provide viewers with nonstop coverage of the events that took place over the next four days. Television drew people together in their shock and grief, and an amazing 90 percent of American citizens tuned in to the TV news over the course of that weekend.

The aftermath of the Kennedy assassination marked the first time that the presence of television cameras changed the course of history. Lee Harvey Oswald (1939–1963) was quickly captured and charged with murdering the president. Recognizing the high level of media

Lee Harvey Oswald, alleged assassin of President Kennedy, was shot while being transferred to jail. TV cameras captured the murder live as it happened. © TOPHAM/THE IMAGE WORKS.

interest in the case, law enforcement officials arranged to move the prisoner to the county jail at a convenient time for news coverage. As police officers escorted Oswald through a hallway jammed with reporters, a Dallas nightclub owner named Jack Ruby (1911–1967) stepped out of the crowd and shot and killed the suspect. The murder of Oswald was the first dramatic news event to be shown live on TV. Afterward, many people blamed the decision to allow television cameras at Oswald's transfer for making the murder possible.

The extensive coverage of the events surrounding Kennedy's assassination and funeral helped turn TV into a trusted source of news and information. Over the course of a single weekend, millions of Americans made the switch from radio and newspapers to TV as their main link to current events.

Television news also provided extensive coverage of the civil rights movement (1955–65), when millions of African Americans engaged in

Television helped bring greater awareness of the civil rights movement to the American public. Here, activist Medgar Evers speaks about race relations during a 1963 TV broadcast. © BETTMANN/CORBIS.

marches and protests aimed at ending segregation (the forced separation of people by race) and securing equal rights for all U.S. citizens. Technical innovations such as videotape technology and portable TV cameras helped bring images of the civil rights struggle to a national television audience. For instance, American viewers watched as federal troops escorted black students past angry white mobs so that they could attend formerly all-white schools in the segregated South. They also saw police forces in several major U.S. cities attack peaceful black protesters with clubs, dogs, and fire hoses. The compelling TV footage expanded public support for the civil rights movement and increased pressure on the federal government to address problems of discrimination and inequality.

In the early years of the civil rights movement, African American participants rarely had an opportunity to express their views on television. Instead, TV news programs mostly showed footage of the most dramatic incidents with an anchor narrating the scenes. By the early 1960s, however, the Reverend Martin Luther King Jr. (1929–1968) had emerged as a spokesman for the movement. From this time on, black civil rights workers were increasingly seen and heard on network television. When King was assassinated on April 4, 1968, riots broke out in more than sixty cities across the United States. Television coverage of the violence helped create a backlash against the civil rights movement. Overall, though, TV news coverage made the civil rights movement seem both valid and urgent, traits that would have been difficult to convey before the television age. TV footage helped generate popular support for national legislation, such as the Voting Rights Act of 1964, protecting the rights of future generations of African Americans.

Another major news event of the 1960s that received significant television coverage was the Vietnam War (1954–75). The United States became involved in this conflict during the Cold War (1945–91), as part of its efforts to halt the spread of communism around the world. The U.S. government sent military troops to Southeast Asia in 1965 to help its ally, South Vietnam, avoid being taken over by its communist neighbor, North Vietnam. But the Communists enjoyed a great deal of support among the Vietnamese people. In fact, South Vietnamese Communists, known as the Viet Cong, joined forces with the North Vietnamese Army to fight against the American and South Vietnamese troops. Even though the United States had superior weapons and equipment, the war turned into a bloody standoff.

Vietnam has been described as the first television war because TV news correspondents provided extensive firsthand coverage of the conflict. Some reporters even went on patrol with American soldiers and sent back footage of the dangerous situations they experienced in the Vietnamese villages and jungles. The bloody combat footage disturbed many Americans and helped turn public opinion against the war. Antiwar protests erupted in large cities and on college campuses across the United States.

As the Vietnam War dragged on, the nation became more deeply divided over U.S. military involvement in the conflict. Some government officials criticized the television coverage, claiming that it hurt the U.S. war effort by presenting only one side of the story. But antiwar activists praised TV journalists for revealing the true nature of the conflict, which they felt the U.S. government had tried to hide from the American people.

In 1968 CBS sent its most respected news anchor, Walter Cronkite (1916–), to Vietnam to give a progress report on the war. Before this

News anchor Walter Cronkite (holding microphone) interviewing troops from the front lines of the Vietnam War. U.S. MARINE CORPS.

time, network news had tried to remain objective—presenting the facts and allowing viewers to form their own opinions about what they saw. But when Cronkite returned home, CBS took the unusual step of allowing him to share his own opinions about the war with American viewers. Speaking before a national audience, Cronkite contradicted positive government reports and expressed his view that the U.S.-led war effort had not made much progress. He said that the government should withdraw U.S. troops and find a way to end the conflict. Cronkite's strongly worded editorial caused millions of viewers to rethink their support for U.S. involvement. It also helped convince President Lyndon B. Johnson (1908–1973; served 1963–68), who had taken office following Kennedy's assassination, not to run for re-election.

A more positive news story—space exploration—also captivated American television viewers during the 1960s. Millions of people tuned in to watch U.S. astronauts make the first manned space flight, the initial orbit of the Earth, and the first moon landing over the course of the decade. When Neil Armstrong (1930–) became the first human being to set foot on the Moon in 1969, the event drew an audience of 130 million in the United States and 600 million around the world—or about one-fourth of the global population at that time.

All three major broadcast networks provided extensive coverage of the historic event. They composed special theme music and poetry for the occasion, and they built scale models of the lunar module (the vehicle that landed on the moon) in their New York studios. Many elements of Armstrong's moon walk were staged for television, as well. For instance, the American flag that he planted on the Moon was made rigid, so that it would look like it was blowing in a breeze. TV producers knew that the Moon has no natural wind, but they felt that a flag that appeared to be rippling in the breeze would provide more compelling pictures for the world's viewers.

Network news faces more competition

TV news coverage continued to expand during the 1970s, as many local television stations began their own daily newscasts. Local news coverage became possible thanks to the development of Electronic News Gathering (ENG) technology. ENG combined several technical inventions—including portable television cameras, videotape systems, and stronger antennas to broadcast signals—to increase stations' ability to cover breaking news stories in a timely manner. Many local stations loaded cameras and videotape editing equipment into vans, which could travel quickly to the site of a news event. The vans were also equipped with telescoping antennas to relay TV signals to the local station's newsroom, making the footage shot in the field available for immediate broadcast.

ENG enabled local TV stations to produce newscasts with a high level of appeal to viewers. It also made news coverage faster, easier, and less expensive for the local stations. In fact, newscasts emerged as an important source of profits for local TV stations. As a result, many local stations expanded their news operations throughout the 1970s, adding morning and afternoon newscasts to schedules that already included early evening programs. The basic format of these local newscasts ended up being similar across the country. They usually featured two anchors—one male and one female—who read the news and chatted with each other between segments. Other reporters appeared on camera to provide weather forecasts, sports updates, and live reports from the field.

A Vice President Complains about the Power of TV News

From the beginning of commercial television broadcasting, TV news coverage has influenced politics in the United States. Since television is the main source of information for many Americans, TV news has the power to affect how voters view political candidates and issues. Television news expanded its influence during the turmoil of the 1960s, when it provided extensive coverage of the Vietnam War and the civil rights movement. During this difficult time in American society, many of the country's leaders were criticized in the news media. Some politicians began to complain about television's ability to shape the opinions of the American people about important issues.

One of the most outspoken critics of TV news was Spiro T. Agnew (1918–1996; served 1969–73), who served as vice president under Richard Nixon (1913–1994; served 1969–74). Agnew believed that the television networks were controlled by a small group of wealthy, powerful men who held liberal political views. He argued that these men had too much influence over the news that was presented to the American people. Agnew claimed that the broadcasters were biased against the president and intentionally slanted the news to make the Nixon administration look bad. He outlined these views in a speech presented on November 13, 1969, in Des Moines, Iowa, which is excerpted below from *American Rhetoric from Roosevelt to Reagan:*

> Tonight I want to discuss the importance of the television news medium to the American people. No nation depends more on the intelligent judgment of its citizens. No medium has a more profound influence over public opinion. Nowhere in our system are there fewer checks on vast power. So, nowhere should there be more conscientious responsibility exercised than by the news media. . . .
>
> They decide what 40 to 50 million Americans will learn of the day's events in the nation and the world. We cannot measure this power and influence by the traditional democratic standards, for these men can create national issues overnight. They can make or break by their coverage and commentary a moratorium [temporary stoppage] on the war [in Vietnam]. They can elevate men from obscurity [being unknown] to national prominence within a week. They can reward some politicians with national exposure and ignore others. For millions of Americans the network reporter who covers a continuing issue— like the ABM [Anti-Ballistic Missile international arms control treaty, which was being negotiated by the United States and Soviet Union at that time] or civil rights—becomes, in effect, the presiding [ruling] judge in a national trial by jury. . . .
>
> The American people would rightly not tolerate this concentration of power in Government. Is it not fair and relevant to question its concentration in the hands of a tiny, enclosed fraternity of privileged men elected by no one and enjoying a monopoly [exclusive control of a business or industry] sanctioned [supported] and licensed by Government?. . . .
>
> A narrow and distorted picture of America often emerges from the televised news. A single, dramatic piece of the mosaic [picture composed of many smaller parts] becomes in the minds of millions the entire picture. . . .
>
> Now, my friends, we'd never trust such power, as I've described, over public opinion in the hands of an elected Government. It's time we questioned it in the hands of a small, unelected elite [ruling class]. The great networks have dominated America's airwaves for decades. The people are entitled to a full accounting of their stewardship.

At first, local newscasts provided an important public service by covering community events and issues that were too local to attract the attention of a national TV network. But the local newscasts also competed fiercely against each other to attract and keep viewers. This competition led many local stations to focus on exciting stories that grabbed viewers' attention—such as traffic accidents, fires, and violent crimes—instead of community news. "Reports on city hall or problems in the schools offered little visual excitement and consistently took a back seat to sensational but unimportant news," Chris Paterson explained in the Museum of Broadcast Communications publication "Local and Regional News." Critics also charged that some stations used exaggeration and gimmicks to promote their newscasts.

The competition from local newscasts created changes in the network news as well. News divisions faced greater pressure to earn high ratings and generate profits for the networks. As a result, network newscasts began shifting their emphasis from hard news on world events and political issues to softer news on celebrities, health issues, and regional events. "We went for the stories that could be illustrated and left alone the ones that required careful examination through text," longtime CBS News anchor Walter Cronkite said in the 1997 book *Glued to the Set*. "This distorted the whole value of television news, to my mind. And distorts it to this day."

The biggest news story of the 1970s involved Richard M. Nixon (1913–1994; served 1969–74), who was elected president in 1968 after Johnson decided not to seek re-election. In the early 1970s the Nixon administration became involved in a political scandal known as Watergate. The scandal developed when burglars with ties to the Republican Party were caught breaking into Democratic Party campaign offices at the Watergate Hotel in Washington, D.C. Nixon initially claimed that he had no prior knowledge of these illegal activities. But in a series of hearings before the U.S. Senate, it became clear that the president and his staff had lied and tried to cover up their knowledge of the crime. Millions of Americans tuned in to watch the hearings live on TV. They also watched in disbelief as the Watergate scandal forced Nixon to become the first U.S. president ever to resign from office in 1974.

CNN revolutionizes TV news

The popularity of national network news broadcasts peaked around 1980. Over the next decade, the networks' nightly news programs lost half of their audience. Competition from local newscasts was one factor in the shrinking audience. A 1996 study by the Pew Research Center for People and the Press found that 65 percent of adults regularly tuned in to local TV news, while only 42 percent regularly watched network news.

The most significant factor in the decline of network news, however, was the creation of the twenty-four-hour cable news channel CNN. Founded by Ted Turner (1938–) in 1980, CNN was so technically inferior to the networks at first that critics called it the "Chicken Noodle Network." Within a few years, though, CNN began attracting large audiences with its extensive coverage of breaking news stories.

In 1986, for instance, CNN was the only TV channel to provide live coverage of the launch of the space shuttle *Challenger*. After the moon walk in 1969, the broadcast networks had stopped paying much attention to the U.S. space program. So when *Challenger* exploded 73 seconds after liftoff, killing all seven astronauts on board, CNN achieved a major scoop on the competition. The cable channel even had a film crew on location at the New Hampshire school where Christa McAuliffe (1948–1986)—a teacher chosen to take part in the space shuttle mission—had worked until her tragic death. The broadcast networks rushed their top anchors into the studios and interrupted regular programming to provide coverage of the accident. Nevertheless, the incident helped make CNN the first choice for many TV viewers when important news broke.

CNN really moved to the forefront of TV news coverage during the 1991 Persian Gulf War. This conflict began when the Middle Eastern nation of Iraq invaded its smaller neighbor, Kuwait. When Iraqi leader Saddam Hussein (1937–) refused international requests to remove his troops from Kuwait, the United States and a group of other countries sent military forces to the Persian Gulf region. The coalition spent several weeks bombing strategic targets in Iraq, then launched a ground attack that forced the Iraqi troops to leave Kuwait.

On the night the coalition bombing raids began, CNN had three anchors stationed in the Iraqi capital of Baghdad. These men—Peter Arnett (1934–), Bernard Shaw (1940–), and John Holliman (1948–1998)—covered the attacks live from the balcony of their downtown hotel room. Their daring footage attracted 11 million viewers—or about twenty times the normal ratings for CNN. When Saddam Hussein ordered all foreign journalists to leave Iraq, Arnett was the only one allowed to remain. He continued reporting for CNN from within Iraq throughout the war. CNN's coverage of the 1991 Persian Gulf War, which was broadcast

CNN correspondent Peter Arnett reporting from Baghdad, Iraq, during the 1991 Persian Gulf War. CNN/GETTY IMAGES.

via satellite, helped the cable network become a prime news source for viewers around the world. Within five years, CNN was more profitable than the three major networks' news divisions combined.

The success of CNN changed the face of television news. Viewers found that they enjoyed having access to news and information twenty-four hours per day. But the demands of filling that much air time forced CNN to adopt a broader definition of what was considered newsworthy. CNN broadcast many live events that had questionable news value, such as funerals and legal trials involving celebrities. Critics also charged that CNN sometimes aired rumors and gossip instead of taking the time to verify information.

The increased competition from CNN caused financial problems for the broadcast networks. All three networks were purchased by large entertainment companies during the late 1980s or early 1990s, and the new corporate owners restructured the network news divisions in order to cut costs. They laid off many employees and reduced news-gathering budgets. In an effort to increase ratings, the network news also started to place a greater emphasis on attention-grabbing stories, such as celebrity scandals and violent crimes. In fact, the network news aired four times more crime stories in 1995 than in 1991, even though the nation's crime rate had actually dropped during this period. At the same time, the networks drew criticism for not keeping the American people well informed about such important issues as the environment, education, and the economy.

The decline of television journalism

Cable television expanded its reach throughout the 1980s. By 1992, about 60 percent of American households subscribed to cable services. CNN continued to be one of the most popular cable channels, even though some critics complained about its increasing focus on celebrities and scandals. Since the broadcast networks tended to follow CNN's lead, many people felt that the overall quality of TV journalism declined throughout the 1990s.

One of the prime examples cited in this argument is the media circus that surrounded the O. J. Simpson murder trial. O. J. Simpson (1947–) was a retired football star who used his fame to launch a successful career as an actor and sports broadcaster. In 1994 Simpson's ex-wife, Nicole, and her male friend were found murdered outside her Los Angeles home. Evidence collected at the crime scene made Simpson the prime suspect, and a warrant was issued for his arrest. When Simpson failed to turn himself in as agreed, the Los Angeles Police Department sent officers to find him. But television reporters got wind of the story, located Simpson's white Ford Bronco on a freeway, and began following the vehicle in helicopters. Local, national, and cable news all interrupted regular programming to cover the slow-motion police chase around Los Angeles.

Simpson finally surrendered to police and was put on trial for murder. The four-month trial was televised live on several channels, including CNN, and the final not-guilty verdict in 1995 drew 100 million viewers. Critics claim that the extensive coverage of the O. J. Simpson case demonstrated the declining quality of TV news, which they say has been obsessed with celebrities and scandals ever since that time.

TV news becomes less objective

In the mid-1990s, the success of CNN led to the startup of several more cable news channels. Microsoft and NBC teamed up to form MSNBC, while the Fox broadcast network launched the Fox News Channel. These cable news channels competed to attract viewers' attention away from CNN and local and network news programming. One way they tried to differentiate themselves was by introducing news programs with loud, brash, opinionated hosts who seemed to enjoy challenging and arguing with their guests.

The signature program on the Fox News Channel, for instance, was *The O'Reilly Factor,* hosted by conservative commentator Bill O'Reilly (1949–). From the beginning, O'Reilly viewed his show as a forum for expressing his own opinion. "Every newspaper in the country has an op-ed [opinion-editorial] page and an editorial page, but broadcasters are afraid to do that," he told Scott Collins in *Crazy like a Fox.* "I'm not. I think people will be interested to hear opinion, especially after you get the news and you want to know what people think about it."

From the 1940s through the 1970s, the FCC had required television broadcasters to make every effort to be objective. An FCC policy called the Fairness Doctrine required the networks to provide balanced coverage of both sides of controversial issues, so that viewers would have enough information to make up their own minds. But the Fairness Doctrine was eliminated in 1987 as part of an effort to reduce the number of government regulations affecting the broadcast industry. Afterward, critics claim that many network and cable news operations became less objective and more biased in their reporting.

Some critics blamed the trend toward less objectivity in TV news on the fact that the major broadcast and cable networks were owned by large parent corporations, such as Time Warner, Walt Disney, Viacom, Seagram, News Corporation, Sony, GE, and AT&T. These major corporations had financial interests in a wide variety of industries, including movies and music, alcoholic beverages, theme parks, professional sports franchises, telephone services, and nuclear power plants. The critics pointed out that the desire to earn profits in one area of the business might create a conflict with the duty to provide fair and unbiased TV news coverage. For example, a network news program might be tempted to downplay its coverage of safety problems in a product manufactured by another division of its parent company.

The declining quality of television news became an issue during the 2000 presidential election, in which Republican candidate George W. Bush (1946–) competed against Democratic candidate Al Gore (1948–). On the night that Americans cast their votes, the TV networks used data collected at the polls to predict the results in various states. As the vote tallies came in, it became clear that the election would be very close. Ten minutes before the polls closed in Florida, the major broadcast networks announced Gore as the winner in the state. A short time later, however, the networks decided that the results were too close to call and placed Florida back into the undecided column. Before the evening ended, the networks had changed their minds once again and predicted Bush as the winner in Florida.

The results in other states eventually made it clear that Florida controlled the outcome of the election. The ballots in Florida were recounted by hand, and even then the results were challenged in court. The 2000 election was ultimately decided by the U.S. Supreme Court, which halted all recounts in December and made Bush the next president of the United States. Afterward, TV news came under harsh criticism for its election-night coverage.

Critics said that the networks behaved in a reckless and irresponsible manner by predicting a winner in Florida before they had enough information to do so correctly. Some analysts claimed that the errors occurred because the networks had been forced to cut back on their political reporting staff in order to reduce costs. In any case, viewers disapproved of the way the networks handled the election results, and many lost faith in the accuracy of network news as a result.

These feelings resulted in increased audiences for cable news channels. By 2001, surveys showed that 45 percent of American viewers turned to cable news first for the latest information on breaking news events, while 22 percent preferred broadcast network news programs, and 20 percent watched local newscasts. Despite declining audience numbers, however, network news continued to draw more viewers than cable news on a day-to-day basis. The combined audience for the three major broadcast networks' news programs in 2001–2002 was over 30 million viewers—more than 10 times the total audience for CNN, MSNBC, and the Fox News Channel during that period.

The power of television news to provide dramatic live coverage of breaking news events became clear once again during the terrorist attacks of September 11, 2001. All of the major broadcast and cable networks switched to live news coverage within a few minutes after an airplane crashed into the North Tower of the World Trade Center in New York City. At first, several anchors speculated that perhaps a private sightseeing plane had flown off course. But it soon became clear that it was a deliberate attack, as TV cameras captured the image of a second jet crashing into the South Tower. Viewers watched in horror as the South Tower collapsed on live television, followed half an hour later by the North Tower. A third airplane controlled by terrorists hit the Pentagon building in Washington D.C., and a fourth airplane crashed in a field in Pennsylvania.

TV news covered the chaos on the streets of New York City as residents tried to flee the destruction and falling debris from the World Trade Center. The news cameras also captured many compelling images of grief and displays of courage. During the coverage of the September 11 attacks, the Fox News Channel introduced a line of text that scrolled across the bottom of the screen to provide viewers with a continuous graphical update on the latest developments. Fox News also tapped into viewers' feelings of patriotism by placing an American flag in the corner of the screen, along with the channel logo.

In the wake of the terrorist attacks in the United States, many analysts claimed that the Fox News Channel became openly biased in its presentation of the news. For instance, Fox News anchors often expressed outright support for President Bush and his war on terrorism. Some American viewers found Fox's conservative slant on the news to be reassuring. As a result, Fox News enjoyed a 43 percent increase in viewers over the next few months, and by 2003 it led CNN in the ratings by a margin of 2:1.

The success of Fox News encouraged other cable news channels to cater to the views of a specific audience with more opinionated, and less objective, news coverage. Some claim that this trend toward biased TV news reporting increased the political divisions in the United States and made it more difficult to resolve important problems in American society.

For More Information

BOOKS

Bliss, Edward J., Jr. *Now the News: The Story of Broadcast Journalism*. New York: Columbia University Press, 1991.

Calabro, Marian. *Zap! A Brief History of Television*. New York: Four Winds Press, 1992.

Collins, Scott. *Crazy like a Fox: The Inside Story of How Fox News Beat CNN.* New York: Portfolio, 2004.

Garner, Joe. *Stay Tuned: Television's Unforgettable Moments.* Kansas City: Andrews McMeel Publishing, 2002.

Hilliard, Robert L., and Michael C. Keith. *The Broadcast Century: A Biography of American Broadcasting.* Boston: Focal Press, 1992.

Kerbel, Matthew. R. *If It Bleeds, It Leads: An Anatomy of Television News.* Boulder, CO: Westview Press, 2000.

McChesney, Robert W. *Rich Media, Poor Democracy: Communications Politics in Dubious Times.* Urbana: University of Illinois Press, 1999.

Nimmo, Dan D. *Nightly Horrors: Crisis Coverage by Television Network News.* Knoxville: University of Tennessee Press, 1985.

Postman, Neil, and Steve Powers. *How to Watch TV News.* New York: Penguin, 1992.

Stark, Steven D. *Glued to the Set: The 60 Television Shows and Events That Made Us Who We Are Today.* New York: The Free Press, 1997.

Whittemore, Hank. *CNN: The Inside Story.* Boston: Little, Brown, 1990.

PERIODICALS

Foote, Joe S. "Television News: Past, Present, and Future." *Mass Communications Review,* Winter-Spring 1992.

Frank, Reuven. "The Shifting Shapes of TV News." *New Leader,* March 2001.

Gitlin, Todd. "We Disport, We Deride: It's All Attitude, All the Time at Fox News." *American Prospect,* February 2003.

Greppi, Michele. "TV Newsmags Tell the Story." *Television Week,* September 1, 2003.

O'Brien, Meredith. "How Did We Get It So Wrong?" *Quill,* January 2001.

Small, William. "Television Journalism." *Television Quarterly* (special issue), Winter 1990.

WEB SITES

Agnew, Spiro T. "Television News Coverage," November 13, 1969. In Ryan, Halford Ross, ed. *American Rhetoric from Roosevelt to Reagan,* 2nd ed. Prospect Heights, IL: Waveland Press, 1987. Also available at *American Rhetoric.com.* http://www.americanrhetoric.com/speeches/spiroagnew.htm (accessed on June 19, 2006).

Kierstead, Phillip. "Network News." *Museum of Broadcast Communications.* http://www.museum.tv/archives/etv/N/htmlN/newsnetwork/newsnetwork.htm (accessed on June 19, 2006).

Paterson, Chris. "Local and Regional News." *Museum of Broadcast Communications.* http://www.museum.tv/archives/etv/N/htmlN/newslocala/newslocala.htm (accessed on June 19, 2006).

10

Television's Impact on American Society and Culture

TV is a constant presence in most Americans' lives. With its fast-moving, visually interesting, highly entertaining style, it commands many people's attention for several hours each day. Studies have shown that television competes with other sources of human interaction—such as family, friends, church, and school—in helping young people develop values and form ideas about the world around them. It also influences viewers' attitudes and beliefs about themselves, as well as about people from other social, ethnic, and cultural backgrounds.

Between the 1940s and 2000s, commercial television had a profound and wide-ranging impact on American society and culture. It influenced the way that people think about such important social issues as race, gender, and class. It played an important role in the political process, particularly in shaping national election campaigns. TV programs and commercials have also been mentioned as major factors contributing to increased American materialism (a view that places more value on acquiring material possessions than on developing in other ways). Finally, television helped to spread American culture around the world.

Racial minorities on TV

Until the 1970s, the majority of the people who appeared on American television programs were Caucasian (white). Being white was presented as normal in all sorts of programs, including news, sports, entertainment, and advertisements. The few minorities that did appear in TV programs tended to be presented as stereotypes (generalized, usually negative images of a group of people). For instance, African American actors often played roles as household servants, while Native Americans often appeared as warriors in Westerns.

Some critics argue that outright racism (unfair treatment of people because of their race) was the reason that so few minorities appeared on television. But television industry analysts offered several other explanations as well. In the 1950s and 1960s, for instance, the broadcast networks tried to create programs that would attract a wide audience. Before research tools became available to gather information about the race and gender of people watching, network programmers assumed that the audience was made up mostly of white viewers. They also assumed that many white viewers would not be interested in watching shows about minorities. In addition, the networks did not want to risk offending viewers—or potential advertisers—in the South who supported segregation (the forced separation of people by race). Whatever the reason, prime-time television programming largely ignored the real-life concerns and contributions of America's racial minorities for many years.

There were a few early TV shows that featured minorities. The popular situation comedy (sitcom) *I Love Lucy,* which aired from 1951 to 1957, co-starred comedian Lucille Ball (1911–1989) and her real-life husband, bandleader Desi Arnaz (1917–1986), who was Hispanic. *The Nat "King" Cole Show,* a musical variety series that began on NBC in 1956, was hosted by the well-known black entertainer Nat King Cole (1919–1965). Even though the program attracted many of the top performers of that time, it was cancelled after one year because it failed to find a sponsor (a company that pays to produce a program for advertising purposes). A very popular early variety program, *The Ed Sullivan Show,* featured a number of black performers as guests. Still, African Americans mostly appeared on TV in the role of entertainers.

This situation slowly began to improve during the civil rights movement (1965–75), when African Americans fought to end segregation and gain equal rights in American society. TV news programs provided extensive coverage of civil rights protests, which helped turn public opinion in favor of the cause of equality. As awareness of racial discrimination (unfair treatment based on race) increased, more social critics began complaining about the absence of minority characters on television. They argued that positive portrayals of minority characters in TV programs could help increase the self-esteem of minority viewers, promote understanding, and improve race relations in the United States.

Breaking the color barrier

In 1965, African American actor and comedian Bill Cosby (1937–) co-starred as a detective on the popular series *I Spy.* He won three Emmy Awards for his role. In 1968 Diahann Carroll (1935–) became the first

Diahann Carroll in the 1960s prime-time TV series Julia.
© BETTMANN/CORBIS.

black woman to star in a prime-time TV series. She played the title character in *Julia,* a sitcom about a nurse raising her young child alone after her husband's death. Since Julia lived in an apartment building with both black and white tenants and never faced prejudice or discrimination due to her race, some critics complained that the show did not reflect the realities of the African American experience. But Carroll claimed that *Julia* was as realistic as any other fictional program on TV. "We all had to realize that television was not representative of any community," she commented in *Ebony.* "It was a make-believe world. Even the white families were cardboard [one-dimensional or flat]."

During the 1970s, television program ratings began using such viewer characteristics as age, income, education, and ethnicity to break down the mass audience into smaller groups. Once the networks could collect more detailed data about the audience, they began creating programs to appeal to specific groups. Around this time, the networks also shifted their general focus away from older, rural viewers and toward younger, urban viewers, who were seen as more likely to spend money on sponsors' products. This change in audience focus led the networks to tackle more frequently debated issues in their programs.

As a result, several programs featuring minority characters and families first appeared in the 1970s. The African American comedian Flip Wilson (1933–1998) hosted a successful variety show that aired on NBC from 1970 to 1974. *The Flip Wilson Show* reached number two in the national TV rankings and won two Emmy Awards. Some historians credit Wilson for leading the way for later black comedians who had successful television careers, such as Arsenio Hall (1955–), Eddie Murphy (1961–), Chris Rock (1965–), and Dave Chappelle (1973–). However, other critics claim that Wilson started an unfortunate trend in which a growing number of African American entertainers on television played the role of comic fool.

Another important minority show of the 1970s was *Good Times,* which aired on CBS for five years beginning in 1974. This situation comedy focused on the struggles of an African American family living in an inner-city apartment building. Each week the Evans family relied on love and humor to overcome discrimination, unemployment, crime, and other problems faced by many black families in the United States. Many TV critics praised the series for dealing with these issues in a realistic way, and many viewers identified with the family's struggles during tough economic times. But some African Americans felt that the character of son J. J., played by Jimmie Walker (1947–), was a ridiculous stereotype. In fact, the actors who played his parents, John Amos (1939–) and Esther Rolle (1920–1998), left the show in protest when its focus shifted from the family to the clownish J. J.

The Jeffersons, which aired on CBS for a decade beginning in 1974, was another important show about an African American family. It was created by Norman Lear (1922–), who also created the popular but controversial show *All in the Family.* The sitcom centered on George Jefferson (played by Sherman Hemsley [1938–]), a successful black businessman

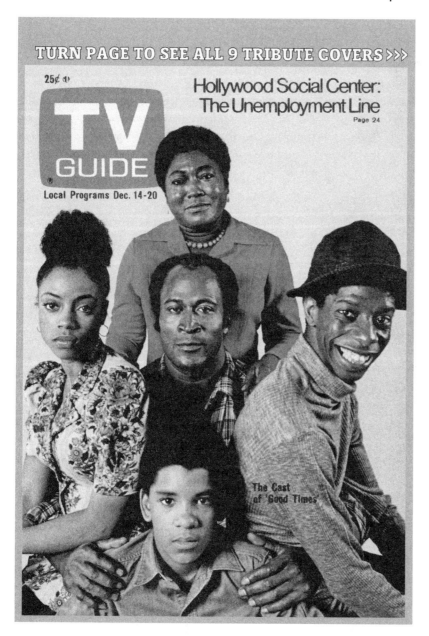

TURN PAGE TO SEE ALL 9 TRIBUTE COVERS >>>

25¢

TV GUIDE

Local Programs Dec. 14-20

Hollywood Social Center:
The Unemployment Line
Page 24

The Cast of Good Times

The cast of Good Times, *who portrayed the Evans family living in inner-city Chicago.* BUSINESS WIRE/ GETTY IMAGES.

who moved his family into a luxury high-rise apartment building in New York City. George often behaved rudely and made a fool of himself, only to be rescued by his patient wife, Louise (Isabel Sanford [1917–2004]). The program reached number four in the annual television ratings in 1974–75, demonstrating that shows starring African Americans could

Television in American Society: Almanac

Freddie Prinze became TV's first Hispanic lead character as the star of the 1970s show Chico and the Man.
© BETTMANN/CORBIS.

achieve widespread, popular success. But it also received criticism during its long run for portraying some characters as stereotypes.

The mid-1970s also saw the launch of the first prime-time TV series centering on a Hispanic character. *Chico and the Man,* which aired on NBC from 1974 to 1978, starred Puerto Rican comedian Freddie Prinze (1954–1977) as Chico Rodriguez. Chico is a talented young mechanic who builds a relationship with a cranky old garage owner, Ed Brown (played by Jack Albertson [1907–1981]). The show was set in a multicultural neighborhood in East Los Angeles, and it received critical praise for presenting a thriving Hispanic culture to national TV audiences. The show continued after the death of Prinze in 1977, but went off the air the following season.

Another landmark program in African American TV history is *Roots,* an eight-part miniseries (a short series of television programs with a continuing story line) that earned some of the highest ratings ever when it aired in 1977. Based on a historical novel by Alex Haley (1921–1992), it followed four generations of an African American family, beginning when the first member was brought to the United States from Africa and sold as a slave. Many people hoped that the miniseries would increase awareness of the impact slavery had on African American families, and thus would help improve race relations in the United States.

The Cosby Show, a sitcom that aired on NBC from 1984 to 1992 and claimed the top spot in the annual TV ratings four times, also had a broad appeal. Created by Bill Cosby, *The Cosby Show* centered on a stable, middle-class black family. Cosby played Dr. Cliff Huxtable, a successful physician and wise and loving father. Phylicia Rashad (1948–) played his wife Clair, a respected attorney and patient mother. Some critics claimed that the program was unrealistic, partly because two professional, working parents could never spend so much time at home with their children. Others complained that the show did not do enough to address issues of importance to African Americans. But many viewers found it refreshing to see the positive image of a comfortable, confident, and loving black family on TV each week.

Cable TV targets minority viewers

During the 1980s and 1990s, American television viewers gained many new channel options. The growth of cable TV services—and the introduction of new broadcast networks such as Fox, UPN, and WB—greatly expanded the amount of programming available on television. Many of the new cable channels and smaller broadcast networks directed their programs toward minorities, since these audiences were not being well served by the major networks. Black Entertainment Television (BET) and UPN focused on African American viewers, for instance, while Univision and Telemundo aimed at Hispanic audiences.

Roots, *a miniseries that followed four generations of an African American family, is one of the highest rated programs in TV history.* AP IMAGES.

Even as shows for and about minorities became more widely available, however, prominent roles for people of color were rare in prime-time programs on the major broadcast networks. There were a few examples of multicultural casts in mainstream series. The police drama *Miami Vice,* which aired from 1984 to 1989, depicted a pair of detectives. One partner was white (Sonny Crockett, played by Don Johnson [1949–]), and the other was black (Rico Tubbs, played by Philip Michael Thomas [1949–]). Similarly, the police drama *NYPD Blue,* which began in 1993, featured a white detective (Andy Sipowitz, played by Dennis Franz [1944–]) partnered with a Hispanic detective (Bobby Simone, played by Jimmy Smits [1955–]). In many cases, though, the minorities who appeared in prime time cop shows were depicted as criminals, gang members, or drug addicts.

In general, television programming became more segregated (separated by race) in the age of cable, with individual shows tending to feature casts that were either white or black. As of 2006 *The Cosby Show* was the last major network program with equal appeal to black and white viewers. Polls showed that black and white Americans tended to watch completely different sets of shows. Most of the programs that attracted large numbers of minority viewers aired on the smaller broadcast networks or on specialized cable networks. Critics argued that these separate viewing patterns prevented people of different races from developing shared interests and common cultural references and thus contributed to the racial divisions in American society.

In 1999 the National Association for the Advancement of Colored People (NAACP) and other minority organizations formally complained about the lack of diversity in network television programs. The networks responded by adding more minorities to the casts of shows and actively recruiting minority employees. By the early 2000s the effort had produced some positive results. Surveys showed that African Americans accounted for 15 percent of the characters in prime-time series. This figure was similar to the percentage of African Americans in the overall U.S. population (12.5 percent).

Hispanics did not fare as well in prime-time TV series. Although Hispanics made up 13.5 percent of the U.S. population, they accounted for only 3 percent of the characters on television in 2003 (Asian Americans and Native Americans each accounted for less than 1 percent of characters). Cable operators targeted the Hispanic market with an increase in Spanish-language programming in the 2000s. But Hispanic activists wanted to see more Hispanic characters in mainstream programming as well. For example, they pointed out that several popular prime-time series were set in Miami, Florida, where as of the early 2000s about 66 percent of the population was Hispanic. Even so, these programs did not feature Hispanic characters in major roles. One of the few successful network series to focus on a Hispanic family was *George Lopez*, which began airing on ABC in 2000. This sitcom starred Hispanic comedian George Lopez (1961–) as the manager of an aircraft parts factory who struggles to deal with his rebellious teenaged children, ambitious wife, and meddlesome mother.

Some experts believe that the key to improving minority representation on television is to increase the number of minorities who work in positions of authority in the TV industry—as station managers, for instance, or as network programming executives. They argue that putting people of color in charge of programming at the major networks and at local TV stations would lead to more frequent, accurate, and respectful portrayals of minorities on screen.

Women on TV

Television has a mixed record when it comes to portraying women and gender roles. Although women made up more than 51 percent of the U.S. population as of 2000, female characters have always accounted for a

The NAACP Fights Racism on TV

The National Association for the Advancement of Colored People (NAACP) has fought against discrimination in the American entertainment industry since its founding in 1909. The organization, which promotes equal rights for African Americans and other minorities, played a role in shaping the content of TV programs from the earliest years of television. In 1951, for instance, the NAACP filed a lawsuit in federal court to stop the CBS network from airing the show *Amos 'n' Andy*, because it portrayed African American characters as stereotypes (generalized, usually negative images of a group of people). Although the lawsuit was not successful, pressure from the NAACP and other organizations helped convince CBS to take the show off the air in 1953.

At the start of every television season, the major broadcast networks release descriptions of the new programs they plan to introduce. Prior to the 1999–2000 season, the NAACP reviewed the TV schedules and pointed out that none of the new prime-time network series featured minority characters in prominent roles. The organization held meetings with television executives about the lack of minorities on TV and reached agreements in which the networks promised to take steps to increase diversity.

After 2000, the NAACP continued to work with the television industry to increase the number of high-profile roles for minorities on screen, as well as to create more employment opportunities for minorities behind the scenes of TV programs. In his introduction to a 2003 report on the organization's progress, NAACP president Kweisi Mfume explained the importance of television in shaping people's views of minorities:

> Ideas and images guide our lives. They create the belief systems that control our individual and societal actions. Television communicates more ideas and images to more people in a single day than [Biblical King] Solomon or [English playwright William] Shakespeare did in their entire lives. More people depend on the medium for news and entertainment, from which they construct their worldview, than on any other venue in the world.
>
> When it comes to forming ideas, reinforcing stereotypes, establishing norms, and shaping our thinking, nothing affects us more than the images and concepts delivered into our lives on a daily basis by television and film. Accordingly there is ample cause for concern about what does or does not happen on television when there is little or no diversity in either opportunities or the decision-making process. . . .
>
> With all the [problems] affecting communities and people across our nation, one might argue that there are more urgent needs and other battles to fight. Although that might be the case in some instances, few if any issues will define us more in the context of who we are, what we think, and how we respond than the medium of television.

Over the years, many other special interest groups have recognized the impact of television on the way Americans think about various issues. Like the NAACP, these groups have increasingly tried to work with the TV industry to make sure that programming reflects their viewpoints.

smaller percentage of the major roles on prime-time TV series—especially drama series. But the history of American television also includes a number of progressive programs that helped viewers come to terms with the expanding role of women in society.

In the 1950s, television programming had a male focus. The most popular shows tended to be Westerns, police dramas, and science-fiction series. These programs usually featured strong male characters that faced danger bravely and used their wits—or their fist-fighting abilities—to solve problems. Most of these types of dramas did not have any regular female characters. Situation comedies often included female characters, but these women appeared almost exclusively in roles as suburban house-wives and mothers.

A few early TV programs included mild challenges to traditional gender roles. Lucy Ricardo, the heroine of the 1950s sitcom *I Love Lucy*, felt dissatisfied with her role as a housewife and wanted to get a job in show business. But Lucy's struggles were presented in a zany, humorous fashion in order to make her ambitious nature less threatening to audiences of that time, when the majority of women did not hold jobs outside of the home. During the 1960s, popular oddball comedies such as *Bewitched* and *I Dream of Jeannie* featured strong female characters who moved beyond their traditional roles with the help of their own magical abilities. Some reviewers claimed that these series helped prepare American society to accept greater empowerment of women.

In the 1970s, feminists (supporters of women's rights) began actively seeking equal rights and opportunities for women in American society. Network TV programming started to reflect the growing women's rights movement by presenting more women in nontraditional roles. The main character in *The Mary Tyler Moore Show*, for example, was a smart, independent, single working woman. The sitcom *One Day at a Time* featured a divorced mother struggling to raise two teenaged daughters on her own. *Maude*, a spin-off from the successful sitcom *All in the Family*, centered on a divorced woman as well. In one of the most controversial sitcom episodes of all time, Maude (played by Beatrice Arthur [1923–]) faced an unplanned pregnancy and decided to have an abortion.

As the broadcast networks gained more information about the viewing audience during the 1970s, they began trying to capture female viewers with dramatic programs as well. Instead of providing nonstop action and adventure, many drama series started to focus on characters' emotional lives. But male characters still dominated these types of shows. In 1972, according to Mary Desjardins in the Museum of Broadcast Communications publication "Gender and Television," 74 percent of the characters in prime-time drama series were male. Little progress was made over the next fifteen years: in 1987, 66 percent of the characters were male.

Such statistics prompted the National Organization for Women (NOW), a women's rights group, to challenge the networks to include more positive representations of women in prime-time programming. Pressure from NOW helped convince CBS not to cancel the original 1980s police show *Cagney and Lacey,* which was the first prime-time drama to star two women. The networks also produced several popular sitcoms starring strong women in the 1980s, including *Roseanne* and *Murphy Brown.*

The rise of cable TV ensured that even more programming for and about women would become available in the 1990s. Several cable channels, such as Lifetime and HGTV, designed their shows for female viewers. Meanwhile, the broadcast networks began featuring women in more diverse roles in entertainment programming. By the 2000s, however, some gaps in coverage remained to be addressed. Women's sports rarely appeared on television, for instance, and news programs used far fewer women than men as expert commentators.

Gays and lesbians on TV

Gay and lesbian characters did not appear on television until the 1970s. Several factors contributed to the introduction of homosexual characters at that time. First, the broadcast networks shifted their focus toward younger, urban viewers, who were thought to hold more accepting social views. Second, a series of rulings by the Federal Communications Commission (FCC) gave independent production companies more control over TV programs. These independent producers tended to be more willing to address frequently debated subject matter than the networks. Finally, homosexuals began to be more visible in American society, and TV shows began to reflect that change.

At first, gay and lesbian characters made occasional appearances in single episodes of ongoing TV series. These characters were usually one-dimensional, or not realistically portrayed, and they typically served the purpose of creating conflict among the regular characters. As more gay and lesbian characters appeared on TV, some critics charged that they were too often presented as stereotypes. In 1978 the National Gay Task Force provided the broadcast networks with a list of positive

The cast and creators of Will & Grace *accept the award for Outstanding Comedy Series at the GLAAD Media Awards in 2006.* FRAZER HARRISON/GETTY IMAGES.

and negative images of homosexuals. The activists encouraged the networks to avoid presenting negative images of gays and lesbians as sexual predators or child molesters. Instead, they asked the networks to present positive images of gays and lesbians as contributing members of society who are comfortable with their sexuality.

In the early 2000s, gay advocacy groups had some success in working with the television industry to promote fair and accurate representations of homosexuals in TV programs. For instance, the Gay and Lesbian Alliance Against Defamation (GLAAD) acts as a resource for the entertainment industry and provides suggestions on how to improve the depiction of homosexuals on TV. GLAAD releases an annual list of gay and lesbian TV characters as part of its mission to eliminate homophobia (fear of homosexuals) and end discrimination against gays in American society.

Some conservative religious and political groups resent gay activists' success in working with the television networks. They believe that homosexuality is abnormal and poses a threat to traditional family values. They view positive portrayals of gay and lesbian characters on TV as promoting immoral behavior. Some groups, such as the American Family Association (AFA), have organized protests against advertisers that sponsor programs that portray homosexuals in a sympathetic or positive way. Television networks thus face pressure from advocacy groups on both sides of the gay rights issue.

For many years, the networks tried to balance these competing interests by including more gay characters in TV series, but strictly limiting any physical or sexual interaction between them. But cable TV channels relaxed these standards in the 1990s, and the broadcast networks had to follow in order to compete. The late 1990s and 2000s saw the introduction of a number of TV programs focusing on gay and lesbian characters, such as *Will & Grace, Queer Eye for the Straight Guy, Queer as Folk,* and *The L Word.*

TV and the American family

In the 1950s, television was considered a form of family entertainment. Most American homes only had one TV set, and many families would gather around it in the evening to watch programs together. Recognizing this trend, the networks produced programs that were suitable for a general audience, such as variety shows and family comedies. From the beginning, fictional TV families have often reflected—and sometimes influenced—the real lives of American families.

TV families of the early 1950s showed some diversity, although they did not represent all American lifestyles. There were traditional, nuclear families composed of parents and children, for instance, as well as childless married couples and extended families living together under one roof. Some TV families lived in cities, while others lived in suburbs or rural areas. But the only ethnic families shown on TV were recent immigrants from European countries such as Ireland or Italy. TV programs did not feature African American or Hispanic families until the 1970s.

By the late 1950s, the increasing popularity of situation comedies (sitcoms) started to make TV families more alike. Most sitcoms featured white, middle-class, nuclear families living in the suburbs. Popular programs such as *The Donna Reed Show, Leave It to Beaver,* and *Father Knows*

The Andy Griffith Show *was a family-oriented program whose lead character was a single father.* HULTON ARCHIVE/ GETTY IMAGES.

Best presented idealized views of suburban families led by a patient, hard-working father. The typical role of women in these shows was as a stay-at-home wife and mother who cooks, cleans the house, cares for the children, and provides constant support to her husband.

During the 1960s, as American women started to break out of traditional roles and seek greater independence and freedom, more TV shows featured different types of families. A number of TV families were led by single fathers, in such shows as *My Three Sons, The Andy Griffith Show, Family Affair,* and *Bonanza.* Since divorce was not widely considered socially acceptable at the time, though, these single fathers were almost always widowers (husbands whose wives had died).

The 1970s was a decade of social change in the United States, with the civil rights movement and feminist movement much in the news. (The civil rights movement sought to secure equal rights and opportunities for African Americans, while the feminist movement sought to secure equal rights and opportunities for women.) The portrayal of family life on television became more diverse during this period. Some TV shows featured working-class families, such as *All in the Family,* and others featured single, working women whose co-workers served the function of a family, such as *The Mary Tyler Moore Show.* Landmark TV programs such as *The Jeffersons* and *Good Times* focused on African American families for the first time. Television also continued to provide sentimental portrayals of nuclear and extended families in programs such as *Little House on the Prairie* and *The Waltons.*

Some of the most popular TV programs of the 1980s were prime-time soap operas about wealthy, powerful families. Shows such as *Dallas* and *Dynasty* presented views of a luxurious, upper-class lifestyle. But the families at the center of these dramas had all sorts of emotional and relationship problems. During the 1990s, television programs in general began featuring more dysfunctional families—from the real-life family feuds on shocking daytime talk shows to the family conflicts on sitcoms such as *Roseanne* and *The Simpsons.* At the same time, many cable TV channels attracted viewers by showing reruns of old shows, such as *Leave It to Beaver* and *The Brady Bunch,* that provided a comforting view of family life in the 1950s and 1960s.

By the 2000s, there were different cable TV channels for every member of a family. Most American homes had at least two TV sets, so families were not as likely to watch television together. Increasingly, the members of a family watched different shows, ones suited to their gender, age group, and interests. Some critics argued that these television viewing patterns had a negative impact on families. They said that separate TV viewing prevented family members from spending time together and engaging in special activities and rituals that created strong family bonds. In addition to reflecting family life in the United States, therefore, television also changed it.

Television concepts of social class

In addition to race, gender, sexual orientation, and family, television has shaped the way that Americans think about the issue of social class. From the 1950s through the 2000s, most characters in TV programs have been upper-middle-class, professional people, such as doctors, lawyers, journalists, and business owners. Working-class and poor characters have appeared much more rarely, and they have often been portrayed in a negative manner.

TV programs have often portrayed working-class men—such as Archie Bunker of *All in the Family* or Homer Simpson of *The Simpsons* — as selfish, immature clowns who have trouble seeing other people's points of view. By contrast, the women in working-class TV families have tended to be more intelligent and sensible than the men. But in the case of middle-class families depicted on television, the fathers and mothers are more likely to be presented as equally mature and responsible parents. In a similar way, television has tended to portray family life in poor or working-class TV families as full of problems and arguments, while middle-class TV families are more likely to be portrayed as emotionally healthy, with all the members contributing and supporting each other. Some critics argue that the positive treatment of the middle class in TV programming sends viewers the message that middle-class values and beliefs are somehow better than those of other social classes.

Religion on TV

Presentations of religion have been relatively uncommon throughout the history of American television programming. In fact, only twenty prime-time entertainment series featured outwardly religious characters in major roles during the first fifty years of TV. Nearly all of these characters were Christian. Jewish and Muslim characters mostly appeared in programs with a historical or biblical focus. Whenever religion did appear in entertainment programs, it tended to be presented as generally as possible in order to avoid offending viewers.

Television has always featured some religious programming on Sunday mornings. These shows have ranged from discussion-based programs to broadcasts of actual church services. Religious shows expanded in number and influence during the 1970s, when satellites orbiting the Earth allowed TV signals to be broadcast nationwide for the first time. Several Christian religious leaders created special programs to take advantage of the wide reach of television and spread their religious messages across the country. This type of religious programming became known as televangelism, and the religious leaders who appeared on TV became known as televangelists.

Some televangelists achieved a great deal of power and influence, such as Pat Robertson (1930–) with *The 700 Club* and Jim Bakker (1939–) and Tammy Faye Bakker (1942–) with *The PTL Club.* Robertson used his popularity on television to begin a political career, including a campaign for president of the United States in 1988. He also began a political organization, the Christian Coalition, and launched the Christian Broadcasting Network (which later became The Family Channel). Overall, though, televangelism fell out of favor during the 1980s, when prominent televangelists Jim Bakker and Jimmy Swaggert (1935–) became entangled in financial and sex scandals.

Religion started to play a more prominent role in entertainment series during the 1990s and 2000s. In the popular series *Northern Exposure,* for instance, several characters explored alternative and Native American religious traditions in their search for spiritual growth. The networks produced a number of other shows that focused on religious themes, such as *Touched by an Angel, Seventh Heaven, Highway to Heaven,* and *Joan of Arcadia.* But while the topic of religion received more attention on TV, it was still usually addressed in a general way and from a Christian perspective.

Television's impact on politics in America

Television coverage has shaped American politics and government in a variety of ways. It has affected the way that political candidates are selected, the way that they campaign for office, and the way that voters decide among them. TV gives the American people a personal look at their leaders and the inner workings of government. But critics claim that television has also affected politics in negative ways. For instance, they say that it has encouraged voters to judge candidates based on their appearance on television instead of on their views on important issues. They also argue that the high cost of political advertising on television has made running for office too expensive for all but the wealthiest Americans.

Almost from the beginning of television, the medium has served as the main source of political news and information. Its influence expanded rapidly during the 1960s, when advances in TV technology allowed viewers to experience major political events, such as debates and nominating conventions, live as they happened. As of 2004, according to research quoted in *American Demographics,* 44 percent of Americans named TV as their top source of political news, while 29 percent named newspapers, radio, or online sources.

Though television is highly influential, surprisingly few regulations govern its role in the political process. A few regulations that applied to politics were included in the Communications Act of 1934, which originally covered radio and was later extended to include television. This act contained an Equal Time Provision, for instance, which required TV stations that gave or sold time to one political candidate to do the same for all other qualified candidates participating in the race.

In 1959 Congress passed an amendment to the 1934 Communications Act. One provision of the 1959 law was the Fairness Doctrine, which required broadcasters to present both sides of hotly debated issues. As part of a larger effort to reduce regulations affecting the broadcast industry, Congress overturned the Fairness Doctrine in 1989. The only part of the law that remained in effect applied to political campaigns. It gave candidates the right to respond to any negative reports contained in broadcast TV programming. In general, however, the FCC did not regulate the content of paid political messages, except to make sure that the sponsor of the message was clearly identified.

Campaign ads on TV

Political campaign advertising got its start on TV in 1952. The Republican candidate for president, Dwight D. Eisenhower (1890–1969), used a series of short commercials to create a friendly, charming image of himself among voters. The TV spots helped Eisenhower win the election, and every presidential campaign since then has relied on TV advertisements to promote candidates to voters. In fact, TV commercials have emerged as the most important form of communication between presidential candidates and voters. These ads allow candidates to reach a wide audience with a message that is under their direct control.

Critics blame television for the rise of negative campaigning (a candidate's use of political messages to criticize his or her opponent). During the first fifty years of political advertising on television, one-third of the commercials were negative. There are a few famous examples of negative ads that influenced the results of an election. In 1964, for instance, Lyndon B. Johnson's campaign ran a controversial TV commercial suggesting that if his opponent, Barry Goldwater (1909–1998), was elected, nuclear war would result. Although the ad was widely criticized, surveys showed that it helped convince voters that the country would be safer with Johnson (1908–1973; served 1963–68) as president. In 1988, George H. W. Bush's campaign ran a commercial suggesting that his opponent, Massachusetts governor Michael Dukakis (1933–), was responsible for the murder of innocent people because he had allowed a dangerous criminal, Willie Horton, to be released from prison. The infamous ad helped put Bush (1924–; served 1989–93) in the White House by convincing voters that he would be tougher on crime than Dukakis.

Many negative political TV advertisements are sponsored by political action committees (PACs) or special interest groups—ranging from associations representing various industries to organizations promoting social and environmental causes. Campaign finance laws limit the amount of money that individual citizens can contribute to support political candidates, but as of 2006 there was no limit on the amount that groups could spend independently to promote a certain candidate or issue. This situation led to the creation of many PACs specifically for the purpose of running negative ads during election campaigns. The PAC is identified as the sponsor of an attack ad, which allows a candidate to benefit from it without being directly associated with negative campaign tactics.

During the 1990s, television news programs and other media began analyzing the content of political advertisements. Many news sources provided a daily or weekly adwatch segment to report on the truthfulness of claims made in campaign commercials. Nevertheless, negative campaign ads continued to flood the airwaves prior to every election. Many of these commercials distorted the records of political opponents in order to win votes. Some political analysts charged that negative campaigning contributed to a decline in public respect for all lawmakers and government institutions.

TV coverage of primaries and debates

Television also plays a major role in the selection of presidential candidates. A large number of candidates typically express interest in being nominated for president by either the Democratic or Republican political parties. Both parties hold a series of primary elections in various states to help them determine which of the many candidates should represent the party in the national elections. Television provides extensive coverage of the primaries. This coverage sometimes gives more attention to some candidates than to others, which can influence voters' opinions about which candidate is the most likely to succeed in the general election. In addition, candidates who do not perform well in the early primaries are often unable to raise funds to pay for continued campaigning.

President George W. Bush, then a presidential candidate, appeared on The Oprah Winfrey Show *during his campaign in 2000.* AP IMAGES.

Once the two major political parties have selected their presidential candidates, television provides extensive coverage of the campaigns. The ability of TV to influence voters' perceptions of the candidates led to the creation of a new position in a candidate's group of advisors called a media consultant or handler. These professionals help shape the candidates' media image through television appearances. The TV appearances can take a number of different forms, including advertisements, interviews, talk show visits, and debates. Televised presidential debates have been a vital part of the campaign process since 1960, when a strong showing in the first TV debates helped John F. Kennedy (1917–1963; served 1961–63) defeat Richard M. Nixon (1913–1994) for the presidency.

TV's influence on voters

A common complaint about television coverage of election campaigns is that it tends to focus on the candidates' personalities, strategies, and political momentum rather than on their opinions about important issues. Television also tends to compress candidate interviews and news events into soundbites of information—or brief, memorable quotes lasting fewer than ten seconds each. Soundbites fit into the limited time available during TV newscasts and commercials, but they do not provide voters with a detailed, in-depth understanding of a candidate's ideas and positions. Some critics also claim that television spends too much time analyzing what is known as the horserace aspect of political campaigns, or which candidate is leading in surveys of voters at a particular time. Overall, critics argue that the emphasis of TV coverage of election campaigns has led more voters to base their decisions on the image the candidates convey on television rather than on the candidates' opinions about various issues.

Television also influences the way that the U.S. government conducts its business. At its best, television coverage acts as a watchdog, constantly observing the activities of the president and Congress and reporting back to the American people. Many politicians have recognized that television puts them under constant observation. Upon taking office in 1968, President Richard Nixon (1913–1994; served 1969–74) created the White House Office of Communication to deal with the media and ensure that his administration delivered its intended message. But television also gives a great deal of free attention to incumbents (people currently holding an elected office) by covering their press conferences, interviews, and public appearances. This attention gives incumbents who run for reelection a big advantage over lesser-known challengers, who must pay for most of their TV exposure via commercials.

Some critics claim that the high cost of advertising on TV makes it too expensive for all but the wealthiest or most politically connected Americans to run for national office. In 1992, billionaire Texas businessman H. Ross Perot (1930–) became an instant presidential candidate by purchasing air time on the major television networks to present his message to voters. But some analysts believe that the Internet had helped make the competition more fair between candidates who may have different amounts of money. The Internet allows candidates to distribute campaign information quickly and raise funds from a wide variety of sources. During the 2004 presidential race, for instance, former Vermont governor Howard Dean (1948–) nearly earned the Democratic Party's nomination by conducting a highly successful Internet fundraising campaign.

As the primary source of political information for American voters, television plays a vital role in shaping campaigns, elections, and government in the United States. It also influences voters' knowledge, opinions, and behavior. For example, studies have shown that TV coverage affects which social and political issues the public considers to be most important. Issues that receive a great deal of TV coverage are generally judged to be more important, while issues that receive little coverage tend to be viewed as less important. At the same time, though, television can overwhelm viewers with an excess of information, especially with the numerous cable channels devoted to politics. Critics argue that this information overload has turned off many viewers and contributed to a decline in the number of eligible voters who actually vote in elections.

Television advertising

In the United States, television operates as a business, with the goal of making money. The broadcast networks earn money by selling commercial time to advertisers. In this way, commercials make it possible for Americans to receive broadcast television signals over the airwaves for free. Cable and satellite TV providers earn money by charging subscribers a monthly fee. Some cable channels also sell commercial time to advertisers, but others only air commercials for their own programs.

Many other nations around the world operate television as a government service rather than as a business. In these countries, viewers pay taxes to support the production and broadcasting of TV programs, and programs appear on the air without commercial interruption. The Public Broadcasting Service (PBS) is the only American network that receives tax money from federal and state governments to support its operations. Most PBS funding, though, comes from donations from individual viewers and charities.

U.S. commercial television is based on ratings, or measurements of the number and type of viewers who watch a particular program. Ratings determine how much money a network can charge advertisers to place commercials on that program. The more viewers from a particular group of people (based on factors such as age, gender, and income) watch a program, the more money the network can charge advertisers for commercial time during that program. In this system, successful programs are those that attract the largest number of viewers who are likely to buy the advertised products. The most successful programs, therefore, are not necessarily those of the highest quality or cultural value.

Since commercials provide the main source of income for the broad-cast networks, advertisers have played an important role in the development of television programming. Advertisers can choose not to sponsor programs that are controversial or that do not support their commercial message. In general, most advertisers want to be associated with programs that put people in the mood to spend money and buy their products. For this reason, shows with sad or tragic elements are less likely to appear on TV than those with happy themes.

The history of TV commercials

The first commercial advertisement appeared on an experimental NBC broadcast in New York City in 1941. The Bulova watch company paid nine dollars for the spot, which only reached a few hundred people since TV sets were not widely available at that time. When TV broadcasting and set ownership expanded in the 1950s, however, advertisers rushed to buy time on the new medium.

In the early years of television broadcasting, commercial sponsors created many of the programs that appeared on the air. Large companies, like the consumer products giant Procter and Gamble, would purchase an hour of air time on a network. Then they would hire an advertising agency to develop an entertainment program to fill that time. The sponsor's name was often made part of the title, as in the *Texaco Star Theater* (sponsored by the Texaco oil company) or the *Camel News Caravan* (sponsored by Camel cigarettes). Advertising messages about the sponsor's products would appear throughout the programs. Most of these early commercials lasted sixty seconds. They typically explained how the product worked and made statements, which may or may not have been true, about the many ways in which viewers might improve their lives by buying it.

In the late 1950s the television networks began taking more control over the production of programs. Rising costs made it more difficult for advertisers to sponsor entire shows. In addition, it was revealed that commercial sponsors had played a role in determining the outcome of several popular quiz shows. They had encouraged producers to give some contestants answers in advance as a way of creating drama and increasing ratings. The quiz show scandal raised concerns about the amount of influence advertisers had over the content of programs.

Around this time, NBC network executive Sylvester L. "Pat" Weaver (1908–2002) came up with the concept of spot advertising. Under this system, which continued to be used in the 2000s, multiple sponsors could purchase small blocks of commercial time on a single program. Within a few years, most advertisers decided to place short commercials in many different programs, rather than pay to sponsor a single program in its entirety.

The broadcast networks then took over the production of programs—building sets and hiring writers, directors, actors, and camera operators. Advertisers had less control over program content, but they could still choose which programs to sponsor. Many advertisers avoided programs that featured unusual characters or hotly debated subjects that might upset their customers, the viewers. As a result, the networks became less likely to produce this sort of program, because they did not want to risk losing potential sponsors.

By the 1960s television commercials could reach a national audience. At the same time, the introduction of color TV systems allowed advertising messages to become more visually interesting. These factors contributed to an increase in television advertising revenues to $1.5 billion per year. Since the cost of air time continued to increase, the typical length of commercials went from sixty seconds to thirty seconds.

During the 1970s, TV advertising began to grow more creative. Instead of providing a straightforward explanation of a product and its benefits, commercials began using the power of television to associate products with more general feelings or moods. A number of new commercials attracted positive attention during this time. One example is the classic 1971 Coca-Cola "Hilltop" ad, in which a diverse crowd of people comes together for a chorus of "I'd Like to Teach the World to Sing." The beverage in this ad was associated with peaceful interaction between different kinds of people. This era also saw the rise of public service advertising. These commercial messages encouraged viewers to take some worthwhile action, such as donate money to charity or quit smoking.

By the 1980s television had made the American advertising industry more powerful than ever before. Companies spent lots of money to develop and test TV commercials in hopes of influencing viewers' attitudes toward their products. Newspapers and magazines began reviewing the latest trends in advertising and presenting awards for the most creative or effective commercials. There were even special TV programs dedicated to showcasing the year's best or funniest commercials.

The late 1980s also saw the introduction of a new type of TV ad called an infomercial. These were half-hour long, sponsored messages

Product placement helps advertisers get their products in front of the viewers during the airing of a show as opposed to during a commercial break. For example, cups of Coca-Cola can be seen in this episode of American Idol. FRANK MICELOTTA/GETTY IMAGES.

that took the form of a regular TV program, such as a celebrity interview or an exercise show. In reality, though, they were an extended commercial for a specific product, such as a diet aid, a certain brand of exercise equipment, or a financial management tool.

Commercial TV and materialist values

In the 1990s and 2000s, TV advertising became a huge business. In 2003, for instance, the television industry attracted an amazing $40 billion in advertising income. Advertisers willingly paid more than $2 million to run a single thirty-second commercial during the Super Bowl. Television advertising also had a tremendous impact on American culture. Characters who appeared in popular TV commercials became celebrities, and numerous advertising slogans (such as Nike's "Just Do It") entered people's conversations.

Yet television commercials also came under widespread criticism. Critics claimed that the seemingly endless strings of commercial messages in TV programs manipulated viewers and promoted materialism (a view that places great emphasis on acquiring things). They argued that commercials made viewers believe that buying consumer goods was the key to happiness and fulfillment. In this way, TV ads encouraged viewers to spend money on things that they did not really need and that would not help them feel more satisfied with their lives. While many Americans disliked the number, loudness, and message of TV commercials, however, few people were willing to pay for broadcast television services through increased taxes, thereby ensuring the continuation of commercials on TV.

The sheer number of advertisements in commercial television programming, meanwhile, has made it more difficult for individual ads to be memorable and effective. More and more American viewers discount the claims made in TV commercials, while others use new technologies to avoid watching them at all. The practice of time shifting, or recording TV programs to watch at a later time, posed a significant threat to commercial television in the 2000s. Digital video recorder (DVR) systems, such as TiVo, made time shifting easier by recording TV programs on a computer hard drive. These systems give users more flexibility in recording and watching programs. Some analysts predict that DVR technology could change the face of television by eliminating network schedules and allowing viewers to watch their favorite programs whenever they want.

For many viewers, a key benefit to using a DVR is that it gives them the ability to skip all the commercials in TV programs. This trend is causing concern among advertisers. Some advertisers have started to find new ways to get their message across on television. For instance, many companies pay to have their products shown during TV programs. In this type of advertising, known as product placement, a character on a TV show might drive a certain type of car or drink a certain type of beverage because a company has paid for this kind of exposure within the program. Some critics argue that understated methods such as product placement are even more dangerous than regular TV commercials, because viewers are less likely to realize that they are receiving an advertising message.

Experts suggest that television viewers constantly remain aware of the commercial nature of television. They emphasize that TV exists not only to entertain and inform, but also to sell things and make viewers think in certain ways. By educating themselves about the ways in which

TV advertising works, viewers can recognize commercial messages and evaluate them carefully.

American TV and the world

By the start of the twenty-first century, improvements in communication technology allowed American television programs to reach distant places around the world. As of 2004, the twenty-four-hour cable news channel CNN broadcast to more than 200 countries around the world, while MTV reached 176 and Nickelodeon was available in 162. The global reach of these cable giants ensured that American TV coverage of wars, political events, and natural disasters—and even music and cartoons— received worldwide attention.

The global reach of television has the potential to make a positive impact on people's lives. For instance, TV programs can help people learn foreign languages and adapt to new cultures. International TV can also help immigrants maintain a connection to their homelands. American television programming has even been mentioned as a factor in the fall of communism (a form of government in which the state controls all property and means of producing wealth) in Eastern Europe during the late 1980s and early 1990s. Many historians believe that TV images of the political freedom and economic growth in the United States and other democratic countries contributed to the political changes that caused Communist governments to fall from power in the Soviet Union, East Germany, and other nations.

American television has also come under criticism, however, for sending mindless entertainment and pushy commercial messages to other countries. Many people and governments around the world have taken offense at the amount of sex and violence shown on American TV. Others have complained that the spread of American popular culture threatens to destroy unique local traditions and ways of life in other countries. In this way, American television programs have contributed to feelings of envy or hatred toward Americans in some parts of the world.

For More Information

BOOKS

Abramson, Jeffrey, et al. *The Electronic Commonwealth: The Impact of New Media Technologies on Democratic Politics.* New York: Basic Books, 1988.

Baeher, Helen, and Gillian Dyer, eds. *Boxed In: Women and Television.* New York: Pandora, 1987.

Bogle, Donald. *Blacks in American Films and Television: An Encyclopedia*. New York: Fireside, 1988.

Diamond, Edwin, and Stephen Bates. *The Spot: The Rise of Political Advertising on Television*. Cambridge, MA: MIT Press, 1984.

Ferre, John, ed. *Channels of Belief: Religion and American Commercial Television*. Ames: Iowa State University Press, 1990.

Gray, Herman. *Watching Race: Television and the Struggle for "Blackness."* Minneapolis: University of Minnesota Press, 1995.

Hart, Roderick P. *Seducing America: How Television Charms the Modern Voter*. New York: Oxford University Press, 1994.

Kubey, Robert, and Mihaly Csikszentmihalyi. *Television and the Quality of Life: How Viewing Shapes Everyday Experience*. Hillsdale, NJ: Lawrence Erlbaum Associates, 1990.

MacDonald, J. Fred. *Blacks and White TV: Afro Americans in Television since 1948*. 2nd ed. Chicago: Nelson-Hall, 1992.

McChesney, Robert W. *Rich Media, Poor Democracy: Communication Politics in Dubious Times*. Urbana: University of Illinois Press, 1999.

Meehan, Diana M. *Ladies of the Evening: Women Characters of Prime-Time Television*. Metuchen, NJ: Scarecrow Press, 1983.

Ranney, Austin. *Channels of Power: The Impact of Television on American Politics*. New York: Basic Books, 1983.

Taylor, Ella. *Prime-Time Families: Television Culture in Postwar America*. Berkeley: University of California Press, 1989.

Twitchell, James R. *Adcult USA: The Triumph of Advertising in American Culture*. New York: Columbia University Press, 1996.

Winn, Marie. *The Plug-In Drug: Television, Computers, and Family Life,* 2nd ed. New York: Penguin, 2002.

Woodward, John, ed. *Popular Culture: Opposing Viewpoints*. Farmington Hills, MI: Greenhaven Press, 2005.

PERIODICALS

Brier, Noah Rubin. "The Net Difference." *American Demographics,* October 1, 2004.

Carroll, Diahann. "From Julia to Cosby to Oprah: Tuning In to 60 Years of TV." *Ebony,* November 2005.

Chunovic, Louis. "The American Dream and TV." *Broadcasting and Cable,* July 4, 2005.

Cox, Craig. "Prime Time Activism." *Utne Reader,* September–October 1999.

Curry, Sheree R. "Little Progress Seen in Diversity." *Television Week,* August 1, 2005.

Rosenzweig, Jane. "Can TV Improve Us?" *American Prospect,* July 1999.

Shrum, L. J., et al. "Television's Cultivation of Material Values." *Journal of Consumer Research,* December 2005.

"What's Wrong with This Picture?" *Time,* May 28, 2001.

WEB SITES

Butsch, Richard. "Social Class and Television." *Museum of Broadcast Communications.* http://www.museum.tv/archives/etv/S/htmlS/socialclass/socialclass. htm (accessed on June 19, 2006).

Buxton, Rodney A. "Sexual Orientation and Television." *Museum of Broadcast Communications.* http://www.museum.tv/archives/etv/S/htmlS/sexualorient/ sexualorient.htm (accessed on June 19, 2006).

Desjardins, Mary. "Gender and Television." *Museum of Broadcast Communications.* http://www.museum.tv/archives/etv/G/htmlG/genderandte/genderandte. htm (accessed on June 19, 2006).

Downing, John D. H. "Racism, Ethnicity, and Television." *Museum of Broadcast Communications.* http://www.museum.tv/archives/etv/R/htmlR/racismethni/ racismethni.htm (accessed on June 19, 2006).

"Hispanics on TV: Barely a Cameo." *CBS News Online,* June 25, 2003. http:// www.cbsnews.com/stories/2003/06/25/entertainment (accessed on June 19, 2006).

Hoover, Stewart M., and J. Jerome Lackamp. "Religion on Television." *Museum of Broadcast Communications.* http://www.museum.tv/archives/etv/R/htmlR/ religionont/religionont.htm (accessed on June 19, 2006).

Kaid, Lynda Lee. "Political Processes and Television." *Museum of Broadcast Communications.* http://www.museum.tv/archives/etv/P/htmlP/politicalpro/ politicalpro.htm (accessed on June 19, 2006).

Mashon, Michael. "Sponsor." *Museum of Broadcast Communications.* http:// www.museum.tv/archives/etv/S/htmlS/sponsor/sponsor.htm (accessed on June 19, 2006).

Mfume, Kweisi. "Out of Focus, Out of Sync: A Report on the Film and TV Industries," November 2003. *NAACP Image Awards.* http://www. naacpimageawards.net/PDFs/focusreport1_master.pdf (accessed on June 19, 2006).

Rutherford, Paul. "Advertising." *Museum of Broadcast Communications.* http:// www.museum.tv/archives/etv/A/htmlA/advertising/advertising.htm (accessed on June 19, 2006).

Spigel, Lynn. "Family on Television." *Museum of Broadcast Communications.* http:// www.museum.tv/archives/etv/F/htmlF/familyontel/familyontel.htm (accessed on June 19, 2006).

11

The Future of Television

While it is difficult to predict the future of technology, many experts claim that the turn of the twenty-first century marked the beginning of a revolution in American television. After 2000, a series of technological breakthroughs changed some of the most fundamental aspects of the TV viewing experience. Home television screens became larger and flatter, for instance, while high-definition broadcasting made TV images sharper and brighter. At the same time, television viewing began moving beyond the home with the introduction of portable video devices and TV programming for mobile phones. The delivery of television signals was being transformed, as well, with the development of Internet Protocol Television (IPTV). By sending TV signals over the Internet—rather than over the airwaves or via cable or satellite—IPTV was expected to expand the number of available channels and provide viewers with access to new interactive features. Finally, advances in digital video recording technology placed the future of network schedules and TV commercials in doubt.

The combination of these new technologies changed how Americans experience television. People could choose not only what TV programs to watch, but also when and where to watch them. Going forward into the second decade of the new century, some viewers may decide to follow traditional TV schedules and watch programs when they are initially broadcast. But many others may take greater control over their TV viewing experience. They may use advanced electronic searching and sorting functions to locate programs from among thousands of available channels, record or download these programs for later viewing, and watch the programs on a television set, a computer, a mobile phone, or some other device that might be invented.

Digital transmission of TV signals

The technology that makes many of these changes possible is the switch from analog to digital transmission of television signals. American TV broadcasting originally developed as an analog technology. Most naturally occurring electromagnetic signals—such as sound and light—are analog, meaning that they are a form of energy composed of waves. Analog signals carry information as continuous, measurable electronic impulses. The main drawback to analog transmission of TV signals is that the waves are subject to interference. Other forms of electromagnetic energy can interact with TV signals and change the shape of the wave, causing the picture to become fuzzy. In order to reduce interference, the Federal Communications Commission (FCC; the U.S. government agency charged with regulating television) gave each television channel in a geographic region a certain amount of space on the airwaves—six megahertz (MHz) of frequency bandwidth—to broadcast its signal.

Communication between computers, by contrast, takes place using digital transmission of electronic signals. In digital transmission, information is stored as a binary code consisting of long strings of the digits zero and one (for example, 1010100010111). These numbers indicate whether tiny electronic circuits should be switched on or off. Digital transmission of TV signals offers a number of advantages over analog transmission. For instance, binary code can be understood by computers and all other types of digital devices, making television and computer technology able to work together for the first time. This means that digital TV signals can be modified or enhanced by a computer. In addition, digital TV sets can interact with computer networks, including the Internet. Digital signals are also less susceptible to interference than analog signals, because binary codes can still be read if a few of the digits get changed.

Another advantage to digital transmission is that signals can be simplified and compressed by computers so that much more data can be sent over the same amount of bandwidth. For television signals, this means that digital technology can provide viewers with movie-quality picture and sound, as well as a variety of interactive features. Digital compression makes it possible to fit high-definition video images into the bandwidth used to transmit regular analog broadcast signals. It also allows networks to squeeze several regular-definition TV channels into the space formerly required to transmit one channel. The main drawback to switching American television to digital transmission is that it forces viewers to upgrade their equipment. Viewers must either buy new digital TV sets or use adapters to convert the digital signals to analog so that they can be seen on regular TV sets.

The Father of Science Fiction Forecasts the Future of TV

Hugo Gernsback (1884–1967) was a famous inventor, writer, and publisher in the first half of the twentieth century. His life's work focused on exploring futuristic ideas and trying out new technologies. Gernsback is probably best known as the person who came up with the term science fiction to describe stories about possible future applications of technology. He published some of the first magazines devoted to this type of literature. The most prestigious honor for science-fiction writing, the Hugo Award, is named after him.

Gernsback also helped launch some of the earliest radio and television technology in the United States. In 1925 he created a radio broadcasting station, WRNY, in New York City. Three years later his station made one of the first experimental television broadcasts, sending a crude image to a few hundred local hobbyists who viewed it on screens the size of a postage stamp.

For much of his life, Gernsback made annual forecasts, or predictions, about the future of various technologies. He published his forecasts in the form of pamphlets that he sent to family, friends, and colleagues around Christmastime each year. Many people saved these pamphlets to see if his predictions would come true. In some ways, Gernsback's ambitious vision of the future helped shape the development of modern communication technologies.

Gernsback's 1956 pamphlet, published on the Web site Hugo.Gernsback.com, concerned the future of television technology. As of 2006, many of his predictions have proven to be accurate. For example, he said that "picture-on-the-wall TV" would be the wave of the future. "The heavy, cumbersome TV sets of today are doomed to extinction," he wrote, "chiefly because they take up too much room in the modern and future home." Just as Gernsback anticipated, giant flat-screen television screens were mounted on the walls of more and more American homes in the 2000s. He also successfully predicted the development of miniature televisions that could fit in a coat pocket or be worn as a wristwatch.

Of course, some of Gernsback's other forecasts seem just as absurd in 2006 as they probably did fifty years earlier. For instance, his 1956 pamphlet also contained a description of "celestial television." Gernsback's vision of this future technology involved an orbiting satellite with a giant, reflective mirror that would allow TV programs, news and weather reports, and commercial advertisements to be projected across the sky. "What would advertisers not pay to get on a monster sky display sign, measuring 60 miles across, with letters from up to 25 to 30 miles high?" he wrote. The mixed results of Gernsback's TV forecasts show that no one can really know what television will look like fifty years into the future.

The FCC originally established a goal of switching all U.S. television broadcasting from analog to digital by the end of 2006, but this deadline was later moved to February 17, 2009. Many cable and satellite TV providers have digitized their systems. Going digital enables these providers to broadcast high-definition pictures over regular channels, engage in multicasting (offering several different programs on a single channel),

or add interactive services such as on-demand movies. But digital cable and satellite services tend to be more expensive than analog, so some customers have been reluctant to make the switch.

High-Definition TV

The change to digital transmission of TV signals makes high-definition television (HDTV) possible in the United States. In order to be scanned by a TV camera and reproduced on a TV screen, a visual image is divided into horizontal lines. The American technical standard (basic rule or guideline), which was established by the FCC in 1941, dictated that TV screens would have a resolution of 525 lines. The term high-definition refers to any TV technology that scans and transmits a visual image at a higher resolution than the U.S. standard. Increasing the number of lines produces images that are much sharper and brighter than those on the previous TV systems.

The first HDTV systems were introduced in Japan in the 1980s. These systems marked a major breakthrough in the visual quality available on a television screen. In 1987 the Japanese national broadcasting company, NHK, demonstrated a 1,125-line HDTV system in the United States. The remarkable picture quality impressed the FCC, which soon began a competition to create an American HDTV system. The main obstacle to creating such a system was that a high-definition picture required 20 MHz of frequency bandwidth, so it would not fit into the 6 MHz of space allowed for a standard-definition TV channel. The FCC felt that the U.S. airwaves were too crowded to allow TV stations to expand their signals for high-definition broadcasting. Instead, the FCC wanted to find a way to squeeze more detailed pictures into the existing bandwidth.

In 1990 a California-based company called General Instrument (GI) solved the problem by creating the world's first all-digital television broadcasting system. After converting analog TV signals to binary code, GI engineers found a way to compress 1,500 megabytes per second (mbps) of information into 6 MHz of bandwidth, which can usually carry only about 20 mbps of data. Their system compares each frame of a visual image and only transmits the parts that move or change. In other words, it provides just enough detail to make the human eye perceive a continuous picture with nothing missing.

The FCC established technical standards for HDTV in 1994. HDTV in the United States has a resolution of up to 1,080 lines, making it more than twice as good as standard-definition images. In addition to sharp picture detail in a widescreen format, HDTV provides for Dolby digital surround sound. This technology separates the audio portion of a TV signal into multiple channels, so that different sounds seem to be coming from different directions. It gives TV viewers a more realistic listening experience, like that found in movie theaters. During the gradual transition from analog to digital TV, American broadcasters were expected to send both digital HDTV and conventional TV signals. In 2009 all analog broadcasting of standard-definition TV signals will end. Once American TV is converted to high-definition digital transmission, the FCC will reassign the old broadcast frequencies to other uses, such as wireless computer and telephone networks or emergency-response services. Analog television sets will no longer be manufactured after 2008. Older analog sets that remain in use after 2009 will require a converter box to decode digital signals.

Interactive TV

For most of its history, television was a one-way form of communication. Broadcast networks sent signals over the airwaves, and viewers received those signals with their TV sets. In the 1990s and 2000s, however, developments in TV technology allowed for more interaction between the sender and receiver of TV signals. Modern interactive TV gives viewers more control over programming. They can select, respond to, and even change the content of some programs. This technology had the potential to redefine the relationship between television broadcasters and viewers.

Interactive TV can take a number of different forms, and it has become increasingly refined over time. Throughout the history of television, several programs have encouraged viewers to participate or interact in low-tech ways. One of the first was the 1950s children's show *Winky Dink and You,* which asked viewers to help a cartoon character overcome problems by drawing on a special plastic sheet that attached to the TV screen. The 1970s saw the introduction of an experimental interactive TV system called QUBE. Created by a cable TV service in Columbus, Ohio, QUBE gave viewers special boxes with buttons that enabled them to play along with game shows, vote in surveys, and even call plays in football games. The audience responses were added up and announced on the air. QUBE and other experimental interactive technologies failed to catch on because they were expensive and because little interactive programming was available.

In the 1980s and 1990s, viewers were encouraged to interact with television by calling in a response by telephone. This approach was used in home-shopping shows, fund-raising telethons (lengthy television shows aimed at raising money for a particular charity), and voting programs such as *American Idol.* TV grew even more interactive in the 2000s with the introduction of digital cable and satellite services. The early digital TV systems featured converter boxes that functioned like small computers on a high-speed network. These boxes offered a direct connection to the service provider, allowing viewers to select or respond to programs instantly. The main application of digital interactive TV technology was video-on-demand services, which allowed customers to select new-release movies and real-time games from a menu.

Internet protocol television

TV was expected to become more fully interactive when signals were delivered over the Internet. As of 2005, according to Kathryn Balint

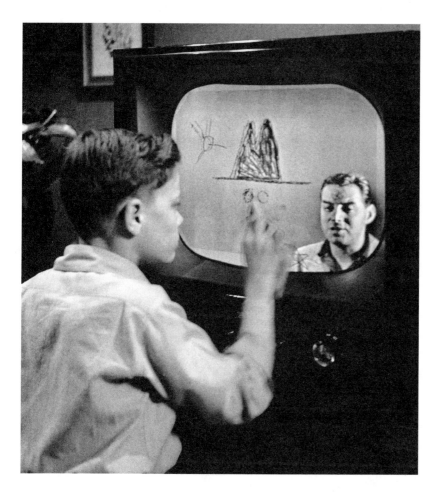

of the *San Diego Union-Tribune,* about one million homes around the world received TV signals through a new service called Internet Protocol Television (IPTV). Internet Protocol (IP) is a set of rules that guide how computers around the world communicate with each other over the vast communication and information network known as the Internet. In the 2000s, faster Internet connections and improved digital compression technology made it possible to adapt IP to carry TV signals.

A number of cable TV companies have tested different methods of sending television signals into American homes through high-speed Internet connections. IPTV services offer a number of potential advantages over traditional broadcast, cable, and satellite delivery methods. For example, cable and satellite TV systems have a limited amount of channel capacity. But the Internet has the capacity to host billions of Web pages, so it may also be able to deliver thousands or even millions of TV channels.

Another advantage of IPTV is that it would allow for greater viewer interaction. People watching television programs on a computer—or on an advanced TV set of the future, which might be a type of computer with a high-definition screen for TV viewing—would also have access to the Internet and all of its resources. This arrangement would allow them to interact with TV programming in many new ways. For instance, viewers could get more information about a person on TV by reading an online biography or buying a book. They could also influence the content of programming by voting in an online poll, participating in an online chat room, or e-mailing the network. If they saw a food commercial that made them want something to eat, they could view a menu on the advertiser's Web site and place an order online.

IPTV services of the future might allow users to watch television programs and receive e-mail or use other Internet functions at the same time. For instance, Internet search engines such as Google might help viewers locate programs on an ever-increasing number of channels. Viewers might also be able to customize the information that scrolls across the bottom of the TV screen on news and sports channels, so that it only provides the information they want to receive, such as local weather or sports scores. Finally, viewers might be able to create their own TV programs and make them available online. IPTV could make producing a TV show as cheap and easy as creating a Web site. Whatever the future holds, by the 2000s it was clear that IPTV had the potential to change television in significant ways.

Digital video recording technology

One of the first technologies to take advantage of the fact that digital TV signals can be understood by computers was the Digital Video Recorder (DVR). Also known as a Personal Video Recorder (PVR), this device records television programs onto a computer hard drive. Although videocassette recorders (VCRs) have long given viewers the option of taping TV programs to watch later, a DVR makes the process much simpler. DVRs take advantage of the electronic program listings offered through digital cable and satellite services to make recording as easy as selecting programs from a schedule with the push of a button. The technology also allows users to view a list of recorded programs, skip through commercials automatically, watch the beginning of a program while the end is still recording, and even pause live programs and return to the same spot in the action. Since DVRs store TV programs as binary code, they also provide a higher-quality reproduction than VCRs.

TiVo founder Michael Ramsay holding a TiVo machine. TiVo was the first digital video recorder (DVR) system to enter the marketplace in the late 1990s. AP IMAGES.

The original DVR system on the market was TiVo, which was introduced in the late 1990s. The success of TiVo convinced many cable and satellite providers, and even computer and telephone companies, to begin offering DVR systems as part of their overall services. DVR technology was increasingly built into the set-top boxes included in cable and satellite TV services in the 2000s, and it might eventually become part of every television set. Many experts predicted that the spread of DVRs would lead to the development of more advanced electronic programming guides. In addition to basic program listings, these guides may offer advanced searching and sorting functions to help viewers find the shows they want to watch. TV listings could be embedded with tags, like Web sites, that allow viewers to search for keywords or even the names of individual cast members.

The growing popularity of DVR technology could have a major impact on the television industry. Through much of the sixty-year history of commercial television, the broadcast networks aired programs according to established schedules. Viewers could only control whether they watched the programs. But DVRs make it easy for viewers to record programs and watch them according to their own schedules. In this way, DVR technology allows people to create their own personal TV channels that show only the programs they want to see, when they want to watch them. Someday viewers might only watch live TV to see real-time events like sports or elections.

For many viewers, a key benefit to using a DVR is that it gives them the ability to skip all the commercials in TV programs. This trend is causing concern among some advertisers. Some advertisers have started to find new ways to get their message across on television. For instance, many companies pay to have their products shown during TV programs—a type of advertising known as product placement. Other advertisers believe that they can use DVR and IPTV technology to their benefit. The computers in these systems can track people's viewing habits, create detailed databases about their lifestyles, and deliver advertising messages that are specifically targeted at viewers' particular needs and interests. In the future, people may have the option of paying less for TV service if they agree to watch commercials, or they may choose to pay a premium for commercial-free television service.

TV whenever and wherever viewers want it

Many people believe that all of these advances in technology will help American viewers gain more control over how and when they watch television. Meanwhile, the introduction of portable video devices and video phones seems likely to make television programming available almost anywhere. Apple Computer, for example, introduced a version of its popular iPod digital music player that also plays videos, and the company's online store sold episodes of TV shows for that system. Several manufacturers of cellular phones incorporated video screens that allowed

An iPod with video capabilities plays an episode of the TV show **Desperate Housewives.** JUSTIN SULLIVAN/GETTY IMAGES.

users to receive TV programming. In the future, increasing numbers of people will be able to watch news updates, sports highlights, music videos, or comedy clips on portable screens, filling spare time while they wait for an appointment or ride public transportation.

With the rapid expansion of TV delivery systems, receiving devices, and channel capacity, some analysts question whether enough creative talent exists to create sufficient numbers of professional-quality programs. They point out that advertising and subscription revenues will be spread thin among all the competitors for viewers' attention, so it will become more difficult for channels to bear the expense of producing good programs. Even if people can watch TV whenever and wherever they want, some critics wonder whether viewers will take advantage of this flexibility if there are only a few programs worth watching.

Despite all the talk about a technological revolution in TV, some analysts believe that many Americans may not change their viewing habits

Cell phones equipped with video screens allow users to receive and view TV programming anytime, anywhere.
JACQUES MUNCH/ AFP/GETTY IMAGES.

very much. After all, by the early 2000s the majority of U.S. households already subscribed to cable and satellite services that offered hundreds of channel options. Yet these households only watched an average of fifteen channels, and the same broadcast networks that had dominated TV in the 1950s continued to attract the largest audiences.

For More Information

BOOKS

Fisher, David E., and Marshall Jon Fisher. *Tube: The Invention of Television.* Washington, D.C.: Counterpoint, 1996.

PERIODICALS

Balint, Kathryn. "For Television via Internet, the Future Is Now." *San Diego Union-Tribune,* July 13, 2005.

Gwinn, Eric, and Mike Hughlett. "TV-for-Phone Content Seen as Having Big Future." *Chicago Tribune,* October 5, 2005.

Levy, Steven. "Television Reloaded." *Newsweek,* May 30, 2005.

Mitchell, Russ. "TV's Next Episode." *U.S. News and World Report,* May 10, 1999.

WEB SITES

Constantakis-Valdez, Patti. "Interactive Television." *Museum of Broadcast Communications.* http://www.museum.tv/archives/etv/I/htmlI/interactivet/interactivet.htm (accessed on June 19, 2006).

"FCC Consumer Facts: Digital Television," February 7, 2006. *Federal Communications Commission.* http://www.fcc.gov/cgb/consumerfacts/digitaltv.html (accessed on June 19, 2006).

Gernsback, Hugo. "Television of the Future," December 1956. *Hugo Gernsback. com.* http://www.twd.net/ird/forecast/1957tvfuture.html (accessed on June 19, 2006).

Grant, August. "Digital Television." *Museum of Broadcast Communications.* http://www.museum.tv/archives/etv/D/htmlD/digitaltelev/digitaltelev.htm (accessed on June 19, 2006).

Karr, Rick. "The Future of Television: Video Programming Wherever, Whenever." *NPR Online.* http://www.npr.org (accessed on June 19, 2006).

Levy, Steven. "Live Talk Transcript: The Future of TV." *MSNBC.com.* http://www.msnbc.msn.com/id/7935605/site/newsweek (accessed on June 19, 2006).

Rose, Frank. "The Fast-Forward, On-Demand, Network-Smashing Future of Television." *Wired,* October 2003. http://www.wired.com/wired/archive/11.10/tv_pr.html (accessed on June 19, 2006).

Seel, Peter B. "High-Definition Television." *Museum of Broadcast Communications.* http://www.museum.tv/archives/etv/H/htmlH/high-definiti/high-definiti.htm (accessed on June 19, 2006).

Smith, Terence. "Transforming Television." *PBS Online NewsHour.* http://www.pbs.org/newshour/bb/media/jan-june00/futuretv_4-5.html (accessed on June 19, 2006).

Where to Learn More

Books

Barnouw, Erik. *Tube of Plenty: The Evolution of American Television.* New York: Oxford University Press, 1975.

Calabro, Marian. *Zap! A Brief History of Television.* New York: Four Winds Press, 1992.

Castleman, Harry, and Walter Podrazik. *Watching TV: Four Decades of American Television.* New York: McGraw-Hill, 1982.

Fisher, David E., and Marshall Jon Fisher. *Tube: The Invention of Television.* Washington, DC: Counterpoint, 1992.

Garner, Joe. *Stay Tuned: Television's Unforgettable Moments.* Kansas City: Andrews McMeel Publishing, 2002.

Gitlin, Todd. *Inside Prime Time.* New York: Pantheon, 1983.

Hilliard, Robert L., and Michael C. Keith. *The Broadcast Century: A Biography of American Broadcasting.* Boston: Focal Press, 1992.

Lichter, S. Robert. *Prime Time: How TV Portrays American Culture.* Washington DC: Regnery Publishers, 1994.

MacDonald, J. Fred. *One Nation under Television: The Rise and Decline of Network TV.* New York: Pantheon, 1990.

McNeil, Alex. *Total Television: The Comprehensive Guide to Programming from 1948 to the Present.* New York: Penguin Books, 1996.

Owen, Rob. *Gen X TV: "The Brady Bunch" to "Melrose Place."* New York: Syracuse University Press, 1997.

Sackett, Susan. *Prime-Time Hits: Television's Most Popular Network Programs, 1950 to the Present.* New York: Billboard Books, 1993.

Schwartz, Evan I. *The Last Lone Inventor: A Tale of Genius, Deceit, and the Birth of Television.* New York: HarperCollins, 2002.

Stark, Steven D. *Glued to the Set: The 60 Television Shows and Events That Made Us Who We Are Today.* New York: The Free Press, 1997.

Stashower, Daniel. *The Boy Genius and the Mogul: The Untold Story of Television.* New York: Broadway Books, 2002.

Web Sites

"Encyclopedia of Television." *Museum of Broadcast Communications.* http://www.museum.tv/archives/etv (accessed on August 9, 2006).

"The FCC History Project," 2003. *Federal Communications Commission.* http://www.fcc.gov/omd/history/tv (accessed on August 9, 2006).

Index

Illustrations are marked by (ill.).

A

ABC (American Broadcasting Company), 18, 47–48, 55. *See also* names of specific television programs; television networks
ABC's Wide World of Sports, 163–66
Academy of Television Arts and Sciences, 93
The Addams Family, 92
Advertising. *See* television advertising
AFA (American Family Association), 209
African Americans
    civil rights movement on television and, 183, 184(ill.)
    family shows, 116, 200–202
    racism, television, and, 197–98
    television portrayals of, 197, 198–204, 205
Agnew, Spiro T., 188
Airwaves, 43–44
Albertson, Jack, 202
Alda, Alan, 100, 101 (ill.)
Ali-Frazier broadcast, 64–65, 65 (ill.)
Ali, Muhammad, 64–65, 65 (ill.)
All-Channel Receiver Act, 46
All in the Family, 98–99, 99 (ill.), 103, 211, 212
All My Children, 149
Allen, Steve, 150
Allen, Tim, 125
AM (amplitude modulation), 4

American Bandstand, 86–87
American Broadcasting Company. *See* ABC (American Broadcasting Company)
American Demographics, 213
American Family Association (AFA), 209
American Idol, 129–30, 129 (ill.), 221 (ill.)
American image worldwide, 223
American Rhetoric from Roosevelt to Reagan (Ryan, Halford, Ross ed.), 188
America's Funniest Home Videos, 128
Amos, John, 200, 201 (ill.)
Amos 'n Andy, 205
Ampex Corporation, 32, 181
Amplitude modulation (AM), 4
Analog signals, 227–28
The Andy Griffith Show, 93, 210, 210 (ill.)
Aniston, Jennifer, 125
Antenna, 45 (ill.), 59, 61 (ill.)
Apple Computer, 236
The Apprentice, 130
Arledge, Roone, 159, 163–64, 169, 171
Armstrong, Neil, 187
Arnaz, Desi, 83–84, 198
Arness, James, 87, 88 (ill.)
Arnett, Peter, 190–91, 191 (ill.)
As the World Turns, 148
Asian Americans, 204
Astronauts, 186–87
The Avengers, 95

B

C